Unkept promises, unclear consequences

Unkept promises, unclear consequences

U.S. economic policy and the Japanese response

Edited by
RYUZO SATO and JOHN A. RIZZO

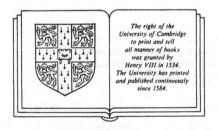

The right of the
University of Cambridge
to print and sell
all manner of books
was granted by
Henry VIII in 1534.
The University has printed
and published continuously
since 1584.

CAMBRIDGE UNIVERSITY PRESS

Cambridge
New York   New Rochelle   Melbourne   Sydney

CAMBRIDGE UNIVERSITY PRESS
Cambridge, New York, Melbourne, Madrid, Cape Town, Singapore, São Paulo

Cambridge University Press
The Edinburgh Building, Cambridge CB2 2RU, UK

Published in the United States of America by Cambridge University Press, New York

www.cambridge.org
Information on this title: www.cambridge.org/9780521352017

First published 1988
This digitally printed first paperback version 2006

A catalogue record for this publication is available from the British Library

Library of Congress Cataloguing in Publication data
Unkept promises, unclear consequences: U.S. economic policy and the
Japanese response/edited by Ryuzo Sato and John A. Rizzo.
p. cm.
ISBN 0-521-35201-0
1. United States – Economic policy – 1981– 2. Balance of trade –
United States. 3. United States – Foreign economic relations –
Japan. 4. Japan – Foreign economic relations – United States.
I. Satō, Ryūzō, 1931– . II. Rizzo, John A.
HC106.8.U56 1988
338.973 – dc19 88–1904

ISBN-13 978-0-521-35201-7 hardback
ISBN-10 0-521-35201-0 hardback

ISBN-13 978-0-521-02766-3 paperback
ISBN-10 0-521-02766-7 paperback

Contents

Preface

Japan–U.S. trade relations are strained at present. They are apt to get worse. The specter of U.S. protectionism is lurking just beneath the surface, and apparently Japan and the United States are putting insufficient effort into preventing its eventual rise.

What has caused this problem? How significant is it, in fact, and what are its possible implications? Is it primarily a U.S. problem, a Japanese problem, something in between, or something else entirely? These are the questions that must be carefully addressed if the bilateral trade imbalance and the resulting trade friction are to be understood and if meaningful solutions are to be found. Insights gleaned from considering these questions should also be useful for improving future bilateral trade relations between Japan and the United States.

In this volume, a distinguished group of economists do battle with these issues. As the problems addressed are often complex and multidimensional, opinions are divided and predictions differ. Of necessity, then, this volume attempts to persuade the reader rather than provide definitive proof on one side or the other of a specific issue. To some extent, this implies that the reader must draw his or her own conclusions from the opinions and available evidence presented here. But such is the task of most public policy decision making. In our view, the information presented in this volume can serve as an important input into the decision-making process.

All of the chapters, with the exception of Chapter 7 (which was originally presented at the conference "Beyond Trade Friction," held in Tokyo on September 1–2, 1986), were sponsored by the Center for Japan–U.S. Business and Economic Studies through a grant from The National Institute for Research Advancement (Japan's National Science Foundation). We gratefully acknowledge the institutes's generous support. We would also like to thank Naotada Kurakake and Shosuke Tanaka for their encouragement of this project.

A number of individuals have assisted us in compiling this volume, but we would particularly like to thank Stephen Figlewski, Karen Lewis, Paul Watchtel, and Akinori Marumo for their suggestions and advice. Thanks are due also to Ann Barrow and Sandra Weren for their typing and editorial assistance. Finally, we would like to thank the review committee of Cambridge University Press for helpful comments and suggestions.

Ryuzo Sato
John A. Rizzo

Contributors

BARRY P. BOSWORTH Senior Fellow, Brookings Institution, Washington, DC 20036.

ROGER E. BRINNER Chief Economist and Group Vice-President, Data Resources, Inc., Lexington, MA 02173.

JOHN A. RIZZO Center for Japan–U.S. Business and Economic Studies, New York University, New York, NY 10006.

PAUL A. SAMUELSON Institute Professor, Massachusetts Institute of Technology, Cambridge, MA 02139; Long-Term Credit Bank of Japan; Visiting Professor of Political Economy, Graduate School of Business Administration, New York University, New York, NY 10006.

RYUZO SATO Center for Japan–U.S. Business and Economic Studies, New York University, New York, NY 10006.

HERBERT STEIN Senior Fellow, American Enterprise Institute, Washington, DC 20036.

LESTER C. THUROW Dean, and Gordon Y. Billard Professor of Economics, Sloan School of Management, Massachusetts Institute of Technology, Cambridge, MA 02139.

CHAPTER 1

Introduction

RYUZO SATO and JOHN A. RIZZO

The two preeminent economies of the world – those of Japan and the United States – are headed on a collision course. The bilateral trade imbalance between the two countries is at a record level and is receiving increasing attention from government officials, business leaders, and the general public. In spite of the perceived importance of the problem, its causes and consequences are still not fully understood. Although there is agreement on some of the more general causes, there is substantial disagreement as to the seriousness of this problem and the likely nature of its resolution. Furthermore, as Japan and the United States become increasingly interdependent, the severity of the problem is likely to escalate.

What happens to Japan – U.S. trade relations and trade imbalances over the next few years will be of critical importance. At stake is nothing less than the future prosperity of the world economy, for adverse economic effects on Japan and the United States can generally be expected to harm each and every country with which these two economic superpowers do business.

This collection of essays evaluates the important issues just mentioned from the perspectives of leading economists in the areas of macroeconomics, international trade, and Japan – U.S. business and economic issues. The book is divided into three sections: Part I focuses on the importance of U.S. macroeconomic policy for the trade imbalance, Part II on the microeconomic causes of the problem, and Part III on Japan's role in the trade imbalance and what actions it is likely to take to help alleviate this problem. What follows is a brief synopsis of each of the author's papers.

Section I

Barry Bosworth discusses the role of U.S. macroeconomic policies over the first half of the 1980s in the current trade imbalance and the lessons to be drawn from those policies. In Bosworth's view, the U.S. current account deficit can be attributed to the failure of supply-side economics. In particular,

1

U.S. government dissaving resulting from tax cuts failed to be offset by an increase in private saving. In fact, the cut in taxes reduced rather than raised private savings.

The combination of monetary restraint and fiscal expansion served to raise interest rates in the United States and thereby increased foreign investment and appreciated the dollar. The stronger dollar, in turn, exacerbated the deficit on current account.

Bosworth believes that the U.S. current account deficit is an unanticipated side-effect of the Reaganomics experiment. Since it is largely a policy-induced phenomenon, however, it is reversible. Predicting declining budget deficits, Bosworth argues that the resulting increase in savings will serve to reduce the current account deficit.

Two lessons in particular can be drawn from Bosworth's analysis. The first and more specific lesson is that supply-side economics appears to be seriously flawed in its ability to stimulate the economy while maintaining budget and trade balances. The second, and more general lesson, is that U.S. macroeconomic policy can no longer afford to take a primarily closed-economy approach. In its early stages, the major concern about supply-side economics was its ability to maintain a balanced budget in the face of across-the-board tax cuts. Much less concern was voiced about the implications of supply-side economics for the U.S. trade position. This proved to be a big mistake, particularly with respect to the enormous trade deficit resulting with Japan. Clearly, future macroeconomic policies must take a more international approach and should possibly include policy coordination efforts between the United States and its major trading partners.

Herbert Stein discusses the historical antecedents of the supply-side economics experiment, which emerged against the backdrop of public dismay over inflation, welfare "cheats," and high taxes. He points out that the plan went far beyond the prescription of liberals and conservatives alike by cutting taxes in areas affecting not only business investments, but also individual income taxes.

Stein notes that "all of the negative possibilities that had existed when the Reagan plan was first announced had become reality." More specifically, the economy had fallen into a recession, with relief nowhere in sight. Interest rates were high and the prospects for long-run growth unpromising.

Even this was only part of the bad news. The rest of the bad news was that the Reagan plan brought havoc on the U.S. trade position, most notably vis-à-vis Japan. Indeed, the budget deficit induced an unexpectedly large capital inflow. Although this had the desirable effect of mitigating the crowding out of private investment, it had disastrous consequences for the U.S. current account, as Bosworth also noted.

Stein echoes Bosworth's sentiment that the possible adverse international consequences of the Reagan plan were never seriously entertained. When they occurred, they came as quite a surprise. Again, the closed-economy approach proved inappropriate in an increasingly open environment.

In terms of economic prospects for the United States, Stein is not an alarmist. Although the outcome of several key factors, including U.S. productivity growth and the resolution of the budget deficit, are unclear, he is confident in America's ability to avoid disaster, even if it appears to be just on the horizon.

Like Bosworth and Stein, Brinner is concerned about the impact of U.S. macroeconomic policy on U.S. economic performance, including the trade deficit. Whereas Bosworth and Stein take a retrospective look at U.S. economic policy, however, Brinner presents and evaluates macroeconomic forecasts of the U.S. economy. He provides three types of forecast: first, a baseline forecast, which ignores budget balancing and tax reform efforts; second, the impact of budget balancing on the forecasts; and third, the effect of tax reform measures.

In Brinner's view, private sector strength is questionable. Consumers are already holding record levels of debt, which clearly limits their ability to finance further spending. On the investment side, spending on increased capacity should be particularly weak. Given America's lagging international competitiveness vis-à-vis Japan, it comes as good news, however, that investment in process innovation is expected to be strong.

With respect to the trade deficit, Brinner predicts that a more competitively priced dollar will cause U.S. exports to grow at a brisk annual average rate of 7–10 percent over the next few years. In contrast, import growth will be negligible and may even decline. The predicted sluggishness in the overall U.S. economy is in part responsible for this expected pattern in imports.

Efforts to balance the budget should also serve to ameliorate the trade deficit. A concern here, however, is that given the overall sluggishness of the U.S. economy, budget balancing may be achieved primarily through "draconian" cutbacks in spending. This could slide the United States into recession.

Brinner argues that, from a macroeconomic standpoint, the impact of tax reform will not be large. Gross output, prices, and interest rates should be little affected. However, he foresees a very unhealthy change in the mix of spending. In particular, tax reform efforts will create disincentives for capital formation by raising the corporate tax burden. This will hurt long-run productivity growth in the United States, since investment in research and development will be diminished. Furthermore, in both the the short run and the long run, growth in GNP will suffer.

Section II

Lester Thurow's discussion focuses more on the U.S. current account deficit than on a review and critique of the macroeconomic policies that led up to this deficit. In this sense, his perspective differs from that of Bosworth, Stein, and Brinner. It also differs in another, more important sense. Thurow considers the U.S. current account deficit not simply as the unfortunate, but easily correctable, outcome of ill-advised macro policy. Rather, he sees the trade deficit as a major crisis, which, even if it is reduced, will have pervasive and painful effects on the United States and its trading partners. What is worse, according to Thurow, there is no guarantee that the problem *can* be corrected and disaster avoided. This view is in sharp contrast to those of Stein and Bosworth.

Why is Thurow so pessimistic? His concern stems from several factors. First and most obviously, the absolute magnitude of the U.S. trade deficit is a reason to be pessimistic. In Thurow's view, the high level of exports to the United States was made possible only by the creation of industrial capacity abroad, for which the only viable outlet is the U.S. market. When the trade imbalance is reduced, this will cause painful industrial restructuring and the loss of millions of jobs.

Another reason for Thurow's pessimism about the prospects for reaching a relatively painless resolution of the U.S. trade deficit is that he thinks the fundamental problem is not so much short- to mid-term macroeconomic policy failures, but long-term microeconomic factors.

In particular, he thinks that the loss in U.S. productivity is the main cause of the imbalance. Many industrialized nations are now surpassing the United States in productivity. It is this loss in productivity that will cause persistent U.S. trade deficits.

One might think that, as the economies of other industrialized nations continue to grow rapidly, they might be able to absorb enough U.S. exports to eliminate the trade imbalance. According to Thurow, however, the world's economies cannot grow fast enough to bring about this scenario, not even if foreign fiscal and monetary policies were to be much more expansionary than they are at present.

Thurow sees U.S. and foreign macroeconomic policies as having exacerbated the U.S. trade deficit, both by speeding up its onset and by increasing its size. He does not, however, believe that a reversal of these policies will cure the problem. Thurow thinks that a reversal in macro policies would by itself have little effect. Basically, his reason for this view is that the U.S. international debt is already so large that any solution not involving severe industrial restructuring efforts on all sides is hard to imagine.

To make a world economy work, Thurow argues, it is necessary for trading partners to limit structural differences among themselves, such as differences in the rates of savings. When large enough, such differences can have an important impact on trade imbalances. As Thurow points out, however, there is no mechanism for coordinating and implementing his proposal.

Samuelson discusses some of the positive aspects of the bilateral trade imbalance between Japan and the United States. Although he recognizes that it is "oversimple dogma" to claim that improved international competitiveness abroad always benefits the United States, he does argue that the import of goods produced more cheaply elsewhere *on the average* improves the well-being of U.S. citizens.

This is one compelling argument for free trade between Japan and the United States. Another is Samuelson's observation that Japan should fully open its markets out of self-interest, for to do so would eliminate allegations that Japan's closed markets are significantly responsible for the bilateral trade imbalance.

Samuelson indicates that the dollar's depreciation reflects determined cooperation by Japan. However, he is fearful that once-and-for-all efforts at dollar depreciation may not result in mid- to long-term reductions in the U.S. trade deficit because once an exchange rate "plateau" is reached, Japanese investors may again attempt to invest in Wall Street securities and thus may drive the dollar back up. The available econometric evidence leads Samuelson to predict that improvements in the trade imbalance will be slow, even assuming an appropriate mix of macro policies in the United States and abroad.

Nevertheless when foreign imports threaten U.S. manufacturing, this is perceived to be an "economic tragedy." The failure to perceive the benefits from free trade magnifies the disdain with which many, if not most, U.S. citizens view Japan's trade surplus. This hardly bodes well for future U.S. – Japan trade relations. Since Samuelson believes that little improvement will occur in the bilateral trade imbalance over the next several years, he predicts that a "protectionist blowoff" in America is a strong possibility. In Samuelson's view, this would be the real economic tragedy, not competition from foreign imports.

Section III

U.S. macroeconomic policy and microeconomic structure have done much to bring about the current record bilateral U.S. trade deficit with Japan. Important as these factors are, however, they provide only part of the story. The rest of the story lies within Japan. Sato and Rizzo investigate those features of Japan's economy and economic policies that have contributed to the bilateral trade imbalance. It turns out that there is no shortage of factors in Japan that have served to exacerbate the imbalance.

Perhaps the most obvious factors contributing to the bilateral trade imbalance are Japan's historically high rate of saving and correspondingly weak domestic consumption. These factors have been reinforced by Japan's macroeconomic policies and industrial structure. On the macroeconomic level, Japan seems at best reluctant to engage in substantial fiscal stimulus. Japan's monetary policy suffers a double "whammy": On the one hand, because of unpleasant bouts with inflation during the early 1970s, Japanese monetary authorities favor modest increases in the money supply; on the other hand, Japan's already low interest rates further mitigate the expansionary effect of monetary policy.

Japan's industrial structure, which of necessity must include a substantial export sector, has become increasingly more export oriented. Such expansion, which came partly in response to the two oil crises of the 1970s, appears to be more dramatic than is necessary for the long-run viability of Japan's economy.

Whereas trade barriers cannot be considered an important contributing factor to Japan's large trade surplus, interest rate regulation and a general failure on Japan's part to fully liberalize its capital markets can be. Thus, Japan's financial sector reinforces the tendency of its industrial structure and macroeconomic policies to promote rather than to diminish its trade surplus.

Despite the numerous features of Japan's economy that have exacerbated the trade imbalance, Japan seems little inclined to take meaningful steps to help resolve the problem unless sufficiently pressured to do so by the United States. This implies that, unless the trade balance improves considerably, trade friction may well increase as U.S. "strong-arm" tactics such as protectionist threats are employed to wrest concessions from Japan.

Conclusion

Clearly, there is no consensus as to where the record bilateral trade imbalance will lead or when it will end. Thurow's primary concern seems to be the absolute magnitude of the trade imbalance and the adverse economic consequences of reducing it. Others, like Samuelson, Sato, and Rizzo, seem more concerned about the trade friction that is apt to arise between Japan and the United States. Still others, like Bosworth and Stein, view the problem more benignly, believing that it can be solved through prudent macroeconomic policy.

Despite the lack of consensus, the chapters collectively suggest that *both* Japan and the United States are significantly responsible for the trade imbalance. As a result, it is not likely to be greatly diminished without considerable cooperative effort on both sides of the Pacific. Another theme to emerge is that, although macroeconomic policy can have a profound effect on the bilateral trade imbalance, microeconomic factors, such as the underlying state of technology in each country, are also critical determinants of the trade imbalance, especially over the long run.

The various views and prescribed solutions focus on three areas: policy, productivity, and politics. By policy we mean macroeconomic stabilization policy. The clear message that emerges from these essays is that U.S. macroeconomic policy has failed to soften the damage. Of these three areas, this is perhaps the easiest to change, and that gives us some hope for improvement.

By "productivity," we mean research and development efforts. Improvements in this area are generally slower in coming than is the case with macroeconomic policy. But come they must if the United States is to maintain international competitiveness with Japan. In recent years, the United States has substantially increased its research and development efforts, and if Brinner's predictions are correct, this trend will continue. So there is cause for hope here as well.

By "politics," we mean the political sentiments of the average citizen in the United States and Japan. These groups tend to view each other's imports with suspicion and distrust. Such sentiments are unfortunate and, moreover, difficult to change.

Directly or indirectly, U.S. macroeconomic policies and funds for investment in research and development are affected by the actions of Congress. If Congress reflects the will of the people, and that will favors a closed-economy, protectionist approach, our macroeconomic policies and our productivity patterns will be those of a nation that is ignoring some basic economic realities.

Like the United States, Japan is ignoring its responsibilities as a large and vital open-economy nation. In failing to increase domestic demand and decrease reliance on exports, Japan is inviting the worst in U.S. trade policy – that is, protectionism – to rear its ugly head. This will in time work to Japan's disadvantage.

Unless things change suddenly and dramatically, serious trade friction seems likely to emerge between the two countries. Now it is probably the case that the absolute magnitude of the trade imbalance is more "eye-catching" than the trade friction associated with that trade imbalance (the reason may be that the former can be quantified). But trade friction is a very serious affair, and, regrettably, the relationship between the trade imbalance and trade friction may be an inverse rather than a direct one. Unless policy makers in both Japan and the United States cooperate with each other rather than attempt to coerce each other, this will be the case. Under such conditions, improvement in the bilateral trade imbalance will be had only at the cost of increasingly strained relations. As long as this remains true, a trade problem will persist between Japan and the United States.

Reaganomic repercussions

PART I

Reaganomic repercussions

CHAPTER 2

The good, the bad, and the unexpected: lessons from American economic policy

BARRY P. BOSWORTH

Developments in the U.S. economy in the first half of the 1980s were dominated by a dramatic shift in the mix of fiscal and monetary policy. A restrictive monetary policy aimed at controlling inflation was combined with a highly stimulative fiscal policy that propped up domestic demand. The major benefit of the policy mix has been a large decline in inflation at less cost in terms of domestic unemployment than would otherwise be the case. The combination of fiscal expansion and monetary restraint also led to an appreciation of the dollar exchange rate, thereby reducing import prices and inflation while sustaining domestic output. The exchange rate revaluation shifted much of the burden of reducing inflation to other countries, as the price of internationally traded goods fell in dollars and rose in other currencies.

The cost has been the decline in the national saving rate and large current account deficits. Thus, the policies placed a burden on future generations, who will inherit less wealth; and the loss of international competitiveness has had a severe impact on U.S. export- and import-competing industries. The federal budget deficit now absorbs nearly two-thirds of net private saving and the United States must borrow 3 percent of its income annually overseas. Between 1980 and 1985 the rise in the exchange rate drove up the cost of producing goods and services in the United States by more than 40 percent in comparison with the cost to its major competitors.

On the domestic front, the response of the U.S. economy to those policy changes has been largely a surprise both to the government and to its critics. The administration expected a supply-side boom led by higher rates of national saving and investment. What it got was, first, a severe recession, followed by a typical Keynesian expansion of domestic demand, as national rates of saving plunged and the economy embarked on a binge of public and private consumption. On the other hand, the critics of the administration

Sheila Murray provided extensive research assistance in the preparation of this chapter and Kathleen Elliott Yinug prepared the manuscript.

expected a surge of domestic interest rates as enormous government budget deficits, in the face of a restrictive monetary policy, forced out private spending – particularly investment. What they got was a general pattern of falling interest rates and domestic investment at or above historical levels.

The new mix of fiscal-monetary policy was also highly controversial overseas. Developing countries, whose debt was denominated in dollars and tied to U.S. interest rates, faced severe debt-servicing problems at a time when worldwide recession sharply reduced export earnings. In addition, an associated rise in the value of the dollar, while lowering import prices in the United States, intensified inflation pressures in other countries whose currencies declined in value. In an effort to wring inflation out of their own economies, those countries followed the shift of the United States toward monetary restraint and many combined it with fiscal restraint. The result was a severe worldwide recession.

In subsequent years, however, the world economy adjusted to this new structure of U.S. economic policy. By the middle of the decade, the United States had replaced the developing countries as the world's largest capital importer. It became a nation critically short of saving, borrowing overseas to finance investments that it was unwilling to provide for itself. Other countries, having overcome the initial inflationary effect of a higher dollar exchange rate, found exports to the United States to be an important source of stimulus to production and employment in their own economies. Perversely, the current imbalance of trade has come to offer benefits both to the United States and to the world economy.

Over the last half of the 1980s, the United States appears to be heading for an equally dramatic reversal of its fiscal-monetary policies. The Congress is committed, through the Gramm–Rudman–Hollings deficit reduction act, to restoring the federal budget to balance by 1991. If the U.S. economy is to adjust to this shift toward fiscal restraint, while avoiding a recession, interest rates and trade with other countries will have to undergo as radical a transformation as the one that accompanied the policy shifts of the early 1980s. This process of adjustment will raise major challenges for economic policy in other countries.

The purpose of this chapter is to assess the effect of the shift in fiscal-monetary policies on the performance of the economy during the first half of the 1980s and to draw lessons for the future. The question of particular interest is: What type of adjustments will be required if the United States acts on its intentions to reduce the federal budget deficit? The issues are complex because these policies have had both benefits and costs. The benefits are most evident in the reduced rate of inflation and the boost that the rise in the exchange rate gave to the standard of living of American consumers. The costs have been a severe recession, a collapse of national saving, and the loss of international competitiveness of American industry.

The chapter is divided into three sections. The first section looks back at the performance of the U.S. economy in the first half of the 1980s. Emphasis is placed on the response of the international capital markets to U.S. domestic policies in accounting for the decline in inflation and the pattern of economic growth that emerged.

The second section contains an assessment of the supply-side response to the economic policies of the Reagan administration. Although the Reagan economic program was originally enunciated as a supply-side policy, in actual practice it became a typical Keynesian program of demand stimulus. Private saving rates did not increase, and the larger government deficit led to a sharply lower rate of national saving. Domestic investment did recover from the depressed levels of the recession, but it plateaued at a level below the investment rate of the 1970s. Productivity growth continued at the depressed rates of the preceding decade.

The concluding section examines the outlook for the remainder of the decade. The major uncertainty arises with respect to the future course of the budget deficit. Elimination of or substantial reductions in the budget deficit are not consistent with the continuation of a large current account deficit. However, although a reduction in the exchange value of the dollar and an improved net export position are necessary for the maintenance of domestic economic activity in the United States, they may be resisted by other countries that will be reluctant to lose the economic stimulus currently being supplied by exports to the United States.

Looking back

A perspective on the U.S. economy can be obtained by comparing its economic performance over the last two decades with that of other major industrial countries – Japan and the European countries of the Organization for Economic Co-operation and Development. Figure 2.1 provides such a comparison in terms of economic growth, unemployment, and inflation. An index of industrial production, divided by the population of labor force age, is shown in the top panel. The sharp contraction of growth after the first oil shock in 1973–4 is clearly evident for all three economies, with per capita economic growth in the United States paralleling that of Europe throughout the remainder of the 1970s. Japan continued a historical trend of faster growth, although the difference was less pronounced than in the 1960s. The severe magnitude of the 1980–2 recession is also apparent in the large drop in production – particularly in the United States. Beginning in late 1982, there

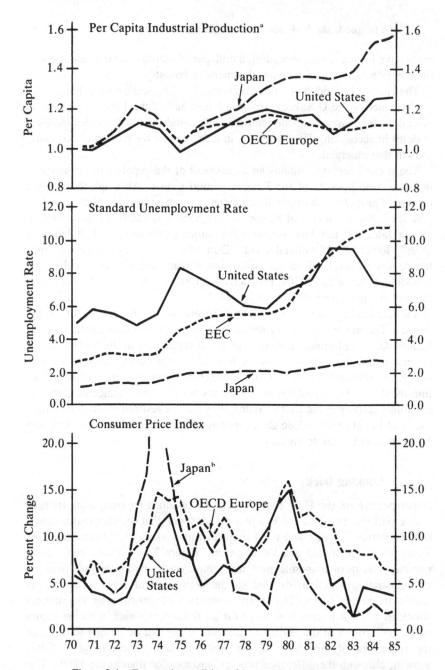

Figure 2.1   Economic condition of Japan, United States, Europe, 1970–85.
Source: OECD Economic Outlook, Main Economic Indicators, Historical
Statistics, Labor Statistics, various issues.
aPopulation of labor-force age.
bJapan's CPI increased by 32 percent in the first half of 1974.

was a strong economic expansion in both Japan and the United States, but growth was virtually at a standstill in Europe.

The differences are more dramatic in terms of unemployment.[1] Although unemployment rates rose over a 15-year period in all three cases, the increase in Japan is quite minimal. Unemployment has been much more cyclical in the United States, peaking at 10.5 percent in 1982; but it has also tended to trend upward over the period as a whole. It leveled out at about 7 percent in 1984–5. On the other hand, Europe has experienced an enormous secular rise in unemployment from about 3 percent of the labor force in the early 1970s to 11 percent in 1985.

Finally, the fall in inflation has been substantial in all three economies. Whereas inflation in Japan is the lowest, the largest decline since 1980 occurred in the United States. Europe continues to experience about 2 percent a year higher inflation than the United States, and there is a wide dispersion of countries around that average.

On the basis of these comparisons, the largest contrast in economic performance is between Europe and Japan, with the United States lying in between. In addition, both the United States and Japan have experienced much better performance since 1982, whereas Europe has lagged far behind. One factor not highlighted in Figure 2.1 is the rapid job growth in the United States – 15.7 percent between 1975 and 1980, and 7.75 percent in 1980–5. Europe, in contrast, has had little or no employment growth. That difference results largely from the much faster growth of the U.S. labor force, a situation that will now change as the United States enters an era of slower growth in the labor supply.[2] In addition, the slow growth of productivity in the United States implies that relatively modest growth in output is sufficient to generate significant increases in the demand for labor.

Inflation

The decline in inflation provides the most dramatic measure of economic improvement in the United States. The rate of increase in the GNP price deflator declined from 10.1 percent in 1980 to 3.5 percent for the four quarters ending in 1985:4 (see Table 2.1). The decline in consumer price inflation was even larger – from 11 to 3.4 percent. Much of this decline was not a suprise, however. It came at the cost of an unusually severe and long domestic recession, which was induced, in turn, by a severe contraction of monetary policy after 1979. Unemployment soared from 6 million in 1979 to over 11 million by the end of 1982. Even with economic recovery, real wages (wage rates adjusted for inflation) have remained below 1978 levels.

On the basis of historical performance, however, the decline in inflation is more than could be expected from the recession alone. The extra gain can be

Table 2.1. *Alternative measures of inflation*

	Year ending					
	1980:4	1981:4	1982:4	1983:4	1984:4	1985:4
Personal consumption expenditure (PCE)						
Fixed price deflator	11.1	9.4	5.9	4.0	3.9	3.4
PCE less food and energy	9.7	8.8	6.4	4.4	4.4	4.2
GNP fixed price deflator	10.0	8.7	5.1	3.6	4.1	3.5
Producer price index (PPI)	12.4	7.2	3.6	0.8	1.7	1.6
PPI less food and energy	10.8	7.6	4.9	2.1	2.2	2.7
Average hourly earnings index	9.6	8.4	6.0	3.9	3.0	3.2
Employment cost index	9.7	9.8	6.4	5.7	4.9	3.9

Source: Department of Labor Statistics, *PPI Detailed Reports* and *Current Wage Developments;* and Department of Commerce, *Survey of Current Business,* various issues.

attributed in large part to the rise in the value of the dollar, which lowered the price of imported and other tradable goods (see Figure 2.2). Existing studies estimate that the lower exchange rate accounted for 1.5–3 percentage points of the decline in inflation since 1980.[3]

It can be argued that the United States achieved that reduction in inflation only through a beggar-thy-neighbor policy, as a rising value of the dollar shifted inflation pressures from the United States to its trading partners – a point that has been made with considerable vehemence by other countries. Furthermore, those gains may be only transitory because, when the dollar returns to more normal levels, the United States will be faced with increased inflation pressures from higher prices for imported goods. However, as long as the unemployment rate remains above the 6 percent rate associated with rising domestic inflation, the economy should be able to absorb some external price shocks without a return to the accelerating path of the 1970s.

Inflation is likely to be much less of a problem in the 1980s than in the 1970s, but not because of a change in the economic relationship between inflation and domestic unemployment. Instead, the major change is a political one: The United States appears content to resolve the problem of inflation simply by maintaining a larger reserve of the unemployed. Although unemployment is far above the historical average, opinion polls reveal little pressure on government to do something about the problem.

Several explanations have been put forth for this changed political environment. First, the generation that had firsthand experience with high levels of unemployment in the 1930s is by and large dead or retired. Second, we may have confused a public concern about the change in unemployment with a

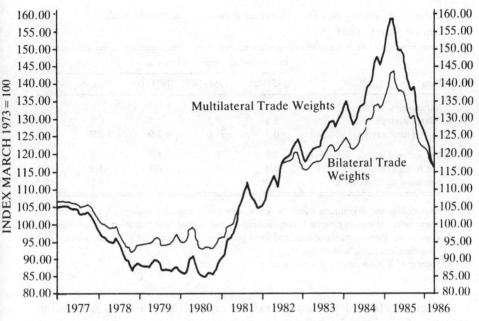

Figure 2.2   The exchange value of the U.S. dollar, 1976–86. *Source:* the Federal Reserve and Morgan Guaranty.

concern about its level. When unemployment is rising, individuals see the threat to their own job as far more immediate; people they know are becoming unemployed. On the other hand, when unemployment is high, but not rising, arguments that the unemployed are unwilling or unable to work become more popular. Third, it has become far more common to argue, even though high unemployment may be undesirable, that government policies cannot reduce it, and that government is not responsible. Fourth, the experience with high rates of inflation in the 1970s heightened public awareness of the cost and it is only natural to expect some shift in the weight of public concern between inflation and unemployment goals. In any case, U.S. policy makers do have political support for a policy that puts primary emphasis on preventing a significant acceleration of inflation.

Saving–investment flows

The costs of the shift in the mix of U.S. fiscal-monetary policies are most evident in the changed pattern of saving and investment in the U.S. economy. A summary of those flows is provided in Table 2.2. All the data are shown on

Table 2.2. *Saving and investment as a share of national product, United States, 1951–85*

Item	Percentage of net national product				
	1951–60	1961–70	1971–80	1981–5	1985
Net saving[a]					
Private saving[b]	8.4	9.2	9.7	8.6	8.8
Government saving	−0.7	−1.0	−2.0	−4.7	−5.4
Net national saving–investment	7.7	8.1	7.7	3.9	3.4
Net foreign investment	0.3	0.6	0.3	−1.3	−3.1
Net domestic investment	7.4	7.6	7.4	5.2	6.5

[a]Net saving and investment equal the gross flow minus capital consumption allowances (the depreciation of existing capital). Net national product equals GNP minus capital consumption allowances. Pension funds of state and local governments are allocated to private saving.
[b]Business and household saving.
Source: U.S. Department of Commerce.

a net basis (after depreciation of existing capital is deducted) and as a percentage of net national output.

Historically, the United States has been a low saving country. The net private saving rate over the postwar period averaged about 8 to 9 percent of income. Contrary to public impressions, however, there has been no tendency toward a secular decline in the saving rate. On the other hand, the government has generally been a net dissaver, and the amount of its dissaving has tended to grow over time, even before 1981. As a result, total national saving has averaged about 7 percent of net output.

Practically all of that saving has been directed into the domestic economy. Approximately one-third has been devoted to residential housing and about two-thirds has been allocated to business investment in plant and equipment. The United States also accumulated a small net creditor position with respect to the rest of the world over the postwar period.

The economic program of the Reagan administration was designed to change this situation through a supply-side program of tax cuts to expand incentives for both private saving and investment. A business tax reduction in 1981 shortened the interval over which capital could be depreciated for tax purposes. Personal income tax rates were reduced in three stages over the 1981–3 period, and individuals were provided with expanded opportunities for retirement saving.

The response of the economy to these policy changes has been a surprise to all concerned. First, from a supply-side perspective, the program has been a failure. There has been, to date, no increase in the private saving rate. Meanwhile, the government budget deficit has risen to a peacetime record. The result has been the lowest rate of national saving since the end of World War II, as over half of all private saving must be devoted to financing the budget deficit.

Economists outside the government, observing the projected budget deficits, expected the shortfall of domestic saving relative to investment demand to place strong pressures on capital markets. The result, they said, would be either (1) inflation, as the monetary authorities would be forced to give way under the pressure on financial markets and expand credit supplies to finance the debt, or (2) sharply higher interest rates, which would crowd out domestic investment.

Those forecasts also turned out to be wrong. Both interest rates and inflation have tended to decline since 1982 and domestic investment is almost comparable to historical levels. The economic forecasts failed to anticipate the ease with which the United States could borrow abroad. Increased foreign demand for dollars to invest in the United States raised the foreign currency value of the dollar by roughly 50 percent (bilateral trade weights) between mid-1980 and the end of 1984. As a result, the competitive position of the United States deteriorated and by 1984 the net inflow of resources (current account deficit) was about 3 percent of income – an amount sufficient to offset fully the decline in national saving and finance a normal rate of domestic investment.

The rise in the value of the dollar and the subsequent trade deficit are the most surprising and controversial aspects of the current economic situation. The causes of the higher dollar are in dispute. Basically, the debate is divided between those who emphasize the budget deficit and the consequent shortage of national saving, and those, particularly in the administration, who argue that foreign capital is attracted by surging opportunities for investment in the United States. In terms of the historical averages shown in Table 2.2, there is little support for the administration's version of the argument: Domestic investment is not unusually high.

Those who emphasize the budget deficit argue that the mix of fiscal and monetary policy raised interest rates relative to those available in other countries, increased foreign demand for dollars, and hence increased the exchange rate. Economic spokesmen of the administration have criticized this explanation on the grounds that (1) there is no historical correlation between deficits and interest rates, and (2) historical experience suggests that countries with large budget deficits experience a fall in their exchange rates.

In part, the administration's arguments are excessively simplistic. First, in the past, government deficits tended to be contemporaneous with domestic economic recessions – periods in which private credit demands were on the decline, the monetary authorities emphasized an easy credit-supply policy, and interest rates were low. The deficits of the 1980s, in contrast, are largely structural in nature, not cyclical, and they occur against the backdrop of a monetary policy stemming from concerns about the inflation risks of excessive growth of domestic production.

Second, budget deficits of the past were associated with falling nominal exchange rates because accommodative monetary policies allowed the deficits to lead to inflation. Thus, falling nominal exchange rates were simply an offset to high rates of domestic price inflation. That pattern of behavior has not recurred in the 1980s, as the Federal Reserve System has continued to be concerned primarily with avoiding an acceleration of inflation.

Finally, the experience with flexible exchange rates is limited to the post-1973 period. Throughout most of that period, governments restricted international capital movements. Before 1980, changes in budget deficits were offset largely within the domestic economy because, outside North America, exchange rates and foreign capital flows were not allowed to respond to changes in the domestic balance of saving and investment. Governments face a much different structure of international capital markets in the 1980s. Regulatory restrictions on international capital flows have been reduced, and new institutions have developed to facilitate the investment of funds in the capital markets of other countries.

It is difficult, however, to explain the full magnitude of the exchange rate increase solely by reference to interest rate differentials between countries. Some account must be taken of developments abroad. This aspect of the issue can be illustrated by asking where else foreigners would have gone with their funds. As a result of the prior recession and the monetary policies in the United States, most developing economies in Latin America encountered severe debt-financing problems and were viewed as highly risky outlets for new investment funds. The Asian countries all have very high domestic saving rates and have little or no need for foreign capital. And the European economies, with excess existing capacity, have experienced low investment demand.

In addition, during the period that national saving was declining in the United States, other industrial countries were engaged in major efforts to reduce their budget deficits, increasing national saving at a time when domestic investment was stagnant or falling as a share of national output. For the OECD as a whole, the rise of the budget deficit in the United States between 1981 and 1985 was almost fully offset by restrictive budgetary actions in other countries. In effect, other countries have been generating a saving surplus at the same time that the United States has been growing short of saving. Thus, in part, the net inflows of capital into the United States should be attributed to a changed economic environment outside the United States.

In some respects the current situation is not unlike the state of affairs after the first OPEC oil crisis. The large current account surplus of OPEC represented a rise in world saving, and international concern focused on the need to recycle the surplus. The situation was resolved by a process in which American and European banks served as financial intermediaries to transfer the excess capital of OPEC to Latin America and the Eastern European economies. Their current account deficits provided the offset to OPEC's surpluses.

Today, the United States has replaced the developing countries as the world's major capital importer, and the other non-OPEC countries have replaced OPEC as the source of the surplus, as they all attempt to use exports to sustain domestic production and employment.

The current high value of the dollar is not surprising if viewed from this perspective, in which saving and investment flows must balance. Given its low national saving rate, plus reasonably good investment opportunities, the United States needs a current account deficit of about 3 percent of its GNP. Such a deficit requires, in turn, a real exchange rate about 30 percent above the level of 1980 in order to hold down exports and raise imports.[4]

Supply-side economics

The 1981 economic recovery program was originally promoted as a major effort to stimulate growth on the supply side of the U.S. economy. Reductions in marginal tax rates were intended to expand incentives to work, save, and invest. The potential economic effects of that program generated substantial controversy among economists and others. The administration, led by supply-side economists, argued that the program would create 3 million new jobs between 1981 and 1986, on top of the increase of 10 million that would result if nothing was done; raise the growth of real output from an annual average of 3.1 percent in the 1970s to 4.4 percent in 1981–6; and increase the share of national income devoted to saving and investment by more than 50 percent (see Table 2.3). Finally, improved productivity growth would enhance the competitive position of U.S. industry in world markets.

Economists outside the administration were more inclined to interpret the tax reduction as a traditional Keynesian program of demand stimulus, albeit under the disguise of a new label. As such, they disagreed with the projected magnitude of the program's impact on the supply side of the economy, particularly the assumption that the personal income tax cut would translate into a major rise in the private saving rate. There was room for disagreement, however: There was no prior history of such major changes in marginal tax rates, and there were no laboratory-type experiments to provide conclusive evidence on either side of the debate.

The passage of time, however, does allow us to evaluate the program on the

Table 2.3. *Supply-side goals and outcomes, 1981–6*

	Projection	Outcome
Employment growth	13 million	10 million
Gain from program	3 million	0
GNP growth (%)	4.4	2.9
Business investment (percentage of GNP)	15.7	12.2
Productivity growth GNP per employed person (annual percentage growth)	2.0	1.1

Source: The projections are taken from budget material prepared in February 1981 by the administration and compared with projections of the Congressional Budget Office prepared in the fall of 1985.

basis of actual developments, rather than conjectures of future events. Of course, other factors have also not been as expected; but, the hypothesized effects were so large that it is unlikely they could have been swamped by offsets in other areas. The issue is also of considerable current interest because Congress is in the midst of another restructuring of the tax system.

Supply-side effects

On the basis of developments through the mid-1980s, it appears that the Economic Recovery Act did expand the demand side of the U.S. economy – providing a powerful stimulus to lift the economy out of the recession of 1980–2. As a stimulus to supply, however, the program has been a failure. Contrary to the original goals, the United States is on a consumption binge, financed by the liquidation of its assets abroad and the lowest rate of national saving and investment since World War II.

First, the economy has fallen far short of the administration's target for output growth – averaging less than 3 percent since 1981 – and the consensus forecast is for more of the same. Second, on the basis of the administration's own forecast, there has been no net gain in employment and labor supply from the tax change. Even with an optimistic forecast for 1986, employment would only achieve the baseline level projected by the administration to exist in the absence of the program (see Table 2.3). Labor force growth is equal to or below earlier projections; and the unemployment rate, at 7 percent, remains far above both the administration's projections and normal historical performance.

It is too early to form any firm judgments about the post-1981 trend in productivity growth because of the importance of cyclical influences. Some economic studies have asserted that the underlying trend in growth has improved, whereas others assert that it has not.[5] In any case, the means proposed to raise productivity – namely, higher saving and investment – can be expected to work only with a long lag. Thus, it is more reasonable to look at the intermediate goals of increasing rates of saving and investment.

The data provided in Table 2.2 and discussed earlier support the following points:

> There has been no major change, either up or down, in the *private* saving rate. It continues to adhere to the long-run historical average net saving rate of about 8–9 percent. In effect, individuals treated the tax reduction of 1981–3 much like any other income gain, spending about 90 percent.
>
> On the other hand, there has been a tremendous decline in the *national* saving rate because of a large increase in the government budget deficit. The net national saving rate has declined from the historical range of 7–8 percent to 3.9 percent in 1981–5 and only 3.4 percent in 1985 (see Table 2.2). Over half of all private saving must be used simply to finance the budget deficit.
>
> Despite the decline in national saving, the rate of net investment in the domestic economy has recovered to a level approaching the historical average of about 7 percent of national output. But that has been possible only by large amounts of borrowing overseas.
>
> Net foreign investment, which has been historically a small positive use of U.S. saving, is now a negative 3 percent of income. In effect, it is foreigners, not Americans, who are doing the investing in the U.S. economy, and it is they, not Americans, who will receive most of the benefits – interest and dividend payments in future years.

Private saving: The failure of the private saving rate to rise after 1981 is the most striking departure from the program's promises. Certainly, there has been a major increase in the after-tax return to savers. We could hardly ask for a more dramatic test of the hypothesis that government policy can influence private saving decisions. The rate of return rose because of (1) lower marginal tax rates, (2) the liberalization of individual retirement accounts, (3) higher real rates of interest in financial markets, and (4) financial deregulation to make those rates available to a much larger number of savers. Further incentives were provided by government statements that created doubts in the minds of the young that they would ever even receive social security, and the creation of a larger public deficit, which some argued would itself lead to higher private saving. All these factors should have increased private saving, but they did not.

A prime example of the difficulty of effecting changes in the overall saving rate through the tax system is that the annual inflow of funds to investment retirement accounts rose from $4.7 billion in 1981 to $32.3 billion in 1983 – a change equal to 0.9 percent of net national product. Yet, the overall private saving rate declined in 1983, even after adjustment for cyclical effects. The tax measures simply led individuals to switch the composition of their wealth, moving from taxable savings accounts to individual retirement accounts (IRAs), foregoing consumption. In fact, we are now faced with bank advertisements urging individuals to borrow funds to invest in IRAs, a gross perversion of the original concept.

Furthermore, a concern for financing capital formation should lead to a focus on the national saving rate, not just private saving. Increases in private saving, if they must be diverted to financing larger public sector deficits, serve little national purpose, and from that perspective, a reduction in the budget deficit would be the most effective means of raising the national rate of capital formation. In the face of the large current and prospective government borrowing, tax incentives pale in significance as a means of increasing the rate of national capital formation.

Investment: The surge in investment spending in 1983–5 would seem to provide the strongest evidence of the positive influence of the economic recovery program. Certainly there is far more agreement among economists that taxes can have a greater impact on investment than on saving decisions. However, again, there was considerable disagreement over the magnitude of the effect projected by the administration.

In a study for the Brookings Institution, I attempted to examine the composition of investment spending in recent years.[6] I found that 93 percent of the rise in equipment spending between 1979 and the end of 1984 was accounted for by two assets: office equipment (mainly computers) and business purchases of automobiles. Yet, the tax rates on these assets were not reduced in 1981. Furthermore, the categories of business investment that benefited most from the new tax code were the ones that grew the least. The benefits of the tax reduction were overwhelmed by the rise in real interest rates.

Much of the recovery in business investment would seem to relate to technological innovation (computers) rather than the tax reduction. Similarly, the growth in business automobile purchases simply reflects a shift in the pattern of spending, as people who used to buy automobiles and called it consumption, now lease those automobiles from private firms who report the automobile purchases as investment. Furthermore, many of the potential benefits of the tax act were offset by increases in the real cost of borrowed funds. Nominal interest rates were far above the levels of the 1970s, while the rate of inflation was far less.

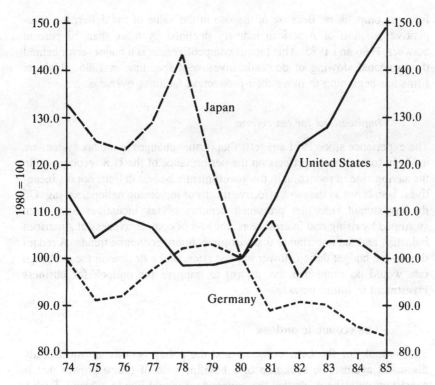

Figure 2.3 Indexes of relative production costs for the United States, Japan, and Germany, 1974–85. *Source:* U.S. Department of Labor.
Note: Indexes of unit labor costs are measured in U.S. dollars and divided by an average of cost indexes for 14 other industrial countries.

International competitiveness: Finally, the budget policies adopted in the 1980s have had a severe impact on the ability of American industry to compete in the world economy. The United States is short of saving, since it uses all but a small fraction of its income to finance consumption – both public and private. Yet, compared with other countries it does have good investment opportunities. The result has been an increase in foreign demand for dollars to finance investments that the United States is unwilling to finance itself. The subsequent rise in the exchange value of the dollar, the fall in import prices, and the rise in the cost of exports simply constitute the process by which goods and services are transferred to the United States. In that sense, the rise in the trade deficit is a direct reflection of the decline in national saving.

The loss of competitiveness is clearly evident in Figure 2.3, which compares the cost of production in the United States with that among its major foreign competitors. Because of the rise in the value of the dollar, the competitive position of American industry declined by more than 30 percent between 1980 and 1985. This loss of competitiveness is a major factor behind the projected slowing of domestic investment spending in 1986. Business firms are beginning to move their production facilities overseas.

Implications for tax reform

The experience since 1981 suggests that further changes in the tax system are unlikely to have major effects on the performance of the U.S. economy. On the saving side, a reduction in the government's budget deficit, not tax incentives, stands out as the most effective means of increasing national saving. On the investment side, the presumed benefits of tax incentives have been swamped by rising real interest rates, the loss of competitiveness of American industry, and the uncertainty that surrounds future economic trends. A reduction in the budget deficit, lower interest rates, and a decline in the exchange rate would do more than tax reform to improve the outlook for business investment in future years.

The economic outlook

The outlook for the U.S. economy and the policy options are most easily discussed against the backdrop of a baseline path of future growth that is consistent with the goals that the government would like to achieve. Such a baseline is provided by the projections used by the Congressional Budget Office to estimate the budget for future years. A summary is provided in Table 2.4. An average annual growth of real GNP of 3–3.5 percent is sufficient, given the anticipated growth in the labor force and labor productivity, to allow for a stable or slowly falling unemployment rate over the remainder of the 1980s. That rate of growth is also judged by most empirical studies to be consistent with a stable rate of domestic inflation in the range of 4–5 percent.[7]

Monetary policy has been and will continue to be the primary policy tool. In the absence of a coherent fiscal policy in recent years, the monetary authorities have taken on the responsibility for regulating the overall level of economic activity. The conduct of monetary policy appears to be guided by a desire to maintain a GNP growth rate similar to that outlined above. Real growth of less than 3 percent, extending over several quarters, is an occasion for an easing of monetary policy; and growth in excess of 4 percent leads to restraint of credit and higher interest rates.

Monetary policy is unusually effective in achieving these goals because of the highly stimulative condition of fiscal policy and the influence of interest

Table 2.4. *Economic outlook for the United States, 1984–90*

Economic variable	Actual	Forecast					
	1985	1986	1987	1988	1989	1990	1991
GNP*a*	3,937	4,192	4,504	4,838	5,214	5,619	6,047
Nominal GNP growth*b*	6.5	6.5	7.4	7.4	7.8	7.8	7.6
Real GNP growth*b*	2.9	3.0	3.3	3.2	3.5	3.5	3.4
GNP deflator*b*	3.6	3.4	4.0	4.1	4.1	4.1	4.1
Unemployment rate*c*	7.2	6.8	6.7	6.5	6.3	6.2	6.0

*a*Billions of current dollars.
*b*Percentage change from year to year.
*c*Annual average.
Source: Congressional Budget Office, *The Economic and Budget Outlook: Fiscal Years 1987–1991. A Report to the Senate and House Committees on the Budget–Part I* (February 1986), p. 7.

rates on the exchange rate and thus the trade balance. It is sufficient for the Federal Reserve to vary the degree of restraint on a basically buoyant economy. Any weakening of domestic production is an occasion for lower interest rates, which will lead, in turn, to a lower exchange rate and a smaller trade deficit. Lags in this process do lead to some fluctuation in the growth rate about the target; but, thus far, the Federal Reserve has been very successful in managing a noninflationary expansion of the domestic economy.

The foreign balance

The current account deficit has played a critical role in the continued expansion of the economy. If the United States were forced to live within its means, domestic interest rates would rise sharply as a budget deficit that absorbs about two-thirds of private saving would compete with and crowd out domestic investment. On the other hand, the United States cannot continue indefinitely with a current account deficit of the present magnitude. A deficit equal to 3 percent of GNP implies a cumulative foreign debt of over $800 billion by the end of the decade. Several factors, however, suggest that the situation may be more sustainable than is often implied by popular forecasts of a near-term crisis.

First, even with a continued current account deficit close to 3 percent of GNP, the foreign debt should not become a major burden until the late 1990s. Several European economies have been able to sustain foreign interest payments equal to 3 percent or more of GNP in recent years – a debt-to-GNP ratio of about 30 percent. The United States began this decade with a substan-

Table 2.5. *Components of U.S. current account balance, 1980–95* (billions of dollars)

	1980	1985	1990[a]
Net balance on:			
Tradable goods and services	−21.3	−128.6	−116.0
Percentage of GNP	0.8	3.3	2.1
Factor income	32.8	17.1	−40.0
Percentage of GNP	1.2	0.4	0.7
Transfers	−5.1	−9.1	−12.0
Percentage of GNP	0.2	0.2	0.2
Current account balance	6.3	−120.6	−168.0
Percentage of GNP	0.2	3.1	3.0

[a]For illustrative purposes, the current account deficit is assumed to remain at 3 percent of GNP after 1985.
Source: United States National Income Accounts.

tial net creditor position, and it will continue to have positive earnings on net foreign assets until about 1987.[8]

Second, the current account deficit is likely to decline in future years. As shown later in this chapter, the federal budget deficit has peaked as a share of the national income and is likely to decline in future years, even without significant action by the Congress. If the private saving rate holds steady, the national saving rate should begin to rise in future years from its current depressed levels. In addition, the high value of the exchange rate is having an increasingly restraining effect on domestic investment, as firms move their production facilities overseas. Thus, the gap between domestic saving and investment is very likely to shrink in the future. Turning back to the saving and investment balance as shown in Table 2.2, it is not difficult to project a current account deficit, required for domestic balance, that declines to 1–2 percent of GNP by the end of this decade. Action to reduce the budget deficit would reduce those borrowing requirements even further.

The value of the dollar should also decline in future years. In the 1980–5 period, a large rise in the real exchange rate was required in order to generate the trade deficit needed to balance saving and investment in the United States. At present, the current account deficit is composed of a large deficit on tradable goods and services, offset in part by a surplus for net factor income (see Table 2.5). As the United States is driven further in the direction of becoming a net debtor nation, a negative balance on factor income will account for an increasing share of the current account deficit and allow for a smaller deficit on merchandise trade accounts. Thus, there will be room for a decline in the dollar even in the face of a current account deficit of present magnitudes. But, as argued above, the current account deficit itself is also likely to shrink.[9]

In summary, a benign outlook for the U.S. recovery, based on the policies that emerged in the first half of the decade, suggests continued real growth in the range of 3–4 percent annually, a slowly falling exchange rate, and a current account deficit declining below 3 percent of GNP. There are, however, major areas of uncertainty, centered around the exchange rate and the potential for change in U.S. budget policies, that could sharply alter the actual pattern of economic growth in future years.

Threats to expansion

The prospect of a collapse in the exchange rate forcing an increase in U.S. interest rates is the most frequently cited threat to the benign scenario of continued future growth outlined above. A large decline in the exchange rate – 20–30 percent – would significantly add to inflation and lead the monetary authorities to adopt a more restrictive policy.[10] In effect, they might decide to abandon a focus on domestic economic balance in order to stabilize the foreign balance – raising interest rates in the United States to stimulate foreign demand for dollars. A rise in interest rates is a major concern because of the potential for a financial crisis in the United States. Domestic savings and loan associations, the farm sector, and foreign debtor nations are all very vulnerable to higher interest rates.

Our understanding of the forces determining exchange rates is not sufficient to rule out the possibility of a precipitous decline in the value of the dollar. The erosion of domestic investment has already initiated a substantial fall in interest rates, as the Federal Reserve struggled in 1985 and early 1986 to sustain economic growth. Those lower interest rates, plus expectations of a continued fall in the exchange rate, reduce the incentives for continued purchases of dollars.

The major pressures for a further decline in the value of the dollar are likely to develop during the second half of the decade when lower interest rates have had time to stimulate investment in the European economies. Many European countries have been under severe political pressures over the first half of the 1980s to reduce budget deficits and thus have been subject to significant fiscal restraint. Their monetary policies were also constrained by fears of worsening inflation during the period of a rising dollar exchange rate. The inflation outlook for Europe is much better in 1986–7. These factors imply improved European growth in future years and increased competition for the investment funds that have been flowing to the United States. If the United States does not act during this period to reduce its own saving–investment imbalance, it will encounter increasing difficulties in attracting foreign resources – which will necessitate higher domestic interest rates.

At the same time, there is some risk that actions to reduce the budget deficit in the United States will themselves precipitate a slowdown in economic growth. The initial impact of any shift toward fiscal restraint is deflationary. Thus, it is important to identify the expected private sector offsets to a reduced budget deficit.

From an American perspective, an easier monetary policy is a critical element of the adjustment to smaller budget deficits. And it is the trade account, responding to a lower level of interest rates and the exchange rate, that is expected to provide an offset to reduced government spending. Thus, if the United States should act to reduce its budget deficit, lower interest rates, a fall in the dollar, and an improving net current account are critical to sustaining domestic economic activity.

From the perspective of the world economy, however, a smaller U.S. trade deficit implies that other countries must be willing to accept a decline in their trade surpluses. If economic activity in the rest of the world fails to pick up, it may be more difficult to eliminate the U.S. trade deficit than is envisioned at present. Other countries may resist the decline in the dollar exchange rate in order to maintain the stimulus that a strong export position contributes to domestic production and employment. Thus, the exchange rate may become a central area of conflict between American and foreign economic policies.

Budget policy

The future course of the federal budget deficit is the major source of uncertainty in projecting the trend of the economy over the remainder of the decade. Serious actions to reduce the deficit from its current high level would begin a process of reversing the saving–investment balance that developed over the first half of the decade, and it would have major implications for world trade flows and growth in other countries.

Current services budget: The projection of the current services budget is designed to show future revenues and outlays on the assumption that tax laws and current expenditure policies remain unchanged. On the revenue side this is a rather clear-cut concept, but it is difficult to apply uniformly to a diverse range of expenditure programs. Those programs can be divided between the mandated programs that operate under continuing resolutions (e.g., Social Security) and those that are subject to annual review through the appropriations process. For the mandated programs, existing laws determine both eligibility and benefits, and substantive change requires new legislation. In this case, the baseline budget assumes that benefit increases will be limited to an adjustment for inflation, but increased caseloads dictate some real growth in outlays. For nondefense programs that are subject to annual review, future increases are limited to adjustments for inflation. For defense spending, in contrast to nondefense spending, there is no clear-cut concept of what it means to continue current policies. Because of a long delay between the approval of new weapons systems (authorizations) and actual expenditures (outlays), funds authorized in one year may not be fully drawn down for several years. The current level of outlays could be adjusted upward in future years to reflect pay and price increases, but that would not allow for the real growth that can be expected from an already existing backlog of unspent appropriations for multiyear programs. Projections of the current services budget allow for the real growth of outlays that would result from spending the current backlog, and they incorporate an assumption that new authorizations will grow at some predetermined rate. Disagreements about the future course of defense spending center around the growth rate that is assumed for new appropriations.

In the February 1986 budget projections of the Congressional Budget Office (CBO) the baseline for defense spending was based on the assumption of zero real growth in future defense authorizations. Actual outlays are then spun out as a delayed response to prior authorizations. Those assumptions are incorporated in the budget projections of Table 2.6.

The figures in Table 2.6 reflect a major change from the budget outlook projected by the CBO in 1985, when the deficit for the remainder of the 1980s was expected to be a constant 5 percent of GNP. The current services deficit is now expected to fall to 2.1 percent of GNP by 1990. The new lower estimate of the deficit is mainly the result of changed assumptions, however, rather than any concrete action by the Congress in 1985. In particular, the 1985 baseline projections incorporated an assumed 5.5 percent annual growth in defense appropriations before allowing for inflation. The new baseline estimates assume zero growth. That change alone reduces the 1990 deficit by $84 billion. The major sources of change in the revised outlook are shown in Figure 2.4.

The baseline outlay estimates are also reduced by the sequestration of appropriations in FY 1986 as the first stage of the Gramm–Rudman–Hollings budget control act.[11] The effects of the sequestration grow to a reduction of outlays of $20 billion in 1990.

Holding defense authorizations to a zero percent annual real growth plus inflation would represent a sharp reversal of the pattern of 1980–5 when authorizations expanded at an annual rate of 15 percent (8 percent in real terms). Because much of the initial buildup was concentrated in procurement of new weapons, future outlays will be dominated by the cost of maintaining a

Table 2.6. *Sources and disposition of government revenues, United States*

	Actual				Projected[a]		
	1960	1970	1980	1985	1986	1988	1990
	Billions of dollars						
Revenues	92.5	192.8	517.1	734.0	778	921	1,068
Outlays	−92.2	195.7	576.7	946.0	986	1,086	1,188
Deficit	0.3	−2.8	−59.6	−212.0	−208	−165	−120
Public debt	237.2	284.9	715.1	1510.0	1,720	2,064	2,326
	Percentage of GNP						
Expenditures							
National defense	9.7	8.4	5.2	6.4	6.4	6.1	5.8
Social Security and Medicare	2.3	3.7	5.8	6.5	6.4	6.5	6.6
Other nondefense	5.2	6.6	9.4	7.8	7.4	6.6	5.9
Net interest	1.4	1.5	2.0	3.3	3.3	3.2	2.8
Total	18.5	20.2	22.4	24.0	23.5	22.4	21.1
Revenues							
Social insurance taxes	2.9	4.6	6.1	6.7	6.7	6.9	6.9
Individual income tax	8.2	9.3	9.5	8.5	8.5	8.7	8.9
Corporate taxes	4.3	3.4	2.5	1.6	1.7	2.1	2.0
Excise taxes	2.3	1.6	0.9	1.0	0.8	0.7	0.6
Other	0.8	1.1	1.0	1.0	0.8	0.8	0.7
Total	18.6	19.9	20.1	18.6	18.6	19.0	19.0
Deficit	0.1	−0.3	−2.9	−5.4	−5.0	−3.4	−2.1
Public debt	47.6	29.4	27.8	38.4	41.0	42.7	41.4

[a]Incorporates an assumed zero percent annual real growth in defense authorizations.
Source: Congressional Budget Office, *The Economic and Budget Outlook: Fiscal Years 1987–1991*, February 1986.

vastly expanded capital stock. It would seem irrational to purchase the new capital, but then fail to provide the funding to operate and maintain it. Thus, it will be difficult to achieve the zero percent growth target unless some existing procurement programs are canceled, an action that, thus far, neither the administration nor the Congress has been willing to take.

Economic assumptions: Medium-period budget projections are notoriously inaccurate. In part, that is to be expected because the president and the Congress do make changes in budget policies between the time of the projection and the actual fiscal year. In addition, however, the projections are very sensitive to variations in the assumed underlying economic conditions – real growth, inflation, and interest rates. The CBO projections shown in Table 2.6

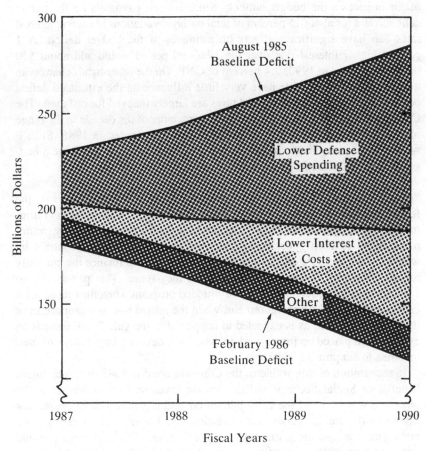

Figure 2.4   Sources of change in baseline deficit projections. *Source:* Congressional Budget Office, *The Economic and Budget Outlook: Fiscal Years 1967–1991. A Report to the Senate and House Committees on the Budget – Part I* (February 1986), p. 66.

assumed a 3.3 percent average annual growth of real GNP over the last half of the 1980s, as summarized in Table 2.4. This growth rate is considerably more optimistic than the 2.7 percent achieved between 1980 and 1985. It is between the 3.1 percent annual growth rate achieved in the 1970s and the 3.9 percent average of the 1960s.

According to alternative budget projections by CBO, a variation in real growth of ½ percent annually over the remainder of the 1980s would raise (or lower) the estimate of the deficit for 1990 by roughly $45 billion, a change equal to about 0.7 percent of GNP. Variations in interest rates also have a major impact on the budget outlook. Since interest payments on the public debt account for about 15 percent of total outlays, variations in market interest rates can have significant effects on estimates of the budget deficit. A 1 percent higher interest rate over the 1986–90 period would add about $30 billion to outlays in 1990, 0.4 percent of GNP. On the other hand, changes in the projected inflation rate have very little influence on the estimated deficit because both revenues and expenditures are largely indexed for inflation. The CBO projections assume inflation for the remainder of the decade in the range of 4 to 4.5 percent annually, the same as that experienced in 1985. Still, it would require very large changes in economic conditions to eliminate a budget deficit that is largely structural in nature.

Social insurance surplus: In one important respect, these projections on the federal budget understate the magnitude of the deficit problem. In its retirement program, the United States does not fully fund the future liability (retirement costs) of each generation, preferring instead an implicit contract by which current workers devote a share of their income to finance the currently retired, in return for equal treatment when they retire. This pay-as-you-go system is roughly equivalent to a fully funded program when the retired are a constant share of the population. But when the retired rise as a proportion of the total population, as is expected to happen after the year 2020, there is an extra burden placed on future workers who must devote a larger share of their incomes to support the elderly.

In recognition of this problem, the Congress acted in 1983 to reduce future benefits of Social Security and to increase taxes on current workers. The objective was to avoid the extra burden on future generations by increasing saving of the current generation, investing in a larger stock of capital, and raising national income in future years. In effect, the current generation would pay a portion of its own retirement costs, avoiding the extra cost to future workers. As a result, the Social Security system will run a substantial surplus for the next three decades, accumulating to about $12 trillion by the year 2030 and declining rapidly thereafter. If, however, the surplus on the trust fund is used to finance the deficit in the rest of the budget and thus consumption of the current generation, no future benefit is obtained.[12] In effect, the United States would simply use a regressive wage tax to finance programs, such as defense, of benefit to the general population.

Over the remainder of the 1980s this extra saving in the trust funds will average about 1 percent of GNP. Thus, validation of the 1983 Social Security amendments requires that the United States aim for a total budget deficit that is smaller by about 1 percent of GNP than it would otherwise be. As an extreme, full balance of the unified budget (exclusive of Social Security) would require a total budget *surplus* averaging about 1 percent of GNP. This is a much more restrictive target for the budget than the historical record in which the United States had a budget *deficit* that averaged about 1–2 percent of GNP.

Budget reduction policies: Although the budget deficit is widely condemned, the basic problem that continues to inhibit action is that doing something – increasing taxes or cutting one's favorite expenditure program – is politically viewed as even worse. If the United States were a closed economy, forced to live within its means, the cost of excessive consumption would be readily within its means, the cost of excessive consumption would be readily apparent in the form of rising inflation or high interest rates. The cost of foreign borrowing, however, involves more subtle considerations that are difficult for the average citizen to understand. The growing trade deficit and the inability of American firms to compete at present exchange rates is one evident cost, but it is more popular to blame the trade policies of other countries, rather than our own budget policies, as the fundamental cause of the problem.

The Deficit Reduction Act of 1986 (Gramm–Rudman–Hollings), by establishing annual targets for a gradual reduction of the budget deficit to zero by 1991, increases the likelihood of a major change in the direction of U.S. fiscal policy. Such a radical shift of policy will, in turn, call for major changes in interest rates and the exchange rate if the United States is to avoid a recession. The reduction in the budget deficit would amount to 5 percent of GNP. Thus, if private saving is assumed to remain unchanged, the offset must be provided by higher levels of domestic investment and an improvement in the current account deficit.

Existing econometric models imply that domestic interest rates would need to decline by 1–2 percentage points simply to raise domestic investment by 1 percent of GNP. In addition, if domestic investment rose from 1985 levels by 2 percentage points of GNP, it would, as a share of GNP, equal or exceed the investment boom of the mid-1960s. It seems evident that much of the adjustment must be reflected in the trade balance. If the United States restores its national saving rate to the level of the 1970s, it will have little need to borrow abroad.

In past years a growing trade deficit provided the major response to the growing budget deficit. So, too, as the process reverses, the trade deficit must decline. The change in the current account will, however, require a decline in the exchange rate far beyond what has already occurred. The United States has lost a net foreign asset position that used to contribute a full 1 percent of GNP to the receipts from abroad. That will have to be offset by larger trade surpluses. In addition, one major market, Latin America, will remain depressed for years to come. On the basis of trends in relative costs, the trade weighted exchange rate would need to return to the level of 1980 – a further

30–5 percent decline from the exchange levels of early 1986 – to restore the current account to balance.

The decline in U.S. interest rates, which is expected to follow a shift in the fiscal-monetary policy mix, will result in lower rates in other countries, and that alone should benefit their economies. Higher growth abroad would, through an income effect, improve U.S. export performance. However, the United States also needs the improvement in competitiveness that would accompany a return of the exchange rate to more normal levels. Therefore, other countries must be willing to allow the dollar to decline, and they must be willing to replace the stimulus that they now receive from exports to the United States with domestic measures. Thus, a successful adjustment to a smaller U.S. budget deficit will require significant changes in economic policy abroad, as much as in the United States.

Notes

1 The unemployment rates shown in Figure 2.1 have been adjusted by the OECD to increase the compatibility of definitions across countries.

2 Howard N. Fullerton, "The 1995 Labor Force: BLS's Latest Projections," *Monthly Labor Review*, vol. 108 (November 1985), pp. 17–25.

3 For references to that research, see Jeffrey Sachs, "The Dollar and the Policy Mix: 1985," *Brookings Papers on Economic Activity*, vol. 1 (1985), pp. 127–47.

4 It is sometimes argued that the trade deficit has caused a loss of as many as 2 million jobs in the United States. This is a fallacious argument because it is unreasonable to suppose that the Federal Reserve would have supported the higher growth of domestic production required to add 2 million jobs. Two million more domestic jobs implies an unemployment rate well below 6 percent. That is a rate of domestic resource utilization that the Federal Reserve would find threatening to its inflation goals. The trade deficit did, however, cause a reallocation of about 2 million jobs from the tradable goods sector to domestic services.

5 There has been some improvement of productivity growth since 1979 in the manufacturing sector; but no such improvement is evident for the nonfarm sector as a whole.

6 Barry Bosworth, "Taxes and the Investment Recovery," *Brookings Papers on Economic Activity*, vol. 1 (1985), pp. 1–38.

7 The growth of potential GNP, labor force plus productivity growth, is believed to be about 3 percent annually, and most inflation studies suggest an unemployment rate above 6 percent would be consistent with a stable or decelerating rate of wage increase.

8 On the basis of recorded transactions, the United States became a net debtor nation in 1985, but that accounting does not reflect the full value of direct investments. It is more meaningful to look at net earnings of investment income, which were about $17 billion in 1985. If the rate of return is assumed to average 10 percent, net assets abroad totaled about $170 billion.

9 In fact, the United States is likely to require a trade surplus simply to balance the current account because of the loss of investment income. In the 1920s the United States could afford a substantial trade deficit because net factor income from abroad equaled nearly 1 percent of GNP.

10 The exchange rate has declined by 20 percent in 1985; but that drop was from a temporary peak that was not fully reflected in import prices, and much of its potential inflation effect has been offset by a decline in oil and other commodity prices.

11 The deficit control act requires that each year's deficit targets be met through cuts in new appropriations – spending from prior year budget authority is exempt. Since, on the average, only half of each year's authorization is spent during the current year, the reduction in new authorizations, required to reduce outlays in 1986 by $12 billion, had a long-run impact on annual outlays nearly twice as large.

12 For further discussion of this issue, see John Hambor, "Social Security Trust Funds in the Unified Budget," Social Security Administration, 1985, mimeographed.

CHAPTER 3

Macroeconomic policy during the Reagan years: 1981–1985

HERBERT STEIN

To explain and evaluate the macroeconomic policy of the Reagan administration, one needs to review the economic situation as it existed in the United States in 1980. The Reagan policy started as a response to what were, or were perceived to be, the problems in the years leading up to the 1980 election. The extent to which those problems were solved is the natural standard for measuring the achievements of Reagan economics; and the extent to which they were not solved, or their "solutions" caused other problems, creates the agenda for economic policy in the years ahead.

Problems seen in 1980

When candidate Reagan asked his famous question in 1980, "Are you better off than you were four years ago?" the statistics gave at best an ambiguous answer. One could certainly have argued that we were better off. Between 1976 and 1980 real output had increased by 3.1 percent per annum, almost exactly the average of the 25 years before 1976. In those four years real per capita disposable income had increased at an average annual rate of 1.5 percent, only a little less than the rate of the preceding 25 years. Total employment had increased greatly – 10 million, or more than 10 percent, in four years. The unemployment rate in 1980 was 7.0 percent, down from 7.6 percent in 1976.

Yet Mr. Reagan could ask that question in 1980 with confidence that most Americans would respond that they were worse off. The basic reason for this unhappy sentiment was inflation. In the two years 1979 and 1980 combined, the Consumer Price Index had risen at an annual rate of almost 13 percent, a rate not experienced in any two-year period in the United States since 1836, except in connection with a war. Energy prices, led by oil, were rising by almost 25 percent a year in 1979 and 1980. There was every reason to think that part of the inflation was temporary. But even without energy prices, the Consumer Price Index was rising by more than 11 percent a year.

In the public mind, inflation was the outstanding economic concern. Most people probably exaggerated the injury that inflation was doing them. They naturally paid much more attention to the rise in the cost of things they bought than in the rise of their own wages, which were also being boosted by inflation. Even if they recognized that their income was keeping up with inflation they were worried about whether it would continue to do so. The anxiety caused by inflation was a real thing that no politician could ignore. Moreover, there were real and disturbing inflationary effects on the distribution of income and taxes and on investment decisions.

The four years prior to 1980 were also a period of greatly increasing consciousness of and resentment toward the rising tax burden. The feeling of being overtaxed was sliding down from the high-income tax groups to the middle-income groups, which included most of the voters. Federal revenues as a percentage of GNP rose from 17.5 percent in 1976 to 19.4 percent in 1980 (fiscal years). All of this increase came from the two taxes that middle-income people were most conscious of – the individual income tax and social insurance contributions. Revenues from these taxes rose from 13.1 percent to 16.1 percent of GNP. Corporate and other taxes remained essentially constant as a share of GNP. A person with $25,000 of income in 1980 was paying about 26 percent of his or her income in individual income and Social Security taxes, if the entire income was from wages and salaries. The same real income in 1975 would have been taxed at about 21 percent. Much of this increase was due to "bracket creep" – the rise of real tax rates as inflation reduced the real value of exemption levels and tax brackets.

Perhaps because of their rising tax brackets, middle-income Americans became more and more dissatisfied with the rise of government spending, especially what was often regarded as spending for the undeserving and idle poor. In fact, however, expenditures directly targeted to poor people were not very large – around 2 percent of GNP – and did not rise as a fraction of GNP during the Carter administration. Transfer payments were rising rapidly, but the bulk of those were for middle-income people, mainly through Social Security or Medicare, and they were accepted as earned and legitimate. The big rise of spending for the poor had occurred during the Johnson and Nixon administrations. By the end of the Carter administration, the earlier enthusiasm or acceptance of the war on poverty had turned to disappointment and anger as the expenditures seemed not to cure, but in some cases even to create, the disease at which they were aimed.

Although inflation, high taxes, and "welfare cheats" topped the list of economic problems perceived by the public in 1980, two other less visible problems were potentially more serious. One was the slowdown of productivity growth, and the other was the lagging relative strength of the U.S. armed forces. From 1976 to 1980, output per hour of work in the private business sector rose by only $\frac{2}{10}$ of 1 percent per annum, whereas in the preceding 25 years it had risen by $2\frac{1}{2}$ percent per annum. This comparison is affected somewhat by cyclical fluctuations in the utilization of productive capacity. A better measure of the change of trend is given by Edward F. Denison's estimates of real *potential* national income per *potential* hour of work – that is real income per hour at constant utilization of the labor force.[1] By this measure, the annual rate of productivity growth fell from 2.45 percent in 1951–76 to 1.37 percent in 1976–80. Continuation of that low rate of productivity growth or, even worse, continuation of a declining trend in the growth rate, would make impossible the rapid improvement of living standards to which Americans have been accustomed.

During the Carter administration, output per capita, disposable income per capita, and consumption per capita rose at about their historic rates despite the slow growth in productivity. This was made possible by an increase in the number of persons employed per capita. In 1980, employment was 44.3 percent of the population; in 1976, it had been 41.5 percent. Much of the increase had been in the employment of women. In 1980, 48.1 percent of all females 20 years of age or older were employed; in 1976, the percentage had been 43.5 percent. So although we were enjoying higher real incomes, we, and especially women, were working more for them. Although an increase of employment is generally regarded as a good thing, there was some unhappiness about this. Complaints were heard that economic conditions were forcing women into the labor force. In any case, the increased employment of women seemed an unreliable and possibly undesirable long-run offset to a declining rate of productivity growth.

The lag in U.S. military forces might not seem to qualify as an economic problem, but it had important economic implications. During the Carter administration, defense spending had been running around 5 percent of GNP – compared with about 10 percent during the Eisenhower and Kennedy administrations. If the attempt to restore America's relative military position should call for raising defense spending to 10 percent of GNP, or even to 7 or 8 percent, that would require restraint of private consumption or investment. Or, as the problem would more usually be put, a substantial increase of defense spending would have complicated the position of a federal budget in which taxes were considered too high and the deficit was worrisome. In 1980, a statement that inflation was too high, taxes were too high, some nondefense spending was too high, productivity growth was too low, and defense spending was too low would have commanded fairly general agreement. But an attempt to specify the magnitude or relative importance of these excesses or deficiencies would have provoked disagreement. Prescriptions for cures were even more controversial.

Policy options in 1980

A discussion of proposals for dealing with these problems that seemed open for consideration in 1980 conveniently starts with inflation, then commonly considered the most urgent item on the agenda. By that date everyone who thought seriously about the matter agreed that the indispensable instrument for dealing with inflation was monetary policy. That, however, left open a number of major issues.

In October 1979, a time of a falling dollar and mounting concern over inflation, the Federal Reserve embarked upon a more determined anti-inflationary policy than had previously been pursued. This change of policy seemed a turn in the direction of "monetarism," but not all the way. The Federal Reserve would try to manage the money supply in a way that would be consistent with a gradual reduction in the inflation rate, given the Federal Reserve's estimates of velocity. Presumably, this would require gradual reduction and then stabilization of the rate of growth of the money supply. On the negative side, it meant that the Federal Reserve would not attempt to stabilize interest rates or exchange rates. However, this was not an all-out commitment to a stable rate of growth of the money supply. The way was left open for departures from the planned path of the money supply when previously unexpected changes of velocity occurred or were predicted.

The "true-blue" monetarists, led by Milton Friedman, welcomed this step by the Federal Reserve, but regarded it as insufficient. The commitment to stable monetary growth was not sufficiently explicit and firm, in their opinion, and too much room was left for disturbing variations in monetary growth as a result of political pressures or simple error. They also thought that the Federal Reserve's operating procedures were inadequate for achieving the desired rate of monetary growth. Thus their prescription for disinflation was a stronger commitment to the steady path of monetary growth and more precise procedures for controlling the money supply.

On the other hand, there was a common view among economists that even this partial step toward monetarism was a mistake. Recognizing the need for a more disinflationary monetary policy, they believed that this could be best achieved by a more flexible adaptation of the money supply to the state of the economy, and more specifically by aiming at the interest rate that seemed most likely to bring about the desired behavior of the inflation rate.

Finally, an increasingly visible group urged that monetary policies aim neither at the quantity of money nor at the rate of interest, but at the stabilization of a particular price – the price of gold. The underlying theory had two ingredients: first, that a fairly stable relationship existed between the price of gold and the general price level, and, second, that stabilizing the price of gold required less skill and judgment by the monetary authority and left the authority less discretion than other monetary rules.

The idea of using monetary policy to get the inflation rate down raised the possibility that disinflation would cause unemployment to rise. Opinions differed as to how serious that problem was and how to deal with it. In one view, the problem would not be serious if the disinflationary policy was credible. If business and labor knew that the government was determined to push the policy through, they would adapt their price and wage behavior to the expectation of a lower inflation rate, which would permit the lower inflation rate to be achieved without much rise of unemployment. This raised the question of how credibility was to be achieved. Some thought that a specific announcement by the president and the Federal Reserve of a target path for gradual disinflation would suffice. Others considered that unlikely and believed that credibility could only be achieved by shock treatment – an all-at-once cut in money growth designed to stop inflation immediately. They believed that after the disappointments of the previous decade, any gradual approach would cause the private sector to discount government's intentions and to expect a revival of inflationary policy.

Another school of thought rejected the whole credibility thesis. They did not believe that sufficient credibility could be achieved by any means to induce business and labor to respond promptly to disinflationary monetary policy and so avoid a rise of unemployment. Their preferred solution was to accompany the tightening of monetary policy with an "income policy" – direct government pressure to slow the increase of prices and wages. They believed this would permit a restriction of demand without a cut in production and employment. They thought that such a policy could be implemented without mandatory price and wage controls, by resorting to "moral suasion."

Thus, in 1980 the range of views about how to deal with the number-one problem, inflation, was wide. It included four kinds of monetary regimes – "soft" monetarism, à la Federal Reserve; "hard" monetarism, à la Friedmanites; more traditional eclectic monetary management, emphasizing interest rates; and the gold standard. Any of these could be implemented gradually or all at once, by shock treatment. In principle, any of these could be accompanied by an incomes policy, although in practice incomes policy was usually recommended by persons who preferred the eclectic monetary policy.

The other problems of 1980 fell mainly within the realm of the budget. Taxes, defense spending, and nondefense spending were themselves part of the budget. The other problem, the slow growth of productivity, was also regarded by many people as a budgetary matter, primarily because of the adverse effect of business taxation on private investment. Or, to put the matter another way, even if taxes were not the chief cause of the productivity slowdown, there were few prescriptions for curing the slowdown other than tax revision. The idea that government could promote a revival of productivity growth by more direct and specific control of the economy, especially with regard to the direction of investment, had some currency but little influence.

With respect to the budget, the differences of opinion were mainly matters of degree. How much should taxes be cut? How much should defense be increased? How much should nondefense spending be cut? These differences depended largely upon attitudes toward the budget deficit, which in fiscal 1980 was about $2\frac{1}{2}$ percent of GNP. Those who worried a great deal about the deficit tended to favor a small tax cut and a slow defense buildup. If the tax cut was to be small, it should be concentrated where it would be expected to do the most good for stimulating productivity, which in the common opinion of the time meant cutting business taxes. The Carter administration took essentially this moderate approach. Others, especially the Reagan team during the campaign, were more daring about the deficit, and accordingly about the size of tax cuts and spending increases, for reasons that will be explained below.

The initial Reagan program

The striking aspect of the Reagan economic program announced after his inauguration in January 1981 was the budget. On the one hand, he proposed to increase real defense expenditures by about $8\frac{1}{2}$ percent per annum from 1980 to 1984, compared with the 5 percent annual increase recommended by President Carter in his last budget. The Carter budget would have raised defense expenditures from 5.3 percent of GNP in 1980 to 5.9 percent in 1984. The Reagan proposal would have raised the ratio to 6.4 percent. At the same time, Mr. Reagan proposed a large tax cut, to be phased in gradually over the next three years. In 1984, the tax cut would reduce revenues by $130 billion, or 14 percent, from the amount estimated by President Carter. This was a cut of $3\frac{1}{4}$ percent of GNP. The Reagan budget also assumed less inflation than the Carter budget, and this also reduced the ratio of receipts to GNP, since indexing for inflation was not part of the plan. All together, the plan would have reduced the ratio of receipts to GNP to 19.3 percent in 1984, compared with 20.3 percent in 1980 and 22.8 percent in 1984 under the Carter budget.

The Reagan plan was intended to bring the budget close to balance by 1984, from a deficit of $74 billion, or 2.8 percent of GNP, in 1980. (These figures include in the total outlays the expenditures that were considered off budget in 1981 but that have since been incorporated in the budget.) Obviously, given the tax cut and the defense increase, the plan depended heavily on cutting nondefense expenditures. The size of the required cut is suggested by Table 3.1.

Thus it would be necessary to cut nondefense expenditures, other than

Table 3.1. *Percentage of GNP*

	1980	1984	
	Actual	Carter budget	Reagan budget
Receipts	20.3	22.8	19.3
Total expenditures	23.1	22.4	19.5
Defense	5.3	5.9	6.5
Nondefense	17.8	16.5	13.0
Net interest	2.0	1.8	1.7
Other	16.8	14.7	11.3
Deficit	2.8	−0.4	0.2

interest, as a percentage of GNP by 28 percent from the actual ratio of 1980 and 23 percent from the ratio projected in the Carter budget. One could reasonably assume that real GNP would be higher in 1984 than it was in 1980, so that a cut of 28 percent from the share of GNP would not be a cut of 28 percent on the real value of government expenditures. Nonetheless, there would have to be an absolute real cut of about 15 percent, at a time of rising population and increasing numbers of Social Security beneficiaries with rising real per capita benefits.

President Reagan did propose a large package of cuts in nondefense expenditures with his economic plan, but even this large package, if fully adopted, would not have been sufficient to achieve the goal of a balanced budget by 1984. The balance was formally achieved by the promise that more expenditure cuts would be proposed later. The cuts that were proposed invaded many programs that were politically sensitive. As it turned out, more of these cuts were accepted than one might have expected. Still, the assumption that they would all be accepted was unrealistic.

From the beginning, many people recognized that the combination of the proposed tax cut, the proposed defense increase, and the proposed balanced budget by 1984 was an improbable one. By the fall of 1981 many more had come to agree. The plan possessed a number of vulnerable points:

1. Some of the required nondefense cuts still had to be proposed.
2. Some of the proposed cuts were unlikely to be adopted.
3. The projections assumed a slow decline of inflation that seemed inconsistent with the administration's ambitions in that respect.
4. The projections assumed a decline of interest rates that might be inconsistent with the projected decline of the inflation rate.
5. The projections assumed a rate of real economic growth in the period

1980–5 that was high relative to the experience of the preceding 15 years.

6. The projections assumed that the economy would rise steadily from 1980 to 1985, with no intervening recession. A recession would increase the budget deficit and add significantly to the projected federal debt on interest charges after the recession had passed. That is, an intervening recession would increase the deficit that would remain even after the recession was over.

One may ask, then, why the Reagan administration proposed such a vulnerable plan. The answer lies in attitudes toward defense, toward taxes, and, most interestingly, toward the deficit.

The Reagan team obviously took very seriously the lag in U.S. defense spending after the Vietnam War, and even the rundown in part of our permanent forces during the war. They were impressed by the Soviet buildup in the 1970s and regarded the Carter response to that as belated and halfhearted. Also, some members of the team thought that public support for increasing defense expenditures would be short-lived and that as much as possible should be achieved quickly, before sentiments changed.

On the tax side, the Reagan plan went far beyond the conventional wisdom that had been shared by conservatives and liberals alike. The conventional wisdom called for concentrating reductions on those taxes considered most harmful to productivity growth, which meant the taxes on the return to business investment. This reduction was to be achieved by increasing the tax credit for investment and accelerating allowable depreciation charges. The Reagan plan added to this a large cut in individual income taxes, initially in the form of a 30 percent reduction of all individual income tax rates. Some people in the Reagan circle believed that these cuts in individual income tax rates would have an important effect in promoting work, savings, and investment, as well as in reducing tax avoidance. Also, they and others believed that winning an election on a program of reducing taxes only for business would be difficult, especially for a Republican who would have to bear the burden of his party's probusiness image. Finally, even if they could get elected on such a tax program, they might be unable to push it through the Congress. The history of previous efforts to enact procapital tax changes showed that they always had to be "bought" by more popular tax reductions.

Still, proponents of a big defense buildup and a big tax cut had to contend with the presence of a budget deficit that most people already considered too large. Various members of the Reagan team dealt with this problem in various ways: Some had confidence that the tax cut they were proposing would generate a rate of economic growth even larger than the budget assumed, so that there would be more revenue than assumed; others counted on the fear of a deficit to force spending down, with the result that cutting taxes would not increase the deficit but only reduce spending; and some were not concerned about the deficit – they denied the usual claims that bigger deficits would cause either inflation or recession and thought that the important objectives were to get spending down and taxes down.

The execution and consequences of this budget program cannot be fully understood, however, without some details of the other part of the macroeconomic plan – monetary policy. The relation of the Reagan administration to monetary policy was, of course, different from its relation to budget policy. The administration was not required, or even expected, to enunciate a monetary policy. That was the province of the Federal Reserve. Yet monetary policy was crucial to the Reagan team's strategy. That was to be the chief instrument for getting inflation down. Mr. Reagan and some of his supporters had an interest in the gold standard, and there was a subdued reference to gold in the Republican platform of 1980. But gold never became a part of the Reagan policy. In 1981, on the initiative of several members of Congress, a commission was established to consider the possible role of gold in the U.S. monetary system. The administration officials who served on the commission made no significant recommendations.

The Reagan policy, as announced at the beginning of 1981, was that the rate of growth of the money supply should move steadily on a declining path until it stabilized at a level consistent with reasonable price stability. The money supply was, at that time, generally understood to be M1 – the narrow definition of money consisting of currency and checkable deposits. There was also an implication that the growth of M1, which had been running at around 6 or 7 percent per annum, should be cut in half over the course of the next four or five years.

The Reagan administration's expectations from this program may be summarized as follows: The inflation rate would be substantially reduced – from the double digits of 1979 and 1980 to 4 percent or less by 1985. The country's military strength would be rebuilt. The growth of productivity, which had been sluggish since 1973, would be revived by the tax changes (as well as by a reduction in government regulations). With productivity rising more rapidly, real output and real income per capita would also rise more rapidly; this would occur with steadily declining unemployment, except for a brief period of softness in the economy in early 1981. This belief that disinflation could be accomplished without even an interim rise in unemployment was one of the most striking features of Reagan economics. Some members of his team simply repeated the conventional wisdom and the statistical evidence on which it was based, holding that a transition to a lower inflation rate would involve a temporary rise in the unemployment rate. Others, while not denying the conventional wisdom, believed that the productivity surge generated by their program could lower costs rapidly and avoid a rise in unemployment.

The evolution of policy in practice

President Reagan was remarkably successful in obtaining enactment of his fiscal program in 1981. The president recommended a 25 percent across-the-board cut in all individual income tax rates, to be phased in over three years, rather than the 30 percent cut that had been discussed during the campaign. He also proposed accelerated depreciation and expansion of the investment credit. Congress enacted these essential features of his program. In addition, Congress cut the top marginal rate of individual income tax from 70 percent to 50 percent immediately and, what is more important, introduced indexing for inflation to take effect beginning in 1985. The president accepted these additions and considered them his.

Congress also approved the enlarged defense program and most but not all of the proposed cuts in nondefense programs that were included in the original Reagan package. Significantly, however, a presidential proposal for rather small reductions in Social Security benefits was overwhelmingly rejected by Congress.

The Reagan budget was enacted in the summer of 1981 without much public concern about the consequences for the deficit. However, by the fall of that year increasing concern was being expressed over it. This concern was reflected in a falling bond market, to which the administration responded by proposing a small deficit-reduction package that included some minor tax increases, euphemistically called "revenue enhancements." None of these were enacted.

The alarm bell about the deficit finally sounded in December 1981 when reports began to surface that the deficit for fiscal 1982 would exceed $100 billion – a figure never seen before. Moreover, 1982 did not look like an exception. Deficits in excess of $100 billion stretched out for years in the future. It appeared that the $100 billion-plus deficit was "structural" – meaning that it would persist even in a prolonged period of high employment.

All of the negative possibilities that had existed when the Reagan plan was first announced had become realities. The economy had fallen into a recession, which was increasing the debt. The prospects for longer-run growth had worsened. Interest rates were not falling as expected. Congress had not accepted all of the expenditure cuts recommended by the administration, and there was little prospect for the additional cuts that the administration had promised to recommend.

Although the appearance of a deficit of $100 billion or more was shocking, there was no clear and agreed view as to the consequences of such a deficit. Some thought the deficit threatened to revive inflation. A more common opinion was that the deficit was depressing the economy and would prevent or delay recovery from the recession then under way. Ironically, this opinion was shared by Keynesian economists who had typically regarded budget deficits as stimulating to the economy.

The opinion that probably had the most support from economic analysis was that the deficit would slow down the rate of economic growth by slowing down the increase in the stock of productive capital. The deficit then in prospect would be 4 or 5 percent of GNP, a ratio not seen since World War II. Net private saving in the United States, both personal and corporate, had been running around 7 percent of GNP. If an amount of saving equal to 4 or 5 percent was to be absorbed in financing the federal deficit, the savings available to finance net private investment in the United States would be very small, and so would net private investment. Economists' estimates differed as to the extent that crowding out of private investment would retard the growth of productivity and total output. Most discussions seemed to assume, however, that the effect on economic growth would be substantial. Moreover, the administration could hardly dispute that crowding out investment would have a substantial negative effect on growth, because its tax policy had been rationalized on the premise that increasing investment would make a dramatic contribution to economic growth.

The prospect of very large budget deficits raised, for the first time during the Reagan administration, the question of the relationship between the fiscal plans and the international economic position of the United States. The suggestion was offered that the deficit would not reduce private investment by an equal amount because the deficit would attract foreign capital to the United States. That is, the increase in the deficit would *tend* to raise interest rates in the United States, which would induce foreigners to invest in the United States. The amount of capital available for private investment is equal to net private saving in the United States, minus the government deficit, plus the inflow of capital from abroad. To the extent that the increase in the deficit increased the inflow of foreign capital, it would not crowd out investment in the United States.

This argument was belittled when first raised at the end of 1981. The United States had never had a capital inflow of more than $15 billion in any year. To rely on capital inflow to offset a significant part of a budget deficit exceeding $100 billion seemed unrealistic. Moreover, if there should be a very large capital inflow there would also be a very large excess of imports over exports. That would provoke strong protectionist pressures and steps would be taken to hold down imports. This discussion was, of course, a hint of what was actually to happen.

Other reasons were advanced, especially by defenders of the administration and of its 1981 tax cut, for not worrying much about the deficit. One was the so-called Ricardian proposition – which Ricardo himself never embraced – that an increased government deficit would itself call for an equal increase in private saving. The argument was that an increase in deficits implied an increase in future tax liabilities, or a decrease in future after-tax incomes. This would induce people to save now to build up a stock of earning assets with which to pay their future taxes or sustain their future after-tax incomes. Another argument was that the tax cuts made in 1981 would increase the after-tax income from saving and induce an increase in private saving sufficient to offset the absorption of savings by the deficit.

The emergence of the large deficit, with possible large political as well as economic implications, set off a vigorous effort by econometricians to discover, empirically, whether budget deficits raise interest rates. The results were inconclusive – some studies saying that they did and others that they did not. One reason for the difficulty in finding empirical proof was that there had been little experience, except in wartime, with deficits of the size being faced in the 1980s. The effects of deficits on interest rates could not be reliably isolated from all the other influences on interest rates. In any case, the effect on interest rates was only a proxy for the real question, which was the effect on private investment. Conceivably, the effect on interest rates could have been small and the effect on investment large.

The deficit was a great embarrassment to the administration. Nothing the Reagan team, or preceding spokesmen in the Republican Party, had ever said prepared the country for the possibility that this administration would have the largest deficit in history. Their reaction was twofold. First, the administration blamed the deficit on the failure of Congress to follow their recommendations for cutting expenditures and tried to use the fear of deficits to put pressure on Congress to cut more. Second, the administration tried to cast doubt on the idea that the deficit caused high interest rates or, later, that it caused the big balance of payments deficit.

The effort to deal with the deficit dominated budget policy, and indeed all economic policy, from the beginning of 1982 until the end of 1985, and will probably continue to do so for some time to come. Whatever it really thought, the administration could not afford to appear unconcerned about the deficit. The opposition in Congress could not afford to miss the opportunity to challenge the Republican administration on the deficit issue. And even some Republicans in Congress felt the need to stake out their own positions as deficit reducers, independent of the president.

The parties differed greatly, however, in their preferred means for dealing with the deficit. The president was determined not to raise taxes and not to cut the defense program; he was left, therefore, concentrating on cutting nondefense expenditures. The congressional liberals, mainly Democrats, supported social programs and wanted to cut defense. A third group in Congress, mainly moderate Republicans, shared the president's concern with defense but also considered some of his proposed nondefense cuts either undesirable or politically unfeasible. Their position was that a package for reducing the deficit would have to include some revenue increases. Thus, there were three options for reducing the deficit – cutting nondefense expenditures, cutting defense, and raising taxes. In the end all of these were done – and the large deficit remained.

A number of measures intended to raise revenues were enacted in 1982, 1983, and 1984. The 1982 revenue increase was initiated by congressional leaders and was at first resisted by the president. He later accepted the increase as part of a package that would also include expenditure cuts. The alleged failure of Congress to deliver on these promised expenditure cuts subsequently became part of the standard argument against increasing taxes, although whether or not Congress actually fulfilled its part of the bargain is still in dispute.[2] The 1982 act was later estimated to have raised 1984 revenues by $36 billion. Also in 1982 gasoline excise taxes were raised, with an expected 1984 revenue yield of $4.2 billion. Amendments to the Social Security Act in 1983 were expected to raise 1984 revenues by $1.8 billion and 1988 revenues by $9.3 billion. In 1984, a Deficit Reduction Act was passed that would have raised less than $1 billion in 1984 but almost $25 billion in 1988. There were other, smaller changes in revenue legislation, some raising and some reducing the revenues.

All in all, by the end of 1984, Congress had enacted revenue increases yielding $54 billion, or 1.5 percent of GNP for fiscal 1984. Nevertheless, revenue in 1984 was 18.6 percent of GNP rather than the 19.3 percent of GNP that the Reagan administration had forecast it would be after the original tax reduction in 1981. This shortfall of revenue despite the subsequent tax increases had three causes. First, inflation was less than had been predicted in 1981, so that the government did not reap the increase in the ratio of revenues to GNP that would result from inflationary bracket creep. The price level rose 31 percent between 1980 and 1984, whereas an increase of 35 percent had been predicted. Second, real output rose less than had been predicted in 1981, so that the government did not get the increase in the ratio of revenues to GNP that would result from real income growth. Between 1980 and 1984, real GNP rose only 9.6 percent, whereas an increase of 15.4 percent had been predicted. Third, the tendency for increasing amounts of income to escape taxation by the use of available legal means seems to have been underestimated. The basic fact was that the 1981 plan had seriously overestimated the revenue that would be yielded with its recommended tax program, and the subsequent tax increases did not fully compensate for the revenue deficiency that resulted from that overestimate.

The second part of the effort to reduce the budget deficit was cutting the defense program. The Reagan program of 1981 had called for annual defense expenditures to rise by 74 percent, in real terms, between 1980 and 1986. As the program stood at the end of 1985, after the annual cuts by Congress, the increase would be only 31 percent. The initial Reagan plan called for defense expenditures equal to 7.1 percent of GNP in 1986. By the end of 1985 it appeared that the ratio would be less than 6.5 percent. But since real GNP would be lower in 1986 than had been estimated originally, real defense expenditures would be about 20 percent below the amount originally estimated. In fact, defense expenditures would be closer to the track projected in Carter's final budget than to the track of Reagan's original budget. It could be argued, however (and was), that, if Carter had been reelected, actual defense expenditures would have been below the track that Carter had projected in January 1981. In sum, cutting the defense program made a small contribution to cutting the budget deficit, but at the price of a substantial reduction in real defense outlays.

As already explained, what I have described as the highly vulnerable Reagan program for bringing the budget into balance by 1984 called for a sharp reduction in nondefense expenditures, other than interest. As a share of GNP, these expenditures were projected to decline from 15.8 percent in 1980 to 11.3 percent in 1984, in contrast to the 14.7 percent projected for 1984 in the last Carter budget. Every year, the Reagan administration engaged in a struggle with Congress over cutting the nondefense part of the budget; and every year the administration won some of this struggle and lost some of it. As it turned out, the expenditure cuts won in this struggle barely offset the built-in increase in the costs of the ongoing programs, mainly Social Security and Medicare, which had been underestimated in the initial Reagan program.

The result of the annual struggles over nondefense spending was that, as a share of GNP, this category (still excluding interest) fell from 15.8 percent in 1980 to 14.3 percent in 1984, well over the 11.3 percent planned by Reagan and not much below the 14.7 percent projected by Carter. The initial Reagan plan had called for a decline of about 15 percent in real terms in nondefense, noninterest spending between 1980 and 1984. In fact, the level of this spending remained approximately constant, as Carter had projected.

Since the deficit turned out to be much larger than the initial Reagan plan had estimated and interest rates were much higher than assumed, federal interest payments were also much higher relative to GNP than had been provided for in the plan. In fiscal 1984 interest was 3.1 percent of GNP, compared with the initial projection of 1.7 percent.[3]

Table 3.2. *Percentage of GNP,*
fiscal 1984

	Initial plan	Actual
Receipts	19.3	18.6
Expenditures	19.5	23.8
Defense	6.5	6.4
Interest	1.7	3.1
Other	11.3	14.3
Deficit	0.2	5.2

The difference between the Reagan initial budget plan and the outcome up to 1984 is summarized in Table 3.2.

The other half of the fiscal-monetary policy – namely, money – should now be brought into the picture. In the early part of 1981, the rise in the money supply seemed quite consistent with the new administration's strategy of gradually reducing the rate of monetary growth in order to achieve a gradual reduction in the inflation rate. Toward the end of the year the rate of increase of the money supply, M1, slowed. But at first this did not cause much concern. The precise path required by the administration's strategy had never been spelled out. Whatever the path was, some temporary deviations from it had to be expected and accepted.

Concern arose as the slow growth of money continued into 1982. Also, and even more worrisome, the rate of growth of nominal GNP was slowing down even more than could be explained by the slower growth of M1. Indeed, the economy was falling into a recession. This meant that velocity was not rising at the pace then considered normal, around 3 percent a year. In fact, velocity was declining.

Serious questions were thus raised for monetary policy. Was it desirable to get up to a rate of monetary growth more consistent with a decelerating but nonrecessionary rate of growth in nominal GNP? Should monetary growth be accelerated even more to compensate for the recent lag? Should it be accelerated still more, perhaps permanently, to compensate for the slower growth of velocity?

One view of these questions, as they looked in the middle of 1982, may be seen in the following paragraphs I wrote then:

In the period since the end of 1979, the rate of inflation has slowed, from 8.6 percent during 1979 to 5.3 percent in the second quarter of 1982. During this same period total output has fluctuated but has made no net gain, being 1 percent lower in the second quarter of 1982 than in the fourth quarter of 1979. Essentially, even though irregularly, the inflation has slowed as the rise of nominal GNP has slowed.

The first question raised by these developments relates to velocity. How is the slow velocity growth of the past three quarters to be interpreted? Is it a random or cyclical fluctuation, which should not be matched by an acceleration of monetary growth because speeding up monetary growth would push nominal GNP above its desired path when velocity returned to its 3 percent trend? Or is it a more durable change, which requires more rapid growth of the money supply if we are to get on the desired nominal GNP path?

This is a large and critical question. In the past three quarters the velocity of M1 fell at an annual rate of 3 percent rather than rising at the 3 percent that is about the historical average. If the growth of the money supply were to be adapted to a 3 percent annual decline of velocity rather than to a 3 percent rise, that would be a big change indeed. But the short-term path of velocity has historically been quite irregular. The slowdown of velocity growth in the past three quarters was unusually large, but more evidence would seem to be required to show that there was a new trend. The argument is sometimes made that the trend of approximately 3 percent per year velocity growth was observed in a period when interest rates and prices were rising which made people want to hold less money in relation to their incomes. On this basis one might expect now to enter a period in which velocity grows more slowly as disinflation proceeds. In countries where there has been an abrupt end to hyperinflation, the demand for money has increased sharply (velocity has decreased sharply). But the connection has not been so clear here, asked from very short-term fluctuations. Velocity has risen at less than its trend rate since the end of 1979, although interest rates are as high now as they were then. If the basic strategy is to stick to the path of monetary restraint unless there is *clear* evidence that the trend of velocity has changed, so as to maximize the predictability of policy, the case for accelerating monetary growth does not seem strong.[4]

These questions were resolved in August 1982 when the Federal Reserve decided to embark upon a course of rapid monetary expansion – leaving behind the policy of a steadily declining rate of monetray growth. This shift was motivated in part by the international debt crisis and in part by the depth of the recession. In August the unemployment rate reached 9.9 percent, the highest rate in 40 years.

From the third quarter of 1982 until the third quarter of 1983, M1 increased by 13.1 percent. The Federal Reserve announced at the beginning of 1983 that it was paying less attention than formerly to M1 as a target of monetary policy. It cited changes in the regulation of interest payments on various kinds of bank deposits as so altering the historical relation between M1 and the behavior of the economy as to make M1 an unreliable guide to policy. The persistence of this high rate of monetary growth became more worrisome, however, as the months passed, especially as nominal GNP was again rising rapidly. Nominal GNP has increased only 3.1 percent from the fourth quarter of 1981 to the fourth quarter of 1982. But in the first quarter of 1983 it rose at an annual rate of 7.0 percent and the rate exceeded 10 percent in the final three quarters.

Reacting to concern over possible overheating of the economy, the Federal

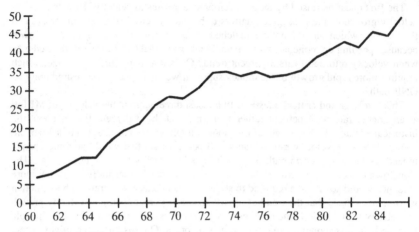

Figure 3.1   Percentage change in M1 over five-year spans.

Reserve in July 1983 resumed its attention to targeting the growth of M1 at a slower rate. From the third quarter of 1983 to the fourth quarter of 1984, M1 increased at an annual rate of 5.5 percent. However, by the third quarter of 1984, the rate of increase in nominal GNP had slowed again. After having increased at an annual rate of 11.2 percent during 1983 and the first half of 1984, M1 increased at a rate of only 6.4 percent during the second half of 1984. Accordingly, the policy of steadily decelerating the rate of monetary growth was again put on the shelf and rapid expansion was resumed. From the fourth quarter of 1984 to the fourth quarter of 1985, M1 increased by 11.5 percent.

Clearly, the monetary policy of the Reagan period had not been one of gradually decelerating growth of the money supply, as initially conceived by the administration. In fact, the rise in M1 from December 1980 to December 1985 had been by far the highest five-year rise of the past two decades, and probably the highest since the Civil War (see Figure 3.1). Moreover, the short-term movements in the money supply were quite variable. They went through four major episodes – deceleration to the summer of 1982, rapid expansion to the spring of 1983, deceleration to the fall of 1984, and rapid expansion to the fall of 1985.

The behavior of the administration's monetary policy could be described as old-fashioned, eclectic, countercyclical leaning against the wind. Money was slowed down when the economy was "felt" by the Federal Reserve to be rising too rapidly, and money was expanded when the economy was "felt" by the Federal Reserve to be rising too slowly. The whole exercise was

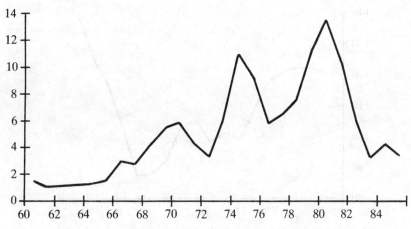

Figure 3.2   Yearly percentage change in Consumer Price Index.

accomplished in an environment of money-supply targets suggesting a monetarist policy. Furthermore, when the Federal Reserve was in its restrictive phase, it lived by the targets, more or less; when in its expansionary phase, it disregarded or revised them. One might say that the monetarist rule was invoked when useful to justify restrictionism but otherwise downplayed.

Results of the policy

At the beginning of the Reagan term, getting inflation down was obviously the most conspicuous, if not necessarily the most important, objective. Considerable success was achieved toward this end, as can be seen in Figure 3.2. By 1983, the inflation rate, as measured by the Consumer Price Index, had fallen to 3 to 4 percent, a rate not previously seen for almost 20 years, except briefly during the Nixon price controls.

When coupled with the rapid increase in the money supply in the period 1980–5, this decline in the inflation rate was a paradox, especially for an administration that tended to identify anti-inflation policy with restrictive monetary policy. Nevertheless, monetary policy played a large role, though not an exclusive one, in this decline. Another important factor to consider, however, is the unmeasurable but real element of expectations, always an important factor in the inflation story.

The inflation experience came in two episodes. The first was the decline in the inflation rate from 13.5 percent during 1980 to 3.2 percent during 1983. The second was the stability of that rate after the middle of 1983.

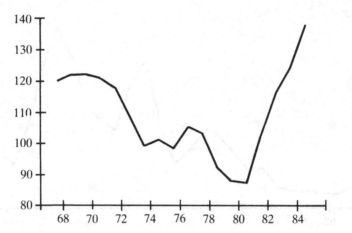

Figure 3.3   Dollar exchange rate, trade-weighted index. March 1973 = 100.

Several factors were at work during the earlier period:

1. This was a period, until April 1982, of declining monetary growth, which contributed to the decline in the rate of increase of aggregate demand (nominal GNP).

2. The rate of increase in nominal demand fell even more than the rate of increase in money. That is, the rate of increase in velocity fell. This is a usual cyclical phenomenon. In 1981 and 1982, however, the slowdown of velocity was exceptionally great, and remained something of a mystery. The velocity decline can be explained at least in part by the decline in inflation rates and interest rates, but that also involves in part explaining the decline in the inflation rate by the decline in the inflation rate.

3. The decline in velocity, as well as changes in the behavior of business and labor, seemed to reflect a belief that a fundamental change had occurred in the tone of economic policy. The president's firmness in dealing with a strike by air traffic controllers contributed to this view. The combination of Reagan and Volker seemed to generate stronger belief that the government would persist in fighting inflation than previous combinations had generated. Some of the benefits attributed to "shock treatment" were achieved without any intention to administer a shock – namely, a change in expectations and attitudes.

4. The exchange rate of the dollar rose sharply after 1981 (see Figure 3.3) for reasons that will be discussed later. This affected the infla-

tion rate in two ways. First, it reduced the dollar cost of imports. Second, it subjected American industries in tradable goods sectors to deflationary pressure in addition to, and probably more enduring than, that resulting from the recession. This contributed to the realization on the part of both management and workers that they could no longer count on being able to pass on all cost increases.

5. Oil prices were not rising rapidly in the 1980–3 period. Whereas energy prices had contributed disproportionately to the rise of the price level from 1978 to 1980, they contributed disproportionately to the slowdown of inflation after 1980.

Although a number of other factors were involved, the 1980–3 decline in the inflation rate was basically a decline associated with a deep recession. Early claims by some Reagan enthusiasts that this time inflation would be overcome without a rise of unemployment were unfounded. There was no sign of the spurt in productivity that some had counted on to cut costs without a recession.

Still, the country had been through declines in the inflation rate during recessions before, and the question was whether inflation would speed up again when the economy recovered. That question was tested during the rapid recovery that began in mid-1983, and the surprise was that inflation remained in the 3–4 percent range. Several factors accounted for this result:

1. The Federal Reserve reduced money growth in mid-1983 and kept the recovery from blowing off into inflation after a high level of economic activity had been reached. Although the economy rose rapidly from mid-1983 to the end of 1984, unemployment never fell below 7 percent, and the rate of increase in nominal GNP, which had been 11.7 percent per annum from the first quarter of 1983 to the second quarter of 1984, was only 5.9 percent from the second quarter of 1984 to the third quarter of 1985. Some people complained that the recovery was choked off before full employment was reached. Whether or not that was true, it *was* restrained before inflation was revived.

2. The dollar continued to rise during most of the recovery period, with the anti-inflationary consequences already described.

3. Oil prices continued to fall.

4. Some of the changes in expectations about inflation that occurred during the recession and were reinforced by the public perceptions of Reagan and Volker persisted into the period of recovery.

After inflation, the second big economic problem for the Reagan administration was the slowdown in the growth of productivity, commonly defined as output per hour. Here the record is much less satisfactory than with respect

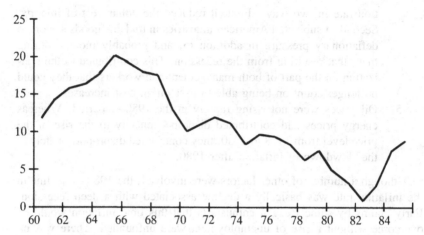

Figure 3.4 Percentage change in output per hour, private business sector, over five-year spans.

to inflation. Actual output per hour worked went through its usual cyclical pattern. That is, the rate of increase fell, and for some quarters turned negative, during the recession and then rose more rapidly during the recovery. A rough attempt to abstract from these cyclical movements is shown in Figure 3.4, which compares changes in output per hour over five-year periods. The increase in the five-year period that ended in 1985 was much higher than in the years that ended in the recession, but also much lower than in the five-year period during most of the 1960s and 1970s. This suggests that, at best, we have regained the disappointing growth rate of the late 1970s.

A more sophisticated attempt to disentangle the trend in productivity growth from its cyclical fluctuations has been made in the study by Edward F. Denison already cited. By Denison's calculations, the rate of productivity growth from 1979 to 1982 was even lower than from 1973 to 1979 and much lower than earlier in the postwar period. Even if productivity growth increased in 1983 to 1985, an extraordinary surge would have been required to bring the rate of productivity increase back to the postwar average or even to the 1973–9 average.

In the initial Reagan plan, a major contribution to stimulating productivity growth was to come from the encouragement to saving and to business investment that would be provided by the 1981 tax cut. But the fact is that private saving did not rise, relative to GNP. The expectation of an increase in saving had not been solidly based from the start. The savings rate had been quite stable in the past and numerous studies had shown the savings rate not to be very responsive to the after-tax return on savings.

Table 3.3. *Net savings and investment*
(percentage of GNP)

	1960–9	1970–9	1985
Net saving available to finance private investment	7.2	7.0	5.8
Private saving	8.1	8.1	6.4
Federal surplus	−0.3	−1.7	−5.0
State and local surplus	0.0	0.8	1.5
Foreign capital inflow	−0.6	−0.2	2.9
Net private investment	7.1	6.9	5.8
Non-residential fixed investment	3.4	3.3	3.3
Residential fixed investment	2.7	2.8	2.3
Inventory increase	1.0	0.8	0.2
Statistical discrepancy	0.1	0.1	0.0

Whereas the savings rate did not increase, the federal deficit did increase, as has already been explained. The rise in the federal deficit was partly offset by a rise in state and local government surpluses. Nevertheless, the combined government deficits were, relative to GNP, at unprecedented peacetime levels. Therefore, the net savings available to finance private investment, after financing the government deficits, were extremely low.

At the same time, the tax changes made in 1981 were encouraging to business investment. However, if the decline in available savings was not to reduce net business investment, there would have to be either a reduction in net residential investment or an inflow of foreign capital, or both. As it turned out, there was a large inflow of foreign capital. This phenomenon, and its consequences, were the most surprising developments in the American economy in the first five years of the Reagan administration. The low level of domestic saving available for private investment, coupled with the incentives in the 1981 tax law, made the United States an attractive place to invest. Also, economic stagnation in Europe discouraged investment there, and the credit problems of the developing countries stopped the flow of capital to them from the developed world. The net result was an enormous inflow of capital, equal in 1985 to 2.9 percent of GNP. This in turn permitted business investment to go on at approximately the ratio to GNP that had been experienced in other years of high economic activity, despite the large federal budget deficit.

The financing of net investment in the United States in 1984, compared with that of earlier periods, is shown in Table 3.3.

Although the capital inflow was essential to sustaining the rate of business investment, a number of problems accompanied it. In the first place, about half of the net increase in the capital stock in the United States during the period belonged to foreigners, and the income earned by this capital would be the income of foreigners, not of Americans. Second, since the inflow of capital was in part a response to conditions in Europe and Latin America, the possibility existed that a change in those conditions would drastically reduce or even reverse the flow.

The immediate and obvious problem was the effect of the capital inflow on U.S. international trade. The capital inflow had to be matched by a net inflow of goods and services – commonly called a U.S. trade "deficit." The mechanism by which this matching was brought about was the exchange rate of the dollar. The demand for dollars by foreigners wanting to invest here raised the exchange rate of the dollar. This raised the price of U.S. goods in foreign markets and lowered the price of foreign goods in U.S. markets, depressing U.S. exports and expanding U.S. imports. The dollar exchange rate had to rise enough to create a trade deficit (more accurately, a deficit on current account) equal to the capital inflow.

This process, of course, injured the U.S. industries that had the greatest stake in exports or were most subject to foreign competition – essentially the industries producing goods that entered most into international trade. Employment in these industries grew less than the average, and in some cases declined. Management and labor in these industries naturally complained, and tended to blame their difficulties on the "unfair" politics of other governments. There was some of that, as always, but it was a small part of the problem. The basic problem – if it should be called a problem at all – was that the policies adopted in 1981 required a shift in the composition of U.S. output. The 1981 policies were intended to raise the devotion of output to defense, to investment, and, via the general tax cut, to consumption. The only way this could succeed, once the economy reached a high level of activity, was to draw more resources from abroad, by net imports, and this implied a shrinkage of certain U.S. industries. Had it been impossible to increase net imports, some other adjustments would have been necessary. In view of the stickiness of the U.S. savings rate, that would probably have meant a shrinkage of U.S. investment industries – especially the construction and equipment industries.

As the trade deficit increased, in 1984 and 1985 (Figure 3.5) an argument commonly heard was that the deficit was causing the loss of many jobs in the United States – three million being the number usually cited. On the basis of this argument, proposals were made, with strong public and congressional support, for severe protectionist measures. In fact, the trade deficit did not reduce total employment in the United States, but only somewhat shifted its industrial location. During the period of the emerging and growing trade deficit, from 1980 to 1985, employment in the United States increased by

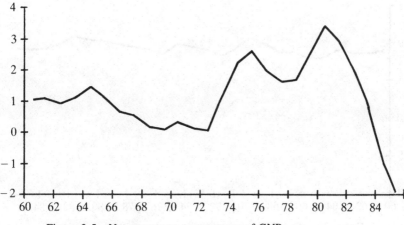

Figure 3.5   Net exports as a percentage of GNP.

eight million. The president resisted the most extensive of the protectionist measures and, at least to the end of 1985, fended them off. However, some more specific measures, affecting steel and textiles, were adopted.

The motivation for the 1981 tax cut was not only to promote savings, investment, and economic growth. Its proponents wanted to give private citizens control over a larger share of their earnings simply on the ground that people who earned income were entitled to it. If achievement of this objective was measured by the share of the GNP collected in federal revenues, it was certainly achieved (see Figure 3.6). But that is not an entirely satisfactory measure. The deficit took earnings from private use as surely as the taxes did. The deficit was the assertion of a claim to collect taxes in the future. Thus, some appraisers of the Reagan fiscal policy prefer to call the deficit just another tax. However, it is not just *another* tax; it is a *different* tax, seemingly voluntary and creating an asset – a federal security – of which people are more conscious than they are of the implied future tax liabilities. Thus the deficit probably has different economic effects than other taxes do. But, like other taxes, it is a subtraction from the earnings of private citizens.

In this sense, the achievement of the Reagan administration's objective of reducing government earned income must be measured by taxes plus the deficit, which amounts to total expenditures. On this score, the objective has not been achieved. Total expenditures during the Reagan administration have been higher, as a share of GNP, than ever before in peacetime (Figure 3.7). The cuts achieved in nondefense spending, other than interest, were not sufficient to offset the rise in defense spending and interest payments.

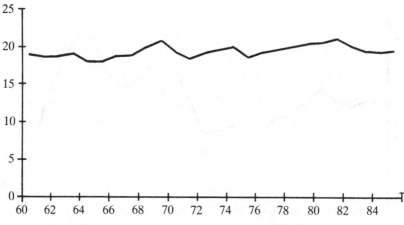

Figure 3.6   Federal revenue as a percentage of GNP.

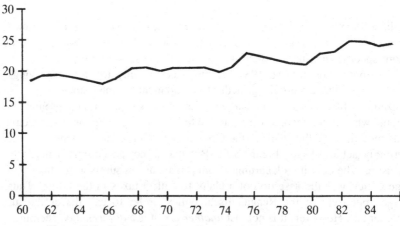

Figure 3.7   Federal outlays as a percentage of GNP.

Present position and prospects

The state of the economy, by the end of 1985, may be summarized as follows:

1. The rate of inflation had been substantially reduced. Even after this
    reduction, however, the rate remained at 3 to 4 percent, which 15
    years ago would have seemed intolerably high.
2. There was not solid evidence of any durable noncyclical upturn in the
    rate of growth in productivity.

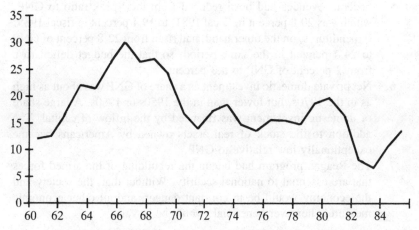

Figure 3.8   Percentage change in real GNP over five-year spans.

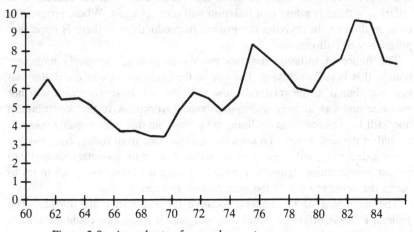

Figure 3.9   Annual rate of unemployment.

3. Total output had increased substantially from the recessionary lows
    of 1982, but the increase over the five-year period 1980–5 was not as
    large as it had been over the five-year spans during most of the 1960s
    and 1970s (Figure 3.8).
4. The unemployment rate, 7.0 percent, was just about where it had
    been at the beginning of President Reagan's term and has been ex-
    ceeded since the Depression of the 1930s only in the recession years
    1975 and 1976 (Figure 3.9).

5. Federal revenues had been reduced from their peak ratio to GNP, which was 20.8 percent in fiscal 1981, to 19.1 percent in fiscal 1985. Expenditures, on the other hand, had risen from 22.8 percent of GNP to 24.4 percent in the same period, so that the budget deficit rose from 2 percent of GNP to 5.3 percent.

6. Net private domestic investment as a share of GNP was about as high as in the 1970s, but lower than in the 1950s or 1960s. A large share of domestic investment was financed by the inflow of capital. The addition to the stock of real assets owned by Americans became exceptionally low relative to GNP.

7. The Reagan program had begun the rebuilding of the armed forces that are essential to national security. Without that, the society and the economy would be in constant danger, and all other economic measures, however beneficial, would be in vain.

The outlook for the future of the American economy is a compound of fear and hope. Where the most progress has been made – in the reduction of inflation – there is a fear that inflation will turn up again. Where progress is most in doubt – in reviving the growth of productivity – there is hope that progress will still come.

The future of inflation depends mainly on policy, expecially monetary policy, that is still uncertain. The rise in the exchange rate of the dollar that has contributed to the relatively low inflation rate in recent years will not continue and has already undergone some reversal. A further contribution may still be realized from declining oil prices, but that will probably come to an end in the near future. To keep the inflation rate from rising, and possibly to get it declining, will depend on the willingness of the monetary authority to persist in restraining demand. This may require not being too quick to try to pump the economy out of the next recession when it comes.

The intentions of the Federal Reserve on this matter are unclear. The Federal Reserve offers no indication, and even if it did, one could not tell for how long its indication would be relevant, since the Board of Governors' membership is in flux. But insofar as one can infer a policy from recent behavior, one can say that the Federal Reserve will resist a rise in inflation above its recent 3–4 percent rate, unless that rise is accompanied by high or rising unemployment, but will feel no great need to try to get the rate down. At the same time, concern can be observed in the country about what some would call a disinflationary policy. Concern is expressed about the debt burdens of farmers, businesses, and developing countries, with the suggestion that the world economy would be better off if the United States had a more expansionary monetary policy. Some dissatisfaction is voiced that the unemployment rate has not been pushed down below 7 percent and this, too, is blamed on an insufficiently expansionary monetary policy. Moreover, some people seem to believe that a more expansionary monetary policy would help solve the country's budget difficulties. Whether the Federal Reserve will respond to any of these pressures and interests is uncertain. On balance, however, more inflation seems likely.

Opinions about the prospects for productivity growth are sharply divided. Although I have said that there is little or no evidence of any upturn so far, some people do see signs of that. And those who see evidence of a pickup are optimistic that there will be more in the future. They point to a likely increase in capital investment under the tax changes made in 1981, tax incentives for research and development, the increased age and experience of the work force, and the benefits of a lower inflation rate. Others claim that all these favorable factors have already been at work for several years, with no visible net results.

In recent years more of the discussion of productivity and of policy to promote productivity growth has focused on the rate of net investment and on government initiatives, especially tax and budget initiatives, to affect investment. As Denison has pointed out, this discussion has tended to exaggerate both the contribution of investment to growth and the contribution of public policy to investment. But, given the size of the federal deficit that we start with, one of the most obviously relevant policy variables is the deficit. A reduction in the deficit would increase the domestic savings available for private investment, and the relative size of this effect could be large. But this effect would probably be offset to some extent by a contrary change in the capital inflow, as the effect of the rising budget deficit had been offset earlier. The reduction in the deficit will reduce the capital inflow, lower the exchange rate of the dollar, reduce net imports, and increase net investment in the United States *owned by Americans*. Whether it reduces *total* net investment in the United States or reduces consumption or government purchases of goods and services will depend upon *how* the deficit is reduced.

Will the budget deficit actually be reduced? Late in 1985 Congress enacted a law (Gramm–Rudman–Hollings) intended to reduce the deficit to zero by 1991. Whether this will work, whether the government will adhere to it, and even whether it is constitutional are all unanswered questions at this time. In any case, the enactment of Gramm–Rudman–Hollings reflects a strong feeling that the public wants the deficit reduced, and if that particular mechanism is not effective, some other will be found. The best bet is that the deficit will be reduced, if not to zero at least enough to stabilize the ratio of debt to GNP and to keep the ratio of federal interest to GNP from exploding.

Probably the most realistic thing to say about the American economy and economic policy is that the economy is strong enough to withstand much folly and that the political process is strong enough to avoid disastrous folly. We may seem to be headed for the edge of the cliff, but we draw back in time: We have drawn back from the edge of disastrous inflation. We have drawn back from the edge of disastrous deterioration of our armed forces. We will draw back from the edge of disastrous budget deficits. The future is uncertain, but the range of uncertainty does not include disaster.

Notes

1 Edward F. Denison, *Trends in American Economy, 1929 to 1982*, Brookings Institution, 1985.
2 David Stockman, in his book *The Triumph of Politics* (Harper & Row, 1986), maintains that Congress did its part but the administration did not.
3 All of these calculations use the GNP estimates as they were before the 1986 revision in order to preserve comparability with the budget estimates made in 1981. The new GNP estimates are 3–3½ percent above the old ones for the years 1980–4.
4 Herbert Stein, "Problems in the Conduct of Monetary Policy," *AEI Economist* (July 1982), pp. 6–7.

CHAPTER 4

Repercussions of grand experiments in U.S. economic policy

ROGER E. BRINNER

Introduction

The past decade has seen major changes in U.S. macroeconomic and micro-economic policies. The large magnitude of these changes reflects fundamental changes in philosophy rather than countercyclical adjustments of policy. Such grand-scale experimentation with the economy has produced gross imbalances, which became indisputable in 1984 and 1985: (1) a federal deficit so large that it could not be cured by growth alone; (2) a dollar exchange rate so strong and a domestic market so open to international trade that most U.S. manufacturing sectors experienced recession-like conditions, even as national spending continued to rise strongly; and (3) monetary policies so narrowly focused on reducing inflation that surprisingly sharp and negative growth and trade consequences occurred.

At the same time, the trading partners of the United States pursued independent courses that proved to be very much at odds with U.S. policy. The government deficit reduction that was sought in Europe and Japan posed substantial problems for U.S. exporters and hence for national income and employment. The dollar rose sharply to reduce the market share of American goods, while fiscal restraint simultaneously reduced the growth of the total market. Finally, the consequent weakness in overseas labor markets prevented dismantling of protectionist barriers to U.S. exports of agriculture, technical products, or basic manufactured goods.

Now, in late 1985 and early 1986, policies are about to change course radically once more. The Federal Reserve explicitly broadened its objectives to include management of the exchange rate and support of real growth as at least equal priorities with inflation control. The U.S. Congress and the Reagan administration are seriously pursuing expenditure restraint, and a major restructuring of the federal tax code is simultaneously being debated. These

The opinions and analyses presented here are the sole responsibility of the author. The references to particular events in 1986 as forecasts reflect the fact that the chapter was prepared in late 1985.

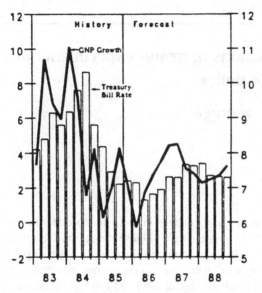

Figure 4.1   Real GNP growth (left, percentage change, annual rates) and the three-month Treasury bill rate (right scale).

policy initiatives are contemplated against a background of questionable private sector strength.

This chapter discusses a baseline forecast that includes the new monetary policy but excludes a full shift to budget balance or major tax reform. In addition, it presents a range of alternative scenarios that lay out some potential courses toward full budget balance in 1991, as required by the Gramm–Rudman-Hollings amendment to the federal debt ceiling legislation. The uncertainties here include the extent to which supportive domestic monetary policy, as well as expansionary foreign monetary, fiscal, and trade policies, will be implemented to complement reduced federal expenditures. The chapter concludes with some thoughts on the impacts of tax reform legislation.

Baseline forecast 1986–1988

Consumers, business executives, and Washington politicians are all extremely sensitive to changing economic conditions, spending freely when good opportunities present themselves and pulling back abruptly when risks arise. Until a broad recovery can be established, this behavior may imply an erratic course for individual sectors of the economy. It may also mean another year of very low inflation as intense competition restrains wage demands and industrial price increases.

The third anniversary of the U.S. economic recovery, which began in 1983, carried with it mostly good memories: Inflation had been brought under control, nominal interest rates were less than half what they had been just four years earlier, and more than eight million people were back at work since the unemployment peak at 10.7 percent in 1982 (Figure 4.1). The stock market liked what it saw during this period, and so did foreign investors. The optimism surrounding the Reagan–Gorbachev summit in Geneva suggested that world tensions, both economic and political, might ease by the end of 1985.

The forecast of slow growth in 1986 is based on the belief that problems left untreated in the earlier years of this expansion – namely, the large federal and trade deficits – all but assured continued anemic growth for the next six months (Tables 4.1 and 4.2). Inflation should remain low, rising only when growth resumes and the dollar's decline in exchange markets percolates through to domestic prices and costs.

Inflation-adjusted spending is more likely to be weak than strong in 1986 because neither consumers nor business nor the federal government is expected to lead domestic spending. Spending will rise less rapidly than income in these sectors, forcing residential construction and exports to rise rapidly enough to keep the recovery alive.

Consumer demand after its autumn peak

American households responded to the August-September 1985 automobile financing offers as the chance of the decade (Figure 4.2). As a result, real spending on autos and parts jumped by $8.9 billion (1972 prices) in the third quarter, contributing one-half of the total expansion in national output ($17.6 billion), compared with a normal share of about 4 percent of spending or 10 percent of cyclical changes in spending. Consumers also managed to raise real nonauto spending by $5.6 billion, even though disposable income fell by $13.2 billion. The personal saving rate thus hit an all-time low of 1.8 percent in September and 2.7 percent for the third quarter.

Although it might be argued that households were just getting around to spending their delayed tax refunds or that collapsing farm income was skewing the data, the fact remains that savings averaged only 4.1 percent of income in 1985. Consumer surveys in late 1985 indicated that households felt that was a good time to buy, and they backed up this sentiment with actual purchases (Table 4.3). Because a conventional recession is unlikely and because interest rates and inflation are only expected to rise modestly from their 1986 troughs, confidence should remain relatively firm (Figure 4.3).

Table 4.1. *Summary table for the U.S. economy: baseline*

	1986			1987				Years				
	II	III	IV	I	II	III	IV	1985	1986	1987	1988	1989
				(Annual rate, seasonally adjusted)								
Real GNP growth rates												
Gross National Product	0.6	2.9	2.6	1.5	3.0	3.9	3.7	2.7	2.6	2.5	3.4	2.0
Total consumption	6.2	6.5	-3.8	2.5	2.6	2.6	2.5	3.5	3.8	2.0	2.4	1.2
Nonresidential fixed investment	-0.9	-0.1	4.6	-12.9	5.4	0.1	10.2	9.3	-0.7	-1.0	4.9	1.8
Residential fixed investment	14.5	9.7	-11.7	-5.8	1.0	6.2	6.3	3.9	8.2	-0.5	3.1	1.8
Total government	9.7	7.6	2.7	-6.5	-0.6	0.2	2.9	6.8	3.5	0.4	0.1	0.7
Civilian unemployment rate (%)	7.2	6.9	6.9	6.9	6.9	6.9	6.7	7.2	7.0	6.9	6.4	6.4
CPI–all urban consumers[a]	-1.7	2.6	3.6	4.5	3.9	4.3	4.5	3.5	2.0	3.6	4.6	4.7
Producer price index–finished goods	-5.2	0.2	4.4	2.9	3.3	3.6	3.0	0.9	-1.3	2.5	4.0	4.0
Compensation per hour[a]	2.3	2.5	3.4	3.0	3.1	3.7	4.2	4.0	3.1	3.2	4.6	4.5
Federal funds rate (%)	6.92	6.21	5.90	5.54	5.21	5.52	5.83	8.10	6.71	5.53	5.73	4.96
New high-grade bond yield (%)	8.53	8.46	8.54	8.23	8.30	8.38	8.47	11.03	8.65	8.34	8.56	7.94
Inventory investment (billion $)	14.5	-8.0	15.5	23.2	18.9	27.6	15.4	11.1	16.4	21.3	27.8	27.4
Net exports (billion $)	-104.5	-108.2	-102.8	-96.4	-88.6	-85.4	-83.1	-78.9	-102.3	-88.4	-76.8	-59.9
Federal budget surplus	-221.1	-188.9	-177.4	-196.5	-188.0	-178.5	-175.1	-198.0	-193.0	-184.5	-152.1	-144.5
Profits after tax[b]	-6.4	-6.7	1.8	21.2	22.4	25.6	12.4	-6.3	-4.8	20.1	8.5	17.4
Real disposable income[a]	7.1	-2.3	-0.4	4.6	1.5	1.7	2.2	2.3	3.1	1.8	2.6	1.2
Industrial production[a]	-2.1	2.3	1.0	-3.2	5.2	8.4	4.2	2.0	0.9	1.8	4.0	1.8
Car sales (mil. unit)	11.2	13.2	10.3	10.2	10.8	11.1	11.2	11.0	11.3	10.8	11.1	10.4
Housing starts (mil. units)	1.91	1.74	1.65	1.66	1.68	1.72	1.77	1.74	1.83	1.71	1.76	1.78

[a] Annual rate of change.
[b] Four-quarter percent change.

Table 4.2. *Industrial production growth rates: baseline*

	1985			1986				Years				
	II	III	IV	I	II	III	IV	1984	1985	1986	1987	1988
Total production	1.3	1.6	0.6	-0.5	-1.4	2.2	4.4	10.5	2.1	0.6	4.1	3.5
Manufacturing	2.0	3.2	1.5	-0.6	-1.9	2.3	4.6	11.3	2.6	0.9	4.3	3.6
Consumer goods	2.5	3.5	1.9	-0.6	-1.1	1.1	2.9	6.5	1.9	0.9	2.7	1.9
Business equipment	3.9	2.5	2.3	-5.1	-4.5	5.6	4.1	17.3	5.1	-0.3	5.2	6.1
Defense and space equipment	10.9	9.8	9.6	9.9	6.2	6.8	8.4	13.1	9.8	8.7	7.9	5.2
Intermediate products	8.5	3.0	0.2	-2.1	-3.0	-0.5	2.1	10.7	4.3	-0.1	2.3	1.7
Utilities	-2.3	-8.6	4.6	-0.3	4.8	1.8	2.4	3.6	1.7	0.7	2.2	2.4
Oil and gas extraction	-6.5	-2.6	-8.1	-2.2	-3.2	-2.1	-2.5	4.6	-2.6	-3.9	-1.0	-0.7
Other mining	13.0	-11.1	-9.5	-1.7	0.6	1.6	3.0	14.3	-0.9	-2.5	3.2	1.8

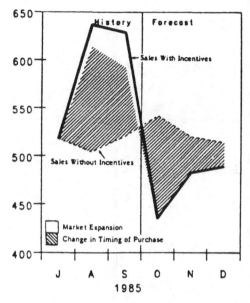

Figure 4.2   Impact of incentives on Carline sales (thousands of units).

Of all the excesses that typically occur at this stage of a cycle, none is more potentially damaging than the accumulation of consumer debt. Just before three of the last four economic downturns, consumer installment credit reached a new high as a share of disposable income. In the current cycle, this ratio has soared from 14.6 percent to an all-time record of 19.2 percent (Figure 4.4). Credit usage has not, however, reached crisis proportions. Debt service as a share of disposable income has risen less than usual because of the decline in interest rates. Moreover, consumers are increasingly using charge cards as cash substitutes, paying their bills before they accrue interest. According to the Federal Reserve Board, about 40 percent of all bank card usage ("debt") never incurs interest expenses, compared with 30 percent in 1980. This means that measured consumer debt can increase without raising the actual debt burden.

Figure 4.4 also shows an adjusted credit-to-income ratio based on surveys of banks, department stores, and oil companies, as well as unpublished Federal Reserve Board data. It is clear that effective debt burden levels are lower than published measures suggest. Nevertheless, consumers are holding a record level of adjusted debt relative to their incomes, and their ability to finance further spending is clearly limited.

Table 4.3. *Consumer opinions regarding buying conditions*
(Why do you think now is a good or a bad time for people to buy?)

	Large household goods		Houses		Cars	
	October 1985	Change from 1 year ago	October 1985	Change from 1 year ago	October 1985	Change from 1 year ago
Good time to buy—selected reasons						
Prices are low; good buys available	34	+5	22	+7	23	+5
Prices won't come down; are going higher	15	−6	7	−2	10	−7
Interest rates low; credit is easy	15	+4	55	+20	41	+27
Total, all reasons	69	−1	68	+16	65	+11
Bad time to buy—selected reasons						
Prices are high	11	−1	15	−1	19	−4
Interest rates are high; credit is tight	3	−2	15	−18	6	−2
Lack of purchasing power	8	+1	10	0	6	0
Total, all reasons	21	+1	28	−15	28	−6
Good−bad	48	−2	30	+31	37	+17

	October 1985	October 1984	Change
Interest rates expectations for next 12 months			
Rates will rise	44	45	−1
Rates will fall	21	18	+3
Stay the same	33	33	0
Expected inflation rate	4.8	5.3	−0.5

Source: Survey Research Center, University of Michigan, Survey of Consumer Attitudes (October 1985).

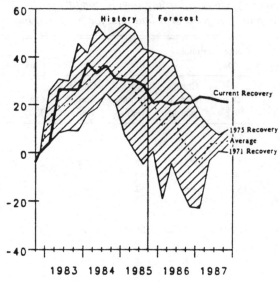

Figure 4.3   Consumer attitudes: a cyclical comparison (trough = 0.0).

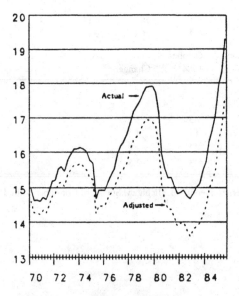

Figure 4.4   Consumer credit outstanding as a share of disposable income.

Table 4.4. *Business fixed investment outlook*
(annual rates of change)

	85:4	86:1	86:2	1985	1986	1987	1988
Nonresident investment	3.8	−4.0	−3.8	6.4	−0.5	4.2	5.4
Durable equipment	−0.9	−3.3	−1.3	5.3	0.0	5.8	6.6
Structures	16.7	−5.7	−10.0	9.1	−1.7	−0.1	2.1
Imports of capital equipment[a]	−7.1	−12.4	−15.2	13.7	−7.7	−1.7	6.9
Capacity utilization rate (%)	80.0	79.1	78.2	80.3	78.5	79.5	79.8
Real net cash flow	1.5	−8.1	1.9	7.7	1.7	0.7	2.1

[a]This category includes 15 percent of auto imports.

Investment under pressure

Businesses invest capital to expand capacity or reduce costs, but only the latter objective is driving investment plans today. With the manufacturing utilization rate down to 80.0 percent from a weak (81.8 percent) high in August 1984, expansion is hardly a top priority.

In normal business cycles, operating rates often hit 87 percent at the peak. During expansions, as much as 40–50 percent of non-utility structures spending and 30–35 percent of equipment spending typically goes toward greater productive capacity; during recessions, these shares fall to about 20 percent for structures and 10–15 percent for equipment. Today's spending priorities therefore put at risk up to 20 percent of investment, the typical change in share during a cycle.

Since a full recession is unlikely, however, the decline will be less drastic. Nevertheless, inflation-adjusted outlays for producers' durable equipment are expected to fall at a 1.8 percent annual rate from the third quarter of 1985 through mid-1986 and then gradually regain strength (Table 4.4); outlays for nonresidential construction, in contrast, are projected to fall at a rate of 2.5 percent through the fourth quarter of 1986 (Table 4.5).

Since the House Ways and Means Committee has amended the already negative presidential proposal, tax reform legislation may be even more discouraging to fixed investment. Business cannot shrug off a $25 billion average annual increase in corporate taxes, the elimination of investment credits, and the dilution of depreciation allowances. Even those firms whose average tax rates could be cut would encounter problems because their customers face a much heavier tax burden. Since the response of the full House and of the Senate is still unclear, the baseline forecast includes no explicit reform package.

Table 4.5. *Investment plans (percentage change)*

	1985 forecasts			1986 forecasts		
	Spending =	Volume +	Inflation	Spending	Volume	Inflation
Commerce Department Survey						
(9/85)	8.3	5.8	2.4	na	na	na
(6/85)	9.2	6.2	2.9	na	na	na
McGraw-Hill Survey (5/85)	9.9	4.6	5.1	−1.9	na	na
(10/85)	8.4	na	na	−1.0	−5.4	4.7
DRI Control						
Total nonresident fixed investment	9.4	6.4	2.9	2.5	−0.5	3.0
Producers' durable equipment	7.7	5.3	2.3	2.7	0.0	2.7
Nonresident structures	12.6	9.1	3.2	2.2	−1.7	4.0
Public utilities	0.7	−1.4	2.1	−0.2	−2.8	2.7
Excluding public utilities	15.9	12.3	3.2	2.7	−1.4	4.3

The most supportive factors for capital spending are declining interest rates and fairly solid balance sheets. Corporate balance sheets are in better shape than they were in 1984 and in slightly better shape than usual for this stage of an expansion. The heavy use of short-term debt during the past two years was a correct bet that rates would come down; the high leverage ratios reflect the torrent of mergers, acquisitions, and leveraged buyouts that have added strength to share prices. Corporate treasurers have taken advantage of lower long-term interest rates to restructure and strengthen company balance sheets. Even more encouraging is the fact that balance sheets have improved in those industries that need it the most, such as the heavier industrial groups including steel and other metals.

A comparable cycle in inventory spending is already two to three quarters old. After adjustment for inflation, nonfarm inventories rose $20.9 billion in 1984; the annual rate of increase has fallen steadily since then, down from $15.7 billion in the first quarter of 1985 to an actual decline of $2.1 billion in the third.

At this point in an expansion, inventory-to-sales ratios are typically higher than they are today. Five years of high real interest rates, however, have driven target ratios down. Only in the retail sector is there a potential problem: The nonauto segment began the fourth quarter of 1985 with stocks appropriate for a booming Christmas season that is unlikely to materialize; the auto companies are also building stocks at near-record rates (Figure 4.5). Although a traditional inventory cycle is not in prospect, investment in stocks will also do little to help the economy.

Government spending on the wane

Voters have now convinced legislators that the federal deficit is a serious problem requiring an immediate solution. The recognition that the deficit is the cause of high interest rates, the strong dollar, and weak agricultural prices is nearly universal. The congressional response to the rising risk of voter backlash is the Gramm–Rudman–Hollings (G–R–H) proposal for automatic budget balancing in six years. Each year, deficit projections by the Office of Management and Budget (OMB) and the Congressional Budget Office (CBO) for the following fiscal year would be compared to a tight schedule of $172 billion in fiscal 1986 and $144 billion in 1987, with a $36 billion reduction in each succeeding year. Any gap between the CBO/OMB average and the G–R–H schedule must be closed by new legislation or by formula-driven, across-the-board cuts.

The concept is good: both Congress and the president would know that the alternative to thoughtful, program-specific decisions would be arbitrary spending cutbacks rather than the current default option of no change at all.

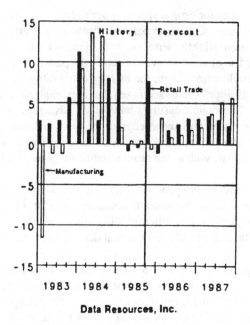

Figure 4.5   Change in inventories, manufacturing, and retail trade (billions of dollars, 1972 prices).

The numerical standards, however, are austere. A target tied to actual deficits rather than to expenditures or to cyclically adjusted deficits is likely to force undesirable fiscal restraint if a recession reduces revenues or raises unemployment benefit outlays. In addition, a zero deficit is not necessarily the best goal. Finally, an assumed deficit of $172 billion in fiscal 1986 is an extremely optimistic starting point.

This legislation is discussed in greater detail later in the chapter. The baseline forecast, however, assumes expenditures in line with prior legislative resolutions (Table 4.6). Even without the new initiatives, federal expenditures excluding interest are projected to rise only 2.8 percent in 1986, 5.7 percent in 1987, and 6.7 percent in 1988. The state local government sector is expected to see its federal grants rise slowly from $99 billion in 1985 to $106 billion in 1988, and must trim its expenditure growth in response because taxpayers are unlikely to tolerate significant tax increases.

Residential construction: a source of strength

Housing is the sector with the highest probability of providing strength to the economy in 1986. There still remains considerable pent-up demand for hous-

Table 4.6. *Baseline government budgets*
(federal fiscal years)

	$Billions					Percentage Change		
	1984	1985	1986	1987	1988	1986	1987	1988
Total spending	1,320	1,445	1,529	1,615	1,729	5.8	5.7	7.0
Federal	859	944	983	1,034	1,106	4.1	5.2	6.9
State and local	461	501	546	581	623	8.9	6.5	7.3
Total receipts	1,200	1,303	1,395	1,505	1,641	7.1	7.8	9.0
Federal	688	750	804	869	955	7.3	8.0	10.0
State and local	512	554	591	636	685	6.8	7.6	7.7
Deficit	−120	−142	−133	−110	−88			
Federal	−172	−195	−179	−165	−150			
State and local	52	52	45	55	62			
Memo								
Real purchases (1972 prices)	297	316	319	320	326	1.2	0.2	1.9
Federal	118	133	132	131	134	−0.8	−0.5	2.4
State and local	178	183	188	189	192	2.6	0.6	1.5
Interest expense	86	103	112	121	131	8.3	7.9	8.2
Federal	111	130	139	151	165	7.2	8.2	9.5
State and local	−25	−26	−27	−30	−34	−2.5	−9.5	−14.7
Full employment federal deficit	−122	−150	−115	−92	−67			

ing, in spite of approximately 1.75 million starts each year from 1983 through 1985, because the number of households has risen rapidly. Given normal patterns of obsolescence and demolition, the net stock of homes has increased by 300,000–400,000 less per year than required to match the underlying demographic potential.

The only puzzle is why these pressures have not led to stronger construction markets in 1985. Permits – authorizations for new construction – have been strong, but starts – genuine construction activity – have been flat. From 1980 through 1984, starts exceeded permits by 7 percent on average. Completely counter to this pattern, starts had been lower than permits from May through September 1985. The departure from historical starts–permits relationships occurred in all three housing classes – single family, 2–4 unit, and 5+ unit structures. The only behavioral explanation is that builders and buyers believe mortgage costs may soon drop another notch. They are apparently obtaining permits now to be prepared to start construction when credit is at its cheapest.

The high and rising level of permits is consistent with the continuing decline in mortgage rates (from 14.5 percent in the third quarter of 1984 to 13.62 percent, 13.07 percent, 12.76 percent, and 12.14 percent in succeeding

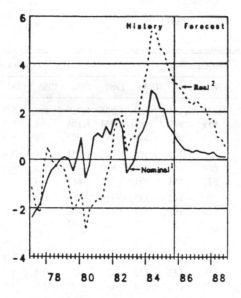

Figure 4.6   U.S. versus rest-of-world interest rate spread.
[1]Ten-year U.S. government bond yield less a composite of industrial trading partners' government bond yield.
[2]Bond yields adjusted by a three-year percentage change in U.S. and foreign wholesale prices.

quarters), a very modest rise (1.8 percent) in new home prices, and strong sales of new and existing units. The drop in housing starts is wholly contradictory, and a correction should be expected.

Better prospects for exports

The expansion of the federal deficit was the prime factor behind the expansion of the trade deficit; impending reductions of the budget imbalance will permit exports to rise once more and will reduce the influx of imports. This optimism is contingent upon the cooperation of foreign governments in the setting of their monetary and fiscal policies such that global interest rate spreads and hence exchange rates return to normal values (Figures 4.6 and 4.7).

The enormous magnitude of U.S. government credit demands dictated a premium of the inflation-adjusted U.S. government bond rate relative to foreign bonds that peaked at 5 percent in 1984 (Table 4.7). This premium provided an entirely logical explanation for the massive overvaluation of the dollar. The exchange markets were not irrational and did not produce a

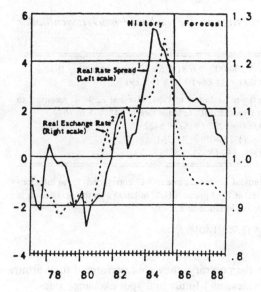

Figure 4.7 Real U.S.–world interest rate spread and the real exchange value of the U.S. dollar.
[1]Nominal U.S.–foreign bond yields less three-year percentage change in U.S. and foreign wholesale prices.
[2]Morgan Guaranty trade-weighted index (1980–2 = 1) adjusted for relative U.S. and foreign wholesale prices.

Table 4.7. *The linkage between bond and exchange rate forecasts*

	1980	1984	1980–4 change[a]	1985	1986	1984–6 change[a]
Government bond yields						
U.S. (10-Year)	11.46	12.44	0.98	10.66	9.34	−3.10
Japan	8.27	6.81	−1.46	6.75	7.35	0.55
Germany	8.50	7.77	−0.73	7.11	6.13	−1.65
Foreign average	11.23	10.08	−1.14	9.26	8.90	−1.18
U.S.–German spread	2.96	4.66	1.70	3.55	3.21	−1.45
Deutschmarks/dollar	1.82	2.85	47.4	2.95	2.37	−21.8
U.S.–Japan spread	3.19	5.63	2.44	3.91	1.99	3.65
Yen/dollar	227.67	236.92	4.0	237.29	193.00	−18.9
U.S.–Foreign average	0.23	2.36	2.12	1.40	0.44	−1.92
Morgan Guaranty Index	0.91	1.22	31.7	1.27	1.09	−13.5

[a]Change reported in percentage points for bond yields, as percentage of base year value for exchange rates.

Table 4.8. *Arbitrage in the exchange market: yen/dollar example*

Option 1: Invest ¥100,000 at 6.81% for 10 years beginning 1984. ¥100,000 × (1.068)^{10} = ¥193,250
Option 2: Convert yen to dollars in 1984, invest at 12.44%, reconvert to yen at hypothetical exchange rate of 142 ¥/$ in 1994. ¥100,000 + 237 (¥/$) = $422 $422 × (1.1244)^{10} = $1,363 $1,363 × 142 (¥/$) = ¥193,250

Note: A 1994 nominal yen/dollar rate of 142 corresponds to an inflation-adjusted rate of 180 at 1984 prices if U.S. inflation over the next decade is 5.5% while Japanese inflation is 3%.

$$142 \times (1.055/1.03)^{10} = 180$$

speculative bubble; on the contrary, they ably performed their arbitrage role among global interest rates, and future and spot exchange rates.

An investor offered a 5 percent premium on the annual return of a 10-year bond could cover a 5 percent depreciation of the U.S. currency for 10 successive years until an equilibrium rate was reestablished. An example using U.S. and Japanese yields and exchange rates readily illustrates this point. In 1984, the U.S. 10-year government bond averaged 12.44 percent, the Japanese bond 6.81 percent, and the dollar was priced at 237 yen. This can be shown to imply an expectation that the long-run (1994) competitive equilibrium value of the dollar was 142 yen (Table 4.8). If 142 yen/dollar seems exceptionally low, it must be noted that Japanese inflation is widely expected to be less than that in the United States. Thus, for example, a 1994 equilibrium value of 142 yen would translate to a real 1984 rate of approximately 180 if U.S. prices rose by 5.5 percent while Japanese prices rose by 3 percent. Not entirely coincidentally, 180 yen per dollar is a reasonable estimate of the exchange rate that would currently equalize U.S. and Japanese manufacturing costs. Similar striking calculations can be made between the United States, and Germany, France, or Korea.

The specific baseline forecast for the trade-weighted dollar exchange rate is a sustained decline. The dollar achieved a peak index value of 1.35 (1980–2 = 1.00) in the first quarter of 1985 and has already fallen to 1.16 as of December 1. By the end of 1986, a further drop of 10.2 percent (to 1.05) is anticipated, followed by small reductions in 1987 and 1988.

In response to more competitive prices, inflation-adjusted goods exports are expected to rise by 8 percent in 1986 and, assuming growth is sustained overseas, 10 percent in 1987, and 7 percent in 1988 (Table 4.9). All major goods-exporting sectors, with the possible exception of agriculture should

Table 4.9. *Real trade flows*
(Percentage change)

	1984	1985	1986	1987	1988
Exports of goods	7.1	−0.2	7.7	10.2	7.0
Foods, feeds, and beverages	−1.8	−14.3	8.0	6.8	5.5
Industrial supplies and materials	4.5	1.9	9.6	7.0	5.6
Capital goods	5.0	2.7	4.0	13.5	10.3
Automotive vehicles and parts	18.4	9.9	10.1	8.3	2.9
Consumer goods	−2.8	−3.8	13.4	21.2	7.1
Other goods	63.8	5.4	8.0	4.6	4.8
Imports of goods	30.1	11.5	−2.2	0.4	3.9
Foods, feeds, and beverages	13.7	7.1	−2.9	−3.6	0.5
Industrial supplies and materials	21.2	2.0	−1.3	0.7	2.9
Petroleum and products	8.1	−11.3	3.4	5.2	7.9
Other supplies and materials	24.6	5.0	−2.2	−0.2	1.8
Capital goods	50.1	13.5	−8.5	−3.0	7.4
Automotive vehicles and parts	28.5	15.7	1.8	12.1	2.4
Consumer goods	30.2	18.0	2.1	−1.2	4.1
Other goods	13.2	16.8	−5.7	−14.7	−3.7

participate in this robust expansion. The highest growth rates may be in the relatively small consumer auto and nonauto categories. The greatest absolute growth should occur in industrial supplies and in capital goods. Equally important for corporate profitability is a prediction of a 2.6 percent average annual increase in goods export prices (excluding foods), a welcome change from the 0.4 percent drop in 1985.

In a symmetric response to a more competitively priced dollar, the volume of goods imports is projected to decline in 1986 by 2.2 percent. The only exceptions are oil imports (following a sharp inventory drawdown in 1985) and automotive vehicles and parts. The modest sluggishness of the overall economy is partly responsible for the general softness in import growth; for example, it will also contribute to a very small increase in auto-related imports in 1986 (1.8 percent versus 28.5 percent in 1984 and 15.7 percent in 1985). By the same token, the good macroeconomic recovery anticipated for 1987 and 1988 produces positive growth in almost all import categories by the last year of the forecast.

Inflation slowly returning

At this point in a recovery, inflation and inflation expectations are often rekindled. Today, however, price growth is modest and likely to remain so. Capacity utilization rates in manufacturing continue to decline and should not

Table 4.10. *Significant wage and employment changes*

	Wage inflation[a]				Employment growth[b]			
	Nov. 1982	Nov. 1983	Nov. 1984	Nov. 1985	Nov. 1982	Nov. 1983	Nov. 1984	Nov. 1985
Private nonfarm sector	5.8	4.0	3.1	2.9	−3.0	4.2	5.1	3.1
Mining	6.2	4.2	3.9	1.6	−15.5	−7.2	2.5	−2.8
Construction	4.4	2.5	1.2	0.8	−6.1	6.7	7.8	7.4
Manufacturing	5.9	2.9	3.3	3.3	−9.3	4.5	3.5	−0.9
Transportation, utilities	6.0	4.2	2.7	2.8	−2.8	0.3	3.9	2.3
Wholesale, retail trade	5.3	4.7	2.7	NA	−0.7	4.5	6.4	3.4
Finance, real estate	6.9	5.4	4.0	4.0	0.8	3.7	3.6	5.0
Services	6.5	4.8	4.0	4.1	1.5	4.9	5.5	5.6

[a]Hourly earnings index, production workers (year-over-year percentage change).
[b]Production workers (year-over-year percentage change).

reach the problematic 85–90 percent zone at any time during the forecast. Foreign recoveries are also too modest to produce shortages that will affect U.S. prices.

The outlook for overall energy prices continues to be favorable. Saudi Arabia and OPEC are moving toward market-determined pricing. On the domestic front, the Federal Energy Regulatory Commission recently approved a new rule that will keep gas prices more competitive with residual fuel as oil prices decline.

In the agricultural sector, the inflation outlook is good from a macro perspective – although not from farmers' perspectives. The reason is simple: abundant supplies. U.S. feed grainstocks (including corn, sorghum, barley, and oats) have increased from 1.9 billion bushels at the end of 1984 to 3.8 billion bushels in the 1985–6 crop year. Pressures on major crop prices will remain weak for some time because of continued increases in per acre productivity. For example, even without further technological breakthroughs or increases in acreage planted, corn yields will expand by 140 million bushels annually.

Labor market conditions are not nearly as tight as they often are after two strong growth years. The unemployment rate continues to hover near 7 percent, reflecting reasonably strong 1.8 percent annual gains in the labor force in 1984 and 1985 and modest economic growth in 1986. There is thus an adequate supply of workers to fill the transitional needs of an economy that is creating far more jobs in service, finance, and retail trade than in manufacturing.

Remarkably enough, the rate of increase in wages is still falling after three

Table 4.11. *Profits, prices, and costs outlook*
(percentage change)

	1985	1986	1987	1988
Post-tax profit growth				
Nominal	−2.3	4.4	12.0	11.5
Inflation adjusted	−5.5	0.9	8.4	7.6
Price inflation				
GNP deflator	3.6	3.4	3.7	4.4
Wholesale prices–all	−0.6	1.0	2.6	3.5
–finished goods	0.8	1.7	2.8	3.5
Unit labor costs	3.7	3.2	3.1	4.1
Dollar exchange rate	3.9	−14.4	−3.8	−1.1
Non-oil imports	−2.7	9.2	8.3	5.1

years of recovery. What is equally surprising is that manufacturing pay increases stabilized at slightly above 3 percent in both 1984 and 1985, whereas wage inflation for all other sectors continued to decline to less than that rate. Such behavior in U.S. heavy industry is likely to mean further employment losses (Table 4.10).

Inflation will continue in the 3.0–3.5 percent range through most of 1986, allowing monetary policy to ease (Table 4.11). As indicated earlier, no domestic wage or cost pressures, bottlenecks, or natural resource problems exist. The dollar's depreciation is the only factor standing between a forecast of stable inflation in 1986 and an alternative scenario of *declining* inflation.

Corporate profits will rise moderately. Although the growth in cash flow will slow as the kick from accelerated depreciation allowances fades, a weaker dollar and lower interest rates will help. As the stock market boom seems to indicate, 1987 and 1988 will be very good years, unless the current tax reform legislation passes without significant changes.

Financial conditions support growth

The Federal Reserve could be logically expected to respond to the previously described macroeconomy by allowing interest rates to continue to drift down (Figures 4.8 and 4.9). The federal funds rate is projected to fall 50 basis points by late summer 1986, while long-term rates decline 40 basis points.

The outlook for domestic monetary policy and interest rates falls into four phases. First, until Congress passes the debt ceiling increase, the Federal Reserve is expected to hold the funds rate in a narrow range just under 8

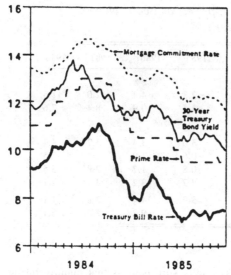

Figure 4.8   Interest rate evidence and outlook (weekly).

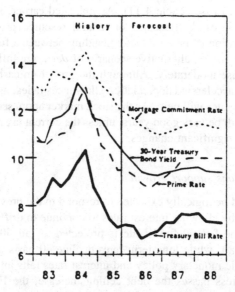

Figure 4.9   Interest rate evidence and outlook (quarterly).

Table 4.12. *Demand for and supply of funds*

	Percentage change, 4th quarter to 4th quarter				
	1984	1985	1986	1987	1988
Real GNP	5.7	2.1	1.9	3.7	2.7
GNP Deflator	3.6	3.8	3.2	4.0	4.5
Nominal GNP	9.5	6.0	5.2	7.9	7.3
Narrow money supply (M1)					
Actual/predicted	5.2	10.9	5.4	5.3	5.0
Fed target range[a]	4–8	3–8	4–7	3.5–6.5	3–6
Broad money supply (M2)					
Actual/predicted	7.7	8.5	6.9	6.9	7.3
Fed target range[a]	6–9	6–9	6–9	5.5–8.5	5–8
Consumer credit[b]	120.3	19.3	6.4	4.8	6.1
Nonfinancial Corp. bank loans[b]	19.0	4.7	4.7	7.1	8.6
Mortgages[b]	11.7	10.4	10.8	10.4	9.5
Federal debt[b]	16.8	15.2	12.9	11.1	9.4
Prime rate[c]	11.8	9.5	9.0	10.0	10.0
Mortgage commitment rate[c]	13.6	11.9	11.0	11.4	11.2
Treasury bill rate[c]	8.87	7.2	6.9	7.6	7.3
10-Year Treasury bond rate[c]	11.7	9.9	9.2	9.5	9.3

[a]1987–8 forecast by DRI.
[b]Percentage change in stock, not flow, of debt.
[c]Fourth-quarter levels.

percent. Given the Treasury's near-zero cash balances, the Fed must use the funds rate as its operating instrument because reserve data are distorted. Second, until M2 growth returns to its target zone, no new relief in rates is likely; indeed, Treasury yields will temporarily rise when the federal government is allowed to return to the market.

Third, the new year will give the Fed the opportunity to set new, steadily achievable monetary growth targets. With a high fourth-quarter 1985 base and without the velocity problems associated with the 1984–5 interest rate drop, there should be no problem matching up actual and targeted money growth in 1986. Specifically, the baseline projection includes a 5.2 percent growth in nominal GNP and a 6.9 percent rise in M2 over the course of 1986 (Table 4.12). As the economy moves away from excessive fiscal stimulus, this forecast implies that long-term rates could drop as much as 100 basis points by the end of 1986.

Fourth, stronger economic activity will bring higher short-term credit costs in 1987 and 1988. A compression of the yield curve is likely as the Treasury's demand for long-term funds subsides and as fears of interest rate volatility abate (Table 4.13). No pronounced rise in bond rates is therefore expected in this final phase of the forecast.

The drive for a balanced federal budget

On December 11, 1985, Congress approved legislation (the Gramm–Rudman–Hollings amendment to a debt ceiling authorization bill) mandating steady progress toward a balanced federal budget in fiscal 1991. In fiscal 1986, the deficit will have to be reduced to $172 billion, followed by reduction to $144 billion for fiscal 1987, $108 billion in 1988, and successive $36 billion reductions for the next three years

One of the sponsors of this legislation has conceded that the legislation is "a bad idea whose time has come." The sponsor was referring to the fact that the legislation mandates arbitrary, across-the-board cuts in a limited set of expenditure categories, instead of a careful program-by-program review as in the normal budget consideration by Congress and the administration. The "bad idea" aspect of the legislation is this substitution of arbitrary rules for responsible legislation. On the other hand, the deficit must be closed; therefore, the "time has come" for this legislation because no compromise could be reached.

The legislation is the only apparent way of eliminating the policy gridlock created by a president determined to cut taxes and raise defense spending, and a House of Representatives determined to preserve domestic programs. Only the Senate has been willing to find a middle ground, making compromises on defense spending, on domestic spending, and on tax increases. Only the Senate has been willing to solve the deficit problem; the House and the president were willing to let the deficit mount year after year on an exponential basis such that the United States was double-, triple-, and quadruple-mortgaging its future.

An optimistic view of the legislation is that the threat of arbitrary program cuts will indeed now force a thoughtful program-by-program pruning of expenditures. The antagonists, namely the administration and the House of Representatives, will be forced to make hard decisions and to reach compromises in order to avoid the arbitrary changes that neither of them desires.

At least three reasonable objections to the legislation can be raised. First, the cutbacks are restricted to a narrow set of programs exempting pensions in particular; social security, government civilian pensions, and military pensions are exempt from the cutbacks that would be required if a deficit target is not achieved. Second, tax increases are not included in the formulas to reduce the deficit to meet the schedule. Third, the numerical standards put forth in the legislation are too austere.

Table 4.13. *The evolving yield curve*

	Level					Spread over bill rate				
	1984	1985	1986	1987	1988	1984	1985	1986	1987	1988
90-Day bill rate	9.52	7.49	6.89	7.48	7.42					
1-Year bill rate	10.89	8.43	7.82	8.33	8.28	1.36	0.95	0.93	0.86	0.86
3–5-year bond yield	12.07	9.94	8.80	9.00	8.90	2.54	2.45	1.91	1.52	1.49
10-year bond yield	12.44	10.66	9.34	9.41	9.36	2.92	3.17	2.45	1.94	1.95
Interest rate volatility index[a]	0.74	0.55	0.54	0.51	0.49					
Full employment budget deficit	−133.7	−144.2	−104.7	−89.3	−60.6					

[a] 48-month moving average of absolute changes in the T-bill rate.

These objections are well understood by the proponents of the legislation. The legislation has these flaws for the same reasons that no compromise could be achieved in the past. The president would not agree to legislation raising taxes, and both the House and the president were unwilling to increase taxes on the politically strong pension recipients in this country. This new legislation simply recognizes political realities and excludes pensions and taxes from the budget-balancing process.

The criticism that the standards are austere relates to the current weakness in the economy. It is unlikely that growth in 1986 will be sufficiently strong to produce the tax revenues hoped for by the legislative sponsors. Government forecasts predict almost 4 percent real growth in the economy, accompanied by 4.5 percent inflation. A more realistic scenario is for 2 percent growth and 3 percent inflation. An economy expanding at 5 percent rather than a 8.5 percent on a nominal GNP basis will produce a revenue shortfall for fiscal 1986 alone of $25–30 billion. Economic weakness of this type will set the stage for a draconian spending reduction for fiscal 1987 to put the deficit back on the targeted path: Major expenditure cutbacks in that year could further weaken the economy, drive revenues even further below the levels hoped for by the sponsors of the bill, and set the stage for yet another round of substantial expenditure cuts in 1988. The legislation thus creates the risk of a vicious cycle: weak economic performance forcing expenditure cutbacks, which further weaken the economic performance, which forces even greater expenditure cutbacks. At some point before the end of the decade, Congress will probably amend or eliminate this legislation to avoid forcing the economy into a conventional recession. This assumption is made in the baseline forecast.

Alternatively, extreme pressure may develop for the Federal Reserve to accelerate the growth of credit in the economy. If the Federal Reserve puts itself in a position where it can be blamed for weak economic growth, it will face a very angry Congress, and an angry Congress would consider legislation to restrict the options for domestic monetary policy. Fearing such a loss of institutional independence, the Federal Reserve may opt to pursue much more stimulative monetary policy in 1986 than it would ordinarily feel comfortable pursuing. It may be forced to take a considerable risk by accelerating inflation in order to avoid the wrath of a Congress that has embarrassed itself by passing a flawed budget-balancing law.

The sensitivity of the outlook to monetary policy is summarized in Table 4.14. In the best of worlds (labeled OPTIM), the passage of the Gramm–Rudman–Hollings legislation calls forth much looser monetary policy and greater private sector confidence in the future. Expectations of both inflation and a potential credit crunch are significantly reduced because fiscal pressure has been removed. The combination of an offsetting monetary stimulus and inherently stronger investment creates better real growth than in the baseline.

Table 4.14. *Comparison of alternative forecasts*

Fiscal policy	Baseline (as in budget resolution)	Gramm–Rudman (as required by Gramm–Rudman amendment)	OPTIM (as in Gramm–Rudman amendment)
Deficit (billions, fiscal 1988)	$169	$105	$94
Monetary policy	Stable	Same open market purchases as baseline	Greater open market purchases
Federal Funds Rate (%)			
Peak	8.4	8.0	7.9
End 1988	8.1	5.5	7.0
Yield Curve	Flattening	Flattening late	Flattening early
Real GNP[a]	Moderate	Late 1986 recession	Strong growth
1985 (%)	2.1	2.1	2.1
1986 (%)	1.9	−1.6	3.1
1987 (%)	3.7	3.1	4.7
1988 (%)	2.7	6.9	2.7
Inflation[a]	Moderate	Lower	Higher
CPI (%, 1986)	3.5	3.3	3.7
Hourly wages (%, 1986)	3.6	3.2	3.8
Productivity growth	Moderate	Stronger	Stronger
Average (%)	1.4	1.6	1.6
Dollar	Declining	Weakening late	Weakening early
End 1988 (%)	Down 13	Down 22	Down 17
Current account deficit end 1988	$99	$54	$77
Consumer confidence	Moderate	Moderate	Strong
Saving rate (average %)	3.8	3.3	3.7
Unemployment rate end 1988 (%)	7.4	7.5	6.6

[a]Percentage change fourth quarter over fourth quarter.

Inflation does rise, but only to 5 percent, and government bond yields retreat to 8 percent. The unemployment rate is down to 6.5 percent, and the exchange rate is approximately equal to its 1980–2 average. A return to normal postwar U.S. economic parameters is therefore achieved by 1988.

Such a favorable picture is certainly not guaranteed. The alternative entitled

Gramm–Rudman is a relatively pure fiscal derivative of the baseline in which no monetary policy or exogenous expectational adjustments occur in 1986 because of the enormous magnitude of the required federal spending cuts. A recession, not additional central bank open market purchases of securities, produces very low interest rates and facilitates a recovery in 1987 and 1988. The extreme economic weakness pushes inflation down below 3 percent and then sends the dollar on a sustained, sharp decline. This does produce a marked improvement in the current account, but at a high price to the United States and its trading partners.

The uncertainties of tax reform

President Reagan declared that the reform of the personal and corporate income tax structure was a major objective of his administration. In response, the Treasury Department drafted an initial framework that was a relatively pure instrument of reform. In May 1985, the president officially endorsed a revised tax reform scheme that accepted numerous political compromises. The Ways and Means Committee of the House of Representatives was then given the task of creating a formal piece of legislation. Table 4.15 summarizes the proposed changes.

Several uncertainties surround these efforts. First, because of the three versions of tax reform, the actual changes in the law are unclear. Second, the set of economic responses to any given change in the tax code is uncertain. Third, timing is an important unknown: If the Senate delays its consideration of a House of Representatives tax bill long into 1986, the effective date might be January 1, 1987. These uncertainties will play havoc with capital spending budgets.

The original legislation was allegedly designed to enhance fairness, simplicity, and growth. Although these plans could enhance the public's perception of fairness, reform proposals are likely to come at a significant cost to business investment and hence to labor productivity growth. Realistically, the measures offer few gains in simplicity.

Fairness and simplicity

The central principle underlying the initial Treasury plan was to treat all income equally, whether its source was labor, equities, bonds, or real estate. To the extent that income represents a multiperiod return, the asset cost would have been indexed to inflation. Incentives to shift income from ordinary tax to capital gains treatment, together with benefits from delayed reporting of current income (such as accelerated depreciation), would have been largely eliminated.

Each taxpayer's comprehensively defined income was to be subject to a

Table 4.15. *Tax overhaul: how various plans compare for the 1986 tax year*

	Current law	Reagan plan	Ways and Means
Individual tax rates	14 rates: from 11% to 50%	3 rates: 15%, 25%, 35%	4 rates: 15%, 25%, 35%, 38%
Personal exemption	$1,080	$2,000	$1,500 for item-izers, $2,000 for nonitemizers
Mortgage interest	Fully deductible for all mortgages	Principal residence deductible	Principal and second residence deduct-ible
Other interest	$10,000 plus amount equal to investment in-come	$5,000 plus amount equal to invest-ment income	$20,000 plus amount equal to investment in-come, cap on tax shelters
Employer-provided health insurance	Not taxed	Taxed up to first $10/month for single; $25 for family	Not taxed
Charitable contribu-tion	Fully deductible	Deductible, but only on itemized re-turns	Fully deductible for itemizers, partly for nonitemizers
State and local taxes	Fully deductible	No deduction	Fully deductible
Capital gains	60% excluded for 20% top rate	30% excluded for 17.3% top rate but few items covered	42% excluded for 22% top rate in 1987
Corporate tax rates	46% top, graduated rates up to $100,000	33% top rate, gradu-ated rates up to $75,000	36% top, graduated rates up to $75,000
Depreciation	Accelerated	Somewhat acceler-ated, but less gen-erous than current law; indexed for inflation	Slower depreciation; very limited in-dexation ($1/2$ of > 5%)

Source: Wall Street Journal, Data Resources, Inc.

simplified rate schedule with only four income brackets: a "zero" bracket not subject to tax, followed by three relatively broad brackets with tax rates of 15, 25, and 35 percent (Table 4.16).

Parts of this approach survived in the President's Tax Proposals for Fairness, Growth, and Simplicity, led by the simplified 15-25-35 rate structure. Inflation adjustments in the measurement of capital gains and of interest

Table 4.16. *Comparison of individual income tax brackets between proposed reforms, by taxable income (1986 dollars)*

Marginal tax rate (%)	President's proposal			House markup		
	Single filer	Joint filing	Head of household	Single filer	Joint filing	Head of household
0	Up to $7,900	Up to $4,000	Up to $3,600	Up to $2,950	Up to $4,800	Up to $4,200
15	Up to $18,000	Up to $29,000	Up to $23,000	Up to $12,500	Up to $22,500	Up to $16,000
25	Up to $42,000	Up to $70,000	Up to $52,000	Up to $30,000	Up to $43,000	Up to $34,000
35	Over $42,000	Over $70,000	Over $52,000	Up to $60,000	Up to $100,000	Up to $75,000
38				Over $60,000	Over $100,000	Over $75,000

Note: Taxable income differs between the two proposals. For example although both provide a $2,000 personal exemption, the House markup would effectively reduce the exemption to $1,500 for itemizers.

Table 4.17. *Income distribution data on the proposed reforms, 1987*

Income class (000s of 1986$)	Percentage change in income tax liability		Percentage change in after-tax income	
	President's proposal	House markup	President's proposal	House markup
Less than $10	−72.4	−76.1	1.0	1.0
$10–20	−18.0	−23.4	1.2	1.5
$20–30	−9.3	−9.9	0.9	1.0
$30–40	−6.6	−8.9	0.7	1.0
$40–50	−7.3	−8.4	1.0	1.1
$50–75	−5.9	−7.2	1.0	1.2
$75–100	−8.9	−5.6	1.9	1.2
$100–200	−10.1	−7.2	2.7	1.9
$200 and above	−15.2	−5.8	4.9	1.9
Total	−10.5	−9.0	1.5	1.3

Note: Preliminary figures from the Joint Committee on Taxation. Released with the caveat.

income and expense were largely removed, probably a wise choice given the complexity that this would add to the code and the tacit acceptance of permanent inflation (of 5 percent or better) that this would signify.

The Ways and Means Committee rejected much of the broadening of the tax base proposed in early Reagan administration drafts. In particular, state and local taxes would be fully deductible, as would interest payments on second homes. In place of the base broadening, the Ways and Means Committee sought to achieve fairness by implementing a tough alternative minimum tax. Changes in tax rates and tax brackets proposed by the House Committee also shifted much of the personal tax savings from middle- and upper-income groups to lower-income groups (Table 4.17). With respect to corporate taxation, no alternative enhances simplicity. It is true that some complicating incentives in the code would be removed (such as the investment tax credit and the accelerated cost recovery system); offsetting this simplification were proposals to index depreciation to the inflation rate and to expand the role of alternative minimum taxes.

Prospects for growth: capital investment and labor force expansion

All of the tax reform plans create large disincentives relative to current law for capital formation by raising the corporate tax burden and by eliminating high-

Table 4.18. *The value of depreciation allowances under current law and proposed reforms*

	Present value of depreciation per $1 [a]				Depreciation rate as a percentage of purchase price in first full year			
	Pre-1981 law	Current law	President's proposal	House markup	Pre-1981 law	Current law	President's proposal	House markup
Producers' durable equipment	0.75	0.84	0.90	0.74	20.4	23.5	28.0	20.8
Utility structures	0.56	0.64	0.87	0.51	8.4	10.0	16.4	7.3
Private structures [b]	0.35	0.53	0.53	0.35	5.0	9.0	4.1	3.3

[a] Current law permits depreciation of the entire (nominal) purchase price of an asset. Because depreciation allowances are spread out over the life of the asset, however, the value of the deduction is less than dollar-for-dollar. The present value of a dollar of depreciation discounts the flow of tax deductions by the Corporate cost of funds. Immediate write-off – full expensing – has a value of 1.00. Calculations assume asset is held for its full depreciable life.

[b] Calculations assume maximum asset life of 19, 28, and 30 years under the three proposals with indexation only in the president's proposal.

Table 4.19. *Depreciation rules under current law and proposed reforms*

Representative asset	Current law		President's proposals[a]			House markup[b]		
	Recovery period	Declining balance parameter	Class	Recovery period	Declining balance parameter	Class	Recovery period	Declining balance parameter
Tuxedos	3	1.5	1	4	2.2	1	3	2.0
Cars, light trucks, computers, race horses, tractors	3	1.5	2	5	2.2	2	5	2.0
Construction machinery, mining, and oil field machinery	5	1.5	3	6	1.98	3	7	2.0
Metal working machinery, general industrial machinery, electrical machinery, machinery NEC	5	1.5	4	7	1.54	4	10	2.0
Railroad equipment, engines, and turbines	5	1.5	5	10	1.7	5	13	2.0
Ships and boats	5	1.5	5	10	1.7	6	16	2.0
Gas facilities	10	1.5	5	10	1.7	7	20	2.0
Very low income housing	15	1.75	6	28	1.12	7	20	2.0
Telephone facilities, electric light and power	15	1.50	5	10	1.7	8	25	2.0
Railroads	15	1.50	5	10	1.7	9	30	2.0
Moderately low-income housing	15	1.75	6	28	1.12	9	30	2.0
All structures	19	1.75	6	28	1.12	10	30	1.0

Note: Details on the House Markup Bill are not available. This table reports our best guess from publicly available information.

[a]In the president's proposals, the basis is indexed for inflation.

[b]In the House markup, the basis is indexed for half of the amount of inflation that exceeds 5 percent, if that figure is positive.

powered investment incentives (Table 4.18 and 4.19). The reductions in the statutory marginal corporate tax rate to 36 percent in the Ways and Means version is insufficient to offset the cash flow losses created by the removal of the specific investment incentives. It is estimated that the corporate tax bill would rise by approximately $25 billion per year as a net result of all changes in corporate taxation. This $25 billion increase is deemed to be politically necessary to pay for personal tax cuts brought about by rate reduction.

What was originally presented by the president as a program of tax reform has evolved into a program of personal tax cuts and corporate tax increases. This is bad enough for capital investment. Even worse, the microeconomic incentives for investment have been reduced. Economists have long acknowledged that for every dollar of tax revenue foregone by the Treasury, investment tax credits and accelerated depreciation stimulate approximately twice the business fixed investment as do cuts in the statutory corporate tax rate. The qualitative logic of this conclusion is quite straightforward. A cut in the marginal tax rate costs the Treasury revenues on old investments as well as new. The corporate tax collected on investments made in prior years, which are now yielding an income stream, is reduced just as much as the prospective tax revenue on current and future investments. By contrast, with investment tax credits and accelerated depreciation, the Treasury only loses revenue on new investments. Hence, the investment "bang for the buck" per dollar of Treasury revenue foregone must be expected to be greater for the special incentive programs than for a normal corporate rate change.

Tables 4.20 to 4.22 and Figures 4.10 and 4.11 quantify and display quite clearly the negative capital formation aspects of the Ways and Means tax reform plan, assuming it is effective January 1, 1987. (The exhibits present the *composite* tax reform package and the impacts of the two logically distinct components: a large personal tax cut and an equally large corporate tax increase. The decomposition clarifies the nature of the spending responses in critical sectors.) Similar criticisms would apply to the president's plan and the Treasury's first draft.

The full reform package would raise consumption by about 1 percent at the end of the first year. This initial strength in household spending would temporarily keep producers' durable spending close to the base case in spite of weaker corporate cash flow. Construction spending, both residential and non-residential, should be expected to fall relative to the baseline from the very beginning of the program. Weakness in investment eventually will force income and consumption back toward baseline values, which further weakens business fixed investment. The negative impacts on capital formation are substantial: By the end of the third year of the tax reform plan, the cumulative effective capital stock would be 1.5 percent lower than in the absence of reform. This translates into a loss of productivity for the nation of 0.5–1.0

Table 4.20. *Composite impacts of the House tax proposal (percentage difference from baseline unless otherwise indicated; all changes delayed until January 1, 1987)*

	1987	1988	1989	1990	1991	1987–91	1992–6
Supply							
Potential man-hours	0.1	0.2	0.3	0.4	0.5	0.3	0.7
Actual man-hours	0.2	0.2	0.2	0.3	0.4	0.2	0.3
Business capital stock	−0.1	−0.7	−1.5	−2.1	−2.1	−1.3	−2.5
Number of homes	−0.1	−0.2	−0.2	−0.3	−0.3	−0.2	−0.4
Full-employment GNP	0.1	0.1	−0.1	−0.2	−0.2	−0.1	−0.1
Actual output per hour	0.1	−0.1	−0.1	−0.1	0.0	−0.1	−1.0
Demand							
Consumer spending	0.6	0.6	0.5	0.6	0.9	0.6	0.8
Fixed investment	−1.1	−3.4	−4.4	−3.7	−1.6	−2.8	−2.9
Residential	−2.2	−3.5	−2.5	−1.3	−0.7	−2.0	−2.2
Nonresidential	−0.7	−3.3	−4.9	−4.3	−1.9	−3.1	−3.1
Equipment	−0.7	−3.7	−5.6	−5.2	−2.3	−3.6	−4.0
Structures	−0.8	−2.4	−2.7	−1.9	−0.6	−1.7	−0.3
Real GNP	0.2	−0.1	−0.2	0.1	0.6	0.1	−0.1
Wages and prices							
Hourly wages	0.0	−0.1	−0.2	−0.3	−0.2	−0.1	0.5
Consumer prices	0.0	−0.1	−0.2	−0.3	−0.2	−0.2	0.5
Real wages	0.0	0.0	0.0	0.0	0.1	0.0	0.0
Wholesale prices	0.0	−0.2	−0.2	0.1	0.6	0.1	2.2
Financial conditions							
Standard & Poor's 500 index	−13.1	−13.4	−12.0	−10.4	−9.2	−11.4	−7.5
Dividend yield[a]	−0.10	−0.28	−0.43	−0.57	−0.71	−0.42	−1.04
Prime rate[a]	0.14	−0.26	−0.82	−1.23	−1.32	−0.70	−0.94
Mortgage rate[a]	0.21	0.29	0.09	−0.08	−0.18	0.06	−0.08
Corporate bond rate[a]	0.24	0.26	0.06	−0.09	−0.18	0.06	−0.08
Post-tax cash flow	−6.5	−8.1	−8.9	−9.7	−11.2	−9.0	−11.6
Other indicators							
Unemployment rate[a]	−0.1	0.0	0.1	0.0	−0.3	0.0	0.0
Employment	0.2	0.1	0.0	0.2	0.6	0.2	0.3
Industrial production	0.3	−0.4	−0.3	0.6	1.7	0.4	−0.3
Capacity utilization rate	0.3	−0.2	0.5	2.0	3.5	1.2	1.5
Federal budget							
Taxes[b]	−3	−14	−8	5	28	2	27
Personal[b]	−26	−34	−35	−37	−38	−34	−42
Corporate[b]	23	20	28	41	62	35	58
Expenditures[b]	0	−1	−3	−7	−11	−4	−6
Interest[b]	0	0	−2	−5	−8	−3	−16
Deficit[b]	2	13	5	−12	−40	−6	−33

[a]Absolute difference in rate.
[b]Absolute difference: billions of dollars.
Source: Data Resources U.S. Review, February 1986.

Table 4.21. *Personal income tax impacts of the House tax proposal (percentage difference from baseline unless otherwise indicated; all changes delayed until January 1, 1987)*

	1987	1988	1989	1990	1991	1987–91	1992–6
Supply							
Potential man-hours	0.1	0.2	0.3	0.4	0.5	0.3	0.7
Actual man-hours	0.3	0.3	0.2	0.3	0.3	0.3	0.3
Business capital stock	0.2	0.4	0.3	0.1	0.0	0.2	−0.3
Number of homes	−0.1	−0.2	−0.4	−0.5	−0.5	−0.3	−0.7
Full-employment GNP	0.2	0.4	0.5	0.4	0.4	0.4	0.5
Actual output per hour	0.4	0.1	−0.1	−0.2	−0.2	0.0	−0.2
Demand							
Consumer spending	1.2	1.5	1.4	1.3	1.3	1.3	1.7
Fixed investment	0.5	−0.2	−1.3	−1.7	−1.5	−0.9	−1.2
Residential	−2.1	−4.9	−5.5	−4.9	−4.4	−4.4	−4.1
Nonresidential	1.3	1.1	−0.2	−0.8	−0.8	0.1	−0.6
Equipment	1.7	1.4	−0.2	−1.0	−0.9	0.1	−0.7
Structures	0.3	0.3	−0.3	−0.4	−0.2	−0.1	−0.2
Real GNP	0.9	0.9	0.5	0.4	0.4	0.6	0.5
Wages and prices							
Hourly wages	0.0	0.1	0.2	0.2	0.3	0.2	0.6
Consumer prices	0.0	0.0	0.1	0.2	0.3	0.1	0.6
Real wages	0.1	0.1	0.1	0.1	0.0	0.1	0.0
Wholesale prices	0.1	0.1	0.1	0.2	0.4	0.2	0.8
Financial conditions							
Standard & Poor's 500 index	−0.1	−3.0	−3.5	−3.1	−2.9	−2.6	−3.4
Dividend yield[a]	0.02	0.00	−0.05	−0.09	−0.11	−0.04	−0.17
Prime rate[a]	0.47	0.92	0.90	0.79	0.75	0.77	1.14
Mortgage rate[a]	0.35	0.85	0.94	0.94	0.98	0.81	1.27
Corporate bond rate[a]	0.41	0.85	0.92	0.92	0.96	0.81	1.25
Post-tax cash flow	0.6	−0.8	−1.6	−1.6	−1.3	−1.0	−2.1
Other indicators							
Unemployment rate[a]	−0.2	−0.3	−0.1	0.0	0.0	−0.1	0.0
Employment	0.4	0.6	0.4	0.2	0.2	0.4	0.3
Industrial production	1.4	0.9	0.2	0.0	0.0	0.5	0.3
Capacity utilization rate	1.4	0.6	−0.2	−0.3	−0.1	0.3	0.4
Federal budget							
Taxes[b]	−26	−31	−34	−34	−33	−32	−33
Personal[b]	−31	−28	−26	−26	−27	−28	−24
Corporate[b]	3	−7	−11	−11	−10	−7	−15
Expenditures[b]	0	5	11	17	23	11	45
Interest[b]	2	7	12	16	20	11	39
Deficit[b]	26	36	46	51	56	43	78

[a] Absolute difference in rate.
[b] Absolute difference: billions of dollars.
Source: Data Resources U.S. Review, February 1986.

Table 4.22. *Corporate income tax impacts of the House tax proposal (percentage difference from baseline unless otherwise indicated; all changes delayed until January 1, 1987)*

	1987	1988	1989	1990	1991	1987–91	1992–6
Supply							
Potential man-hours	0.0	0.0	0.0	0.0	0.0	0.0	0.0
Actual man-hours	−0.1	−0.1	0.0	0.1	0.1	0.0	0.0
Business capital stock	−0.3	−1.0	−1.8	−2.2	−2.1	−1.5	−2.2
Number of homes	0.0	0.0	0.1	0.2	0.2	0.1	0.3
Full-employment GNP	−0.1	−0.3	−0.5	−0.7	−0.6	−0.4	−0.5
Actual output per hour	−0.2	−0.2	−0.1	0.1	0.2	0.0	−0.7
Demand							
Consumer spending	−0.4	−0.8	−0.9	−0.7	−0.4	−0.6	−0.8
Fixed investment	−1.2	−3.2	−3.4	−2.2	−0.1	−2.0	−1.6
Residential	−0.1	0.7	2.4	3.3	3.6	2.0	1.7
Nonresidential	−1.5	−4.3	−4.9	−3.7	−1.1	−3.1	−2.3
Equipment	−1.8	−4.9	−5.8	−4.5	−1.4	−3.7	−3.1
Structures	−1.0	−2.5	−2.4	−1.5	−0.3	−1.5	−0.1
Real GNP	−0.4	−0.9	−0.8	−0.4	0.2	−0.4	−0.6
Wages and prices							
Hourly wages	0.0	−0.2	−0.3	−0.5	−0.5	−0.3	0.0
Consumer prices	0.0	−0.1	−0.2	−0.4	−0.5	−0.3	0.0
Real wages	0.0	−0.1	−0.1	−0.1	0.0	0.0	0.0
Wholesale prices	−0.1	−0.2	−0.2	−0.1	0.3	0.0	1.5
Financial conditions							
Standard & Poor's 500 index	−13.1	−11.5	−9.5	−7.9	−6.8	−9.5	−4.8
Dividend yield[a]	−0.13	−0.32	−0.44	−0.55	−0.67	−0.42	−0.96
Prime rate[a]	−0.22	−1.00	−1.65	−2.02	−2.06	−1.39	−1.95
Mortgage rate[a]	−0.07	−0.42	−0.77	−0.97	−1.11	−0.67	−1.23
Corporate bond rate[a]	−0.09	−0.46	−0.78	−0.96	−1.08	−0.67	−1.20
Post-tax cash flow	−6.8	−7.3	−7.3	−7.8	−9.5	−7.8	−9.5
Other indicators							
Unemployment rate[a]	0.1	0.3	0.3	0.0	−0.3	0.1	0.0
Employment	−0.1	−0.4	−0.4	−0.1	0.3	−0.1	0.0
Industrial production	−0.7	−1.3	−0.6	0.5	1.7	0.0	−0.5
Capacity utilization rate	−0.7	−0.9	0.4	2.2	3.7	0.9	1.2
Federal budget							
Taxes[b]	19	15	22	36	60	30	58
Personal[b]	−1	−6	−9	−11	−11	−8	−16
Corporate[b]	21	24	35	50	70	40	68
Expenditures[b]	−1	−4	−12	−21	−31	−14	−43
Interest[b]	−1	−5	−12	−18	−25	−12	−46
Deficit[b]	−20	−19	−34	−57	−90	−44	−101

[a]Absolute difference in rate.
[b]Absolute difference: billions of dollars.
Source: Data Resources U.S. Review, February 1986.

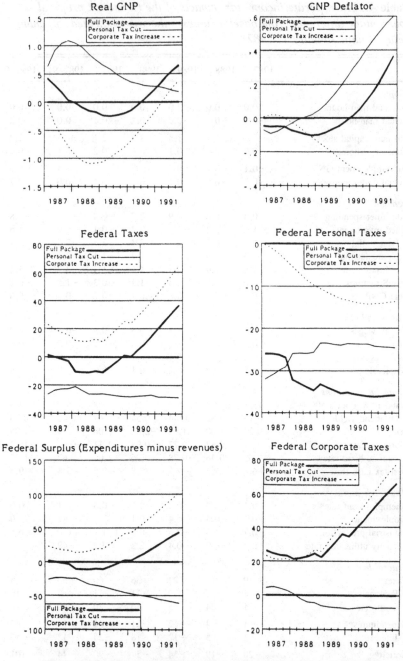

Figure 4.10 The consequences of tax reform. Impacts on output, prices, and government finances (percent difference from baseline stimulated by full package and by the discrete personal and corporate tax components). (Change in billions of dollars.)

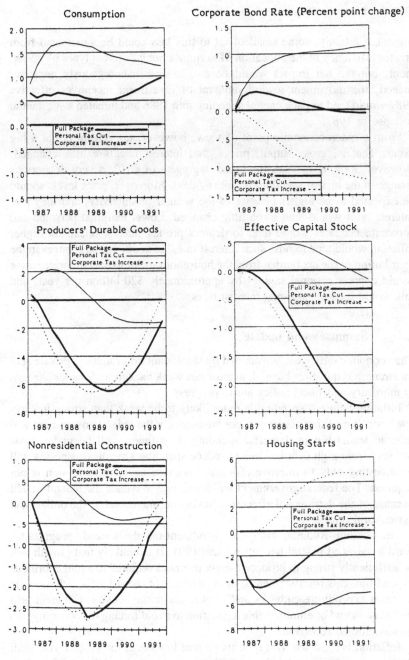

Figure 4.11 Impacts on real spending and capital formation (percent difference from baseline stimulated by full package and by the discrete personal and corporate tax components).

103

percent. Certainly, some small offset to this loss could be anticipated from greater efficiency in the allocation of savings among different types of investment, but the net impact would be clearly and unambiguously negative. Indeed, the movement toward removal of investment incentives effective 1987 would tend to pack capital spending into 1986 and threaten a substantial collapse in 1987.

From a macroeconomic point of view, however, tax reform is not a big event. That is, gross output, prices, and interest rates are little changed. However, looking beneath the broad aggregate of GNP, a very deleterious change in the mix of spending is quite evident. Moreover, price levels should be expected to be higher because of the weaker productivity, and they are. Interest rates would tend to be little changed: Lower marginal personal and corporate tax rates would tend to depress pre-tax interest rates, but higher inflation would tend to raise such interest rates. In addition, the changes in the distribution of the tax burden from the household sector to the corporate sector would depress national savings by approximately $20 billion per year, and this would tend to raise real interest rates.

Summary and update

The economic outlook is surrounded by significant uncertainties. Private sector strength is questionable and, against this weak background, major changes in monetary and fiscal policy are in progress.

Inflation-adjusted spending is more likely to be weak than strong in early 1986 because neither consumers nor business nor the federal government will provide leadership in domestic spending. Consumers will be under some pressure from high debt burdens to reduce spending growth. Businesses will be investing only to improve efficiency because capacity expansion is not required. The federal government will be aiming to reduce the federal deficit because of the detrimental effect it is having on interest rates, the dollar, and agricultural prices.

The Gramm–Rudman–Hollings amendment mandates steady progress toward a balanced federal budget in fiscal 1991. It is unlikely that growth will be sufficiently strong to produce the tax revenues required to avoid enormous expenditure cuts for 1988 and beyond. Because of the risk of a vicious cycle between expenditure cutbacks and weaker economic activity, Congress will probably amend or eliminate this legislation to avoid forcing the economy into a conventional recession.

Inflation is expected to stay in its current low range for another year until the recovery regains strength and the impacts of a weaker dollar are felt. As a result, the Federal Reserve can be expected to respond by allowing interest rates to decline further until midyear; the dollar should continue its decline through 1986. Much looser monetary policy would be called for under Gramm–Rudman–Hollings as fears of both inflation and a potential credit crunch would be significantly reduced.

Tax reform is a major objective of the Reagan administration. Each of the tax reform measures proposed by the Treasury, the president, and the Ways and Means Committee reduces personal taxes at the expense of the corporate taxpayer, thus creating large disincentives for capital formation relative to current law. Expectations of tax reform beginning in 1987 would pack capital spending in 1986 and threaten a substantial collapse in investment in 1987.

Most of this uncertainty will be resolved in the near future. The Federal Reserve will have signaled the degree of its willingness to substitute monetary stimulus for fiscal restraint. The fate of tax reform legislation will be clear. The extent of the near-term capital spending weakness will also be revealed.

An updated reading on the experiments

As of December 1986, the basic economic scenarios have played out much as expected. In addition, the Federal Reserve has been emboldened by the counterinflationary shock of collapsing oil prices to pursue even more expansionary policy than anticipated. Responding to these developments, bond rates are approximately 2 percentage points lower, and consumer spending has evolved more strongly; households responded vigorously to the wealth created by the associated bond- and stock-market rally and to the windfall purchasing power gain from lower oil prices. The foreign exchange value of the dollar logically followed U.S. bond rates down, precisely in the fashion described previously as financial arbitrage.

With regard to the near-term outlook for policies and the economy, tax reform has been passed by the House and Senate and signed by the president. It is widely expected to exert a strongly negative influence on business fixed investment. Real GNP will be depressed almost 0.5 percent in the near term, primarily because of a sustained 4–5 percent drop in capital spending. In the longer term, efficiency gains (per unit of capital) and greater labor force participation will offset a smaller capital stock to permit total output to approximate the economic potential achievable without tax reform. The nation is clearly pushed toward a more labor-intensive economy, and hence toward lower output per labor hour. The new tax bill further reduces America's international competitiveness by raising the cost of capital 10–15 percent: U.S.-made goods will not be as low cost or as technologically advanced as they might have been given this adverse shock.

Equally worrisome is dissipation of the budget discipline hoped for from the Gramm–Rudman–Hollings deficit reduction legislation. In 1986, the Supreme Court crippled its power by curbing its automatic expenditure cuts.

Subsequently, Congress and the president chose to engage in destructive budget timing and estimation games that first bloated the fiscal 1986 deficit, and then evaded the spirit of the law for fiscal 1987. Federal asset sales (which do not reduce federal demands on credit markets) exaggerated revenue forecasts, and "low-ball" expenditure estimates for agriculture allowed elected officials to pretend the fiscal 1987 deficit target of $144–154 billion would be met. Independent observers agree that the budget shortfall will be at least $170 billion and possibly $180–190 billion; it is inconceivable that the fiscal 1988 target of $108 billion can be honestly met. This failure also means that the United States will continue to substitute government spending for investment and imports for domestic production.

Finally, the United States, Japan, Germany, France, and the United Kingdom (the "G-5") did meet to attempt better coordination of monetary and fiscal policies. The first meeting in September 1985 seemed to promise fiscal stimulus outside the United States to complement U.S. fiscal restraint, but only insignificant progress has been achieved. On the other hand, U.S. monetary policy has been so expansive that Japan and Germany have been forced to follow this lead in part to stabilize their currencies.

The global growth outlook is mixed, with all of the major industrial nations facing substantial adjustment problems. Protectionism is a constant threat in an environment with rapidly changing exchange rates and mediocre expansion in total world trade. U.S. growth will then be contingent upon an export rebound and sustained strength in construction markets. The locomotives for U.S. and global growth in the second half of the 1980s will thus be different from those in the first half.

Is there life beyond the trade imbalance?

CHAPTER 5

U.S. economic prospects and policy options: impact on Japan–U.S. relations

PAUL A. SAMUELSON

A Japanese renaissance

One of mankind's oldest myths, long antedating Tchaikovsky's ballet or Grimm's fairy tales, is the legend of the sleeping beauty who is awakened back to life by the kiss of a prince charming. What we are not told is whether, after the princess is brought back to life, the couple really did live happily ever afterward.

Were there no quarrels? Did the wife come to outstrip the husband in earning power? What kept their balance of payments in equilibrium? The tale ends just when the real-world problems begin.

If it is not too fanciful, think of 1945 Japan as the helpless and sleeping beauty. Cast the MacArthur occupation authority in the role of the prince charming. In doing so, no prejudgment is being made about how the credit should be divided for bringing about the postwar Japanese miracle. After all, even in the folk story, it is possible that the princess was already awakening of her own accord and that the prince was merely a lucky passerby who happened to appear on the scene at the critical moment.

The takeoff of the Japanese economy after 1945 might even be considered a second rerun of the sleeping beauty legend. The first would have to be the case of Commodore Perry's opening up of Japan just prior to the Meiji Restoration. Admittedly, the 1950–75 takeoff of Japan does have to be re-

I owe thanks for professional insights to Dr. Ryuzo Sato, Director of the Center for Japan–U.S. Business and Economic Studies, New York University, and Visiting Professor, Kennedy School of Government, Harvard University; also to the MIT Sloan School of Management for a Gordon Y. Billard Fellowship that provided research opportunity; and to Aase Huggins for valuable editorial assistance. More than 50 leading American forecasters provided indispensable inputs relevant to the current econometric scene.

A summary of this project's research findings and relevant viewpoints was presented at the NYU Center for Japan–U.S. Business and Economic Studies on December 4, 1985, under the title "The U.S. and Japanese Economies in the Remaining Reagan Years." This chapter reproduces most of that lecture, with some modifications suggested by the valuable discussions there.

garded as something of a miracle. However, those who know about Japan's progress from, say, 1860 to 1905 ought to have been somewhat prepared for the postwar spurt. A miracle is more surprising the first time it happens than the second time around!

This chapter surveys and analyzes macroeconomic developments affecting Japan–U.S. trade imbalances and trade relationships for the remaining years of the Reagan administration. From these positivistic findings must flow the policy recommendations that are implied.

Such a big topic can never be finally resolved. What I can do, however, is to present some of my tentative findings and hypotheses.

That I shall raise more questions that I can answer requires no apology. For in an inexact science like political economy, posing the right questions to investigate and ponder over is an important part of the battle.

Success story

Americans are alarmed to find that we have a large adverse balance of payments on current account. This is a dramatic reversal from the 1950s, when the rest of the world complained resentfully of a chronic "dollar shortage."

The time interval from dollar shortage to the present is precisely the epoch of the postwar Japanese miracle. In 1950, Japan was a poor oriental country with life expectancies still in the fifties. No wonder the Japanese retirement age became set early.

As best we can estimate, the 1950 per capita real income of Japan, in ratio to that of the United States expressed as 100, was only 17 – or about one-sixth (Table 5.1). Then things changed. And how they did change!

By 1955, Japan was almost at one-fourth of the U.S. living standard. By 1960, it had reached one-third. Some time between 1965 and 1970, Japan went past one-half our level, having already surpassed the Soviet per capita level along the way. After 1970, Japan left Britain behind.

By the time of the 1973 OPEC crisis, Japan had reached two-thirds of the American level of living.

Where does Japan now stand? I suspect that most people have an exaggerated estimate of Japanese productivity. Sometimes Americans think that each Japanese worker is seven feet tall. Moreover, Japanese management is supposed to have secret weapons of compromise and consensus agreement and to possess mysterious procedures that ensure perfect quality control.

At White House meetings, I have heard American businesspeople and trade unionists complain that the Japanese work too hard; in the manner of Benjamin Franklin and Max Weber, they save too much; and to top off the indictment, they are just too damned smart.

The statistical facts do not quite bear this out. As of 1985, Japanese produc-

Table 5.1. *Per capital real incomes*
(expressed as percentage of U.S.)

	1950	1955	1960	1965	1970	1975	1980
United States	100	100	100	100	100	100	100
Japan	17	23	33	43	64	68	72
USSR	30	33	40	42	47	50	48
West Germany	40	54	71	71	79	81	86
South Korea	11(1953)	12	12	12	17	21	25
United Kingdom	56	59	65	63	64	65	65
India	7	7	8	7	7	7	6
China	6½	8⅔	9¾	9¼	10⅔	12¼	14
Taiwan	10	12	13	15	20	24	31

Source: Robert Summres and Alan Heston, "Improved International Comparisons of Real Product and Its Composition: 1950–1980," *Review of Income and Wealth* (June 1984).[1]

tivity still trails U.S. productivity. Calling U.S. per capita real income 100 in 1986, I estimate Japan's per capita income to be somewhere around 80. This puts Japan perceptibly below Canada, Norway, West Germany, France, Sweden, Switzerland, and Denmark.

True, Japanese life expectancies now average out to the high seventies, making them second to none. True, by the end of the century Japan will move toward or beyond the top of the list in per capita real income, provided only that it continues to enjoy annual growth rates that average out 2 percentage points greater than ours. Since the Soviet population is more than double that of Japan, in terms of *total* rather than *per capita* real GNP, by the year 2000 the ordering will still be the United States first, and the USSR and Japan next, without much difference between the second- and the third-place nations. For all China's population size, even if the post-Mao economic reforms work out well, China will still not come close in total economic weight to the Big Three – or, if we include all of Western Europe in a Common Market bloc, China will still trail the Big Four.

Not a zero-sum game

I do not care for the sporting-page way of looking at economic rivalries. From the time in 1870 when Bismarck unified Germany, England and third-party observers could envisage in Germany a rival who eventually would threaten the hegemony of the British Empire.

The German GNP grew faster than the British. Science in the Wilhelmine universities spawned the successful German chemistry and electricity industries. As far as economics is concerned, this could have been a fruitful competition and rivalry. German progress did not have to be bought at the price of British progress any more than nineteenth-century American progress had to be at the expense of the British Empire's standard of welfare.

Otto von Bismarck has much to answer for at the bar of historical judgment. Provoking two wars, against Austria and France, Bismarck bequeathed to the vain Wilhelm II an unstable legacy. World War I was the bitter fruit of Bismarckian adventurism, and Hitler's World War II was part of the total bill.

None of this served an economic purpose or followed inevitably from economic causation.

This basic truth needs emphasizing in our own time. From 1950 to 1975 the mixed economies of Western Europe and the Far East gained mightily on the United States. In 1945 the 6 percent of world population who were Americans must have enjoyed almost half of global GNP. By 1980 this had dropped to only a quarter of global GNP.

Foreigners' gain was not our loss. Their gain was part of the acceleration of global real output that occurred in the third quarter of the twentieth century and that was widely shared by both developing and industrialized regions. The point is that this step-up in global GNP was also shared by us in North America: In terms of U.S. history over two centuries, the 1946–73 years were marked by generous real growth – even though West Germany, Japan, and the Common Market were gaining on us.

Attention should be directed to the remarkable fact that Japan's post-1950 prosperity has owed nothing to military expenditures. Early in this century, Lenin, Hobson, and Rosa Luxemburg propounded a theory of imperialism that has much appeal in Marxian circles. According to their thesis, advancing economies like those of Germany and Japan must necessarily run out of purchasing power as their masses receive too little effective income to keep employment full. Only by imperialistic adventures in colonies and war can the metropolitan center keep itself going.

So much for science fiction. What are the midcentury facts in this age after Keynes? Japan has about the lowest ratio of military personnel to total population of any nation. Indeed, if we adjust for relative wealth, Japan joins with Switzerland and Canada in having *negative* ratios! Japan at the point five-sixths through the twentieth century displays the precise reverse of the Bismarck pattern of Germany at the two-thirds point of the nineteenth century.

This demonstration is good for the world. It is good for Japan. If and when Japan becomes tempted to bring its military might into relation with its economic might, I hope Tokyo and Washington will be reminded of the salutary truth that economic welfare no longer has to depend on political power.

Table 5.2 gives data on the degree to which different economies are "militarized.'' If one divides nations according to whether they are non-Marxist or Marxist, it appears that the latter tend to experience a greater degree of militarization.

The present crisis in U.S.–Japan relations

To recapitulate, the sober truth is the reverse of the proposition that Japan's growth robs America's growth. Here is how I put it in a *New York Times* article of September 15, 1985:

Since 1950 the typical American has had a rise in real income of about 93 percent. A respectable fraction of this gain came from technical progress abroad (the cost cutting lobbyists complain about). Our purchases from abroad give us the benefit of the services of foreign workers and resources; at the same time that this is a bargain to us, it raises the real wage rates of workers abroad as a wider circle of consumers bid for their services. Examine a 1950 Sears catalog and the equipment in a 1950 hospital; do the same for 1985, and realize that much of *our* real gains do stem from cheaper imports.

Although Japan's name is not mentioned in the above paragraph, it, more than any other country, deserves credit for the U.S. standard-of-living progress that is associated with cheaper imports. I am not oblivious to the problems faced by manufacturing industries in America that are associated with new foreign competition and shall address this serious matter. What I want to stress is the beneficent face of the coin.

Good policy for both countries will want to preserve the mutual-benefit aspects while trying to minimize or contain the transitional burdens.

Pure theory of trade

I have written several major articles on the basic economics of the Pacific Basin's challenge to Europe and North America. Since I cannot go into all the fine details, let me merely cite these publications: my 1972 Little Nobel lecture entitled "International Trade for a Rich Country"; my German Symposium piece of 1981 "To Protect Manufacturing?"; my detailed analysis in the recent Saburo Okita *Festschrift*, entitled "Analytics of Free-trade or Protectionist Response by America to Japan's Growth Spurt"; and my brief summary in defense of free trade rather than protection that appeared in the *New York Times* of September 15, 1985.

Two truths need underlining.

1. The living standard of American workers and capitalists is on the average increased when Japan or Korea makes technological advances in producing goods that we characteristically import from them.

Table 5.2. *Marxism and militarism: force ratios of Marxist and non-Marxist regimes*

Selected non-Marxist countries	Force ratio	Wealth-adjusted force ratio	Marxist countries	Force ratio	Wealth-adjusted force ratio
Western Hemisphere			Albania	18.9	19.6
United States	9.1	4.6	Angola	6.4	7.1
Canada	3.3	−0.9	Algeria	6.0	5.2
Mexico	2.0	0.4	Benin	0.8	4.1
Guatemala	2.3	2.8	Bulgaria	19.7	17.6
Honduras	3.9	5.7	Burma	4.9	9.3
El Salvador	5.4	6.8	Cape Verde	10.0	12.9
Costa Rica	1.5	2.6	China (Mainland)	4.3	5.9
Colombia	2.6	2.6	Congo	10.0	10.4
Venezuela	3.2	1.1	Cuba	23.5	22.7
Brazil	3.6	2.7	Czechoslovakia	13.8	10.0
Argentina	6.0	3.9	Ethiopia	8.2	12.9
Chile	10.3	9.2	Germany (East)	14.0	10.0
			Guinea	3.2	6.4
Europe			Guinea-Bissau	5.0	9.4
United Kingdom	5.8	2.0	Hungary	10.5	7.5
France	8.9	4.7	Iraq	32.1	31.7
West Germany	7.8	3.6	Korea, North	38.0	39.1
Sweden	8.4	3.7	Laos	15.8	21.6
Switzerland	3.6	−1.3	Madagascar	2.2	5.3
Austria	5.3	1.5	Mongolia	21.2	21.6
Italy	6.9	3.8	Mozambique	1.5	4.4
			Nicaragua	27.8	28.7
Mid-East			Poland	11.9	9.3
Israel	46.2	43.4	Romania	10.5	8.1
Turkey	13.3	13.5	Somalia	8.9	12.0
Jordan	19.7	19.8	Soviet Union	16.3	13.3
Egypt	10.0	11.7	Syria	30.9	30.4
Saudi Arabia	5.4	0.5	Tanzania	2.7	6.1
Iran	11.4	11.0	Vietnam	21.5	25.8
Libya	16.7	19.8	Yemen (South)	12.5	14.8
			Yugoslavia	10.9	9.3
Africa					
South Africa	2.3	0.9	Mean, 32 Marxist countries	13.3	14.1
Nigeria	1.6	2.5			
Ghana	1.0	0.3	Mean, 109 Non-Marxist countries	6.1	5.9
Zaire	0.9	5.3			
Liberia	3.5	5.8			
Sudan	3.3	5.3			
Asia					
Japan	2.0	−2.0			
India	1.6	5.3			
Indonesia	1.7	3.7			

Table 5.2. (*cont.*)

Selected non-Marxist countries	Force ratio	Wealth-adjusted force ratio	Marxist countries	Force ratio	Wealth-adjusted force ratio
Asia					
Thailand	4.8	5.1			
Taiwan	27.2	25.8			
Australia	4.8	0.5			
Philippines	3.0	4.3			

Note: The force ratio is the number of active, full-time military personnel per 1,000 population (data are for 1982). The adjusted force ratio is based on the relationship between national wealth and the force ratio. Each country's figure represents the deviation of its actual force ratio from the force ratio it would be expected to have given its level of wealth.
Source: World Military Expenditures and Arms Transfers, 1972–1982, U.S. Arms Control and Disarmament Agency, 1984.

2. But it is oversimple dogma to argue that free trade *always* entails a boost in America's well-being. When Pacific economies develop new technical advances in goods that we previously produced at low cost, this dynamic change in comparative advantage most definitely will subtract from America's consumers' surplus from trade and thus from our average real incomes. Those Americans hurt are not merely the workers and factory owners in the export industries that have lost visibility; most U.S. incomes may have to come down to clear markets in the new equilibrium. That can imply a slowdown in the trend of mean real wage rates, or can even entail an outright decline.

I should add that the necessary drop in European real wage rates can be as great as or greater than the implied drop in American wages. There is perhaps some evidence that post-1973 European real wage rates have been even more inflexibly resistant than ours have been; this may help explain why we have been able to create more than 30 million new jobs in the last decade, whereas western Europe has barely been able to maintain the same total of jobs.

When noneconomists learn that dynamic free trade can hurt America's living standards, they have one first natural reaction: "Avoid free-trade's hurt by putting quotas and tariffs against the low-cost foreign imports."

Economists who are expert in the analysis of international trade cannot agree. Their system deduces that, on top of the new harm that innovation under free trade brings, there is likely to be superimposed a second harm from the protectionist measures. Yes, some old high-paying jobs can be subsidized into existing ones; however, the accompanying new market-clearing spread of American real wages in other places will average out to a lower overall standard of U.S. earnings. What holds for the factor of production labor can hold also for capital or for U.S. natural resources. That is why experts advise: "Don't react to decline in our effective productivity, brought about by innovation abroad, by gratuitously shooting ourselves in the foot through the device of import quotas."

Qualifications

That, in a nutshell, is basic trade theory. Are there no exceptions and qualifications? Yes, here are a few that are possibilities but that don't stand up as being significant under quantitative measurements.

1. If American firms have a lot of unexploited monopoly power, then some cleverly allocated modest tariffs might force foreigners to pay more for the products we alone can supply. Note that this does not suggest tariffs where lobbyists and senators are most eager to put them – namely on auto, steel, shoe, and textile industries, where the United States no longer has competitive viability much less unexploited monopoly power.

2. There is a new second argument associated most recently with the name of Dean Henry Rosovsky of Harvard University. Schumpeterian innovators, he points out, typically make large temporary profits in the time period when rivals have not learned to imitate their new productivity. However, the Japanese are alleged to collusively rob American entrepreneurs of these Schumpeterian rents from innovation by erecting "unfair" trade barriers. Professor Rosovsky in effect counsels: "An eye for an eye. Let's put on quotas as a bargaining chip to force Japan to play the free trade game fairly."

If we study the Rosovsky point, we shall ultimately find that it belongs with the earlier point alleging that America does have some monopoly power, in the sense that we can legislatively alter the mean terms of trade at which we sell our exports relative to the prices we pay for our imports.

Does America have great power over its international terms of trade? Under pure-competition theory, where rivals and potential rivals exist in many regions, the answer is, only within narrow limits.

Under realistic workable competition, where Fortune-500 companies here and abroad do learn by doing and where economies of large-scale production are important, one cannot be so dogmatically negative.

However, what is it that is actually being proposed by the protectionists? They have no way of calculating the maximal terms of trade as called for by the "scientific tariff" of the advanced textbooks. In fact, they are not proposing tariffs or quotas for Schumpeterian infant industries and processes. Either they favor across-the-board surcharges against all Japanese exports, or against all Pacific-Basin exports; or, primarily, they favor ad hoc quota relief for old industries that have for a long time been losing market share – textiles, shoes, steel, autos, sugar, and so forth.

Almost all economic experts, here and abroad, will doubt that quotas on routine American manufacturers can succeed in a bootstrap operation of raising mean U.S. real incomes or in preserving them. A few experts do hold out hopes for an industrial policy. The Late Lord Kaldor of the U.K. Labor Party was a rare theoretist who believed that U.K. protection would actually raise U.K. incomes. Miyohei Shinohara is a Japanese economist who has investigated how a MITI-like industrial policy might succeed in dynamically altering a nation's comparative advantages. Both on the liberal left in the American labor movement, and at that West Point of American capitalism – the Harvard Business School – there is a similar belief by Professor Bruce Scott and others, that abandoning free trade would have a useful role to play as part of a new American industrial policy.

To make more precise statements about the merits of free trade with technologically advancing Pacific Basin countries like Japan, we need to examine some simple models of trade with foreign innovation. We begin the discussion by considering the Ricardian model. Let our traditional export be good 1, which has unit labor costs here of a_1 and a_1^* in Japan. Good 2 has respective labor costs of a_2 and a_2^*, and good 3 has costs of a_3 and a_3^*. Good 3 is traditionally our import because we postulate the following initial comparative-advantage inequalities:

$$a_1/a_1^* < a_2/a_2^* < a_3/a_3^*. \tag{1}$$

It must depend on reciprocal demand whether good 2 is an import or an export for us. (If Japan begins with a relatively "small" population and labor supply, so that

$$L^*/L \ll 1, \tag{2}$$

it is probable that we do export good 2 initially.)

What is the effect of a Japanese innovation that lowers its a_3^*? Now Japan supplies our import good at lower real costs in terms of its labor; now its workers get an increased real wage in terms of good 3. Once Japan is big enough to supply *all* of our good-3 needs, competition will bid down the relative price of our import relative to the other goods that we do produce. This illustrates two principles:

> *Rule 1.* Innovations abroad in goods we continue to import tend to benefit Americans.

Rule 2. Such innovations will also benefit Japanese if, but only if, our demand for those goods is "sufficiently" elastic.

With more than two goods in the model, the full analysis of this becomes complicated. However, the above qualitative results can be illustrated well by the easy-to-manage case of two Ricardian goods that people everywhere spend their money on in the same fixed proportions (the Millian and Cobb–Douglas case). Suppose the two regions have comparable labor supplies in the sense that each is able to specialize completely as the sole producer of the good in which it has a comparative advantage.

In this case, both before and after the Japanese innovation, the regions keep as shares of combined income the respective fractions in which their own good attracts income. As long as this is the case, the Japanese innovation that raises *aggregate* real income must raise *each* nation's per capita income by the same percentage. Rule 1 is confirmed; and, in this case, so is Rule 2.

This Mill–Ricardo two-good case suggests some of the needed qualifications. When Japan is so small that it can't fill our entire needs for its export good, Japan faces infinitely elastic demand and we get *none* of the joint benefit from the innovation; this consequence is the limiting edge of Rule 1. When Japan is so large that we can't fill all its need for our export good, Japan's comparative costs determine all prices and our labor shares with its labor in getting higher real wage after the innovation, confirming both rules.

When the increased potential supply for her favored good causes people everywhere to spend a smaller fraction on it – as is the case when inelasticity of uniform homothetic demand prevails – increased plenty can be absolutely immiserating to Japan, confirming the contingent second part of Rule 2.

Are these conclusions robust under departures from Ricardo's labor-only model? Little that is unambiguous can be said about a truly general model involving any number of goods and factors of production, nonhomothetic taste differences among people by regions, and possibly negative income elasticities. However, even in a Heckscher–Ohlin world,[2] or a Viner–Ricardo–Samuelson–Jones technology like that in Samuelson,[3] there remains a presumption that the industry and region wherein an innovation takes place will have the prices of its goods cheapened; people elsewhere are probably benefited. People there may well benefit, save that inelasticity of demands for their goods may make the innovation entail a net loss to them.

The reader can work out the two-factor model in which every good in each place is producible by transferable labor there working with fixed lands specialized for each of the goods. Every good might be produced in some positive amounts in both places. With ignorable transport costs, each good is being exported by the region that is favored to concentrate on it. Now let Japan undergo an innovation that reduces its costs in one of its export goods. Presumably that cheapens it relative to other goods: The American land specific to that good will now have less labor working on it, and the U.S. real wage in terms of that good rises, whereas this land's real rent falls. The U.S. labor displaced from this industry gets spread over the other industries, thereby raising land rents there a bit and lowering U.S. real wage rates measured in terms of the other goods. There still remains a presumption that U.S. factors of production as a whole now earn a higher real income in toto. In Japan it depends on elasticities of demand whether the innovation has raised or lowered the remuneration of total factors. Unless inelasticity is great, there is a presumption toward a net Japanese gain. Gains, however, are unevenly distributed.

To the degree that the prices of other goods will have risen relative to Japan's new market-clearing wage, labor will be shifted to them, and their lands will share in the gain via higher land rents. (However, the reverse allocations between lands and labors in other industries could occur.)

How innovations abroad can harm our free-trade well-being

Now for the more subtle part of the problem, the part so often misunderstood by naive free traders:

> Rule 3. Innovation abroad that enables producers there to displace producers here who previously exported abroad (and provided for domestic needs here) will tend *to reduce American living standards*.

This displays the usefulness of the Ricardian three-good scenario. Suppose that, before the innovation, we produce good 1 and they produce good 3, and that both of us competitively produce good 2. In that case, the ratio of our real wage level to theirs, measured in any units – both in $, both in yen, both in terms of good i as numeraire – will equal the a_2^*/a_2 ratio of the borderline good produced in both places.

$$W/W^* = a_2^*/a_2. \tag{3}$$

Now introduce a small innovation in Japanese production of good 2, which reduces a_2^* a little. Until the cost reduction becomes so large as to drive out of existence *all* U.S. production of q_2, the relation (3) still obtains. Clearly, then, our real wage will fall when a_2^* drops!

Fall relative to the Japanese wage? Or fall absolutely? Actually, *both!* Here is why. As before, a unit of American work buys the same amount of good 1 (namely, a real wage of $1/a_2$). As before, the U.S. real wage in terms of good 2 stays at $1/a_2$. But now each American worker must work longer to get 1 unit of good 3 by importing. While both regions produce good 2, we must have:

$$W/P_3 = (P_2/P_3)(W/P_2) = (a_2^*/a_3^*)/a_2. \tag{4}$$

From (4) it is clear that a reduction in a_2^* must reduce America's real wage expressed in terms of the good obtainable only by importing. Since the other real wages for the goods we continue to produce at home are unchanged, it is manifest that America's *overall real wage* has indeed been hurt by the Japanese innovation.

Warning: This hurt has nothing to do with induced transitional unemployment. All markets clear always. However, the real wage at which our labor market clears has been hurt by innovation abroad, which makes Japan more cost-competitive in goods we did previously (and perhaps still do) produce. Thus, Rule 3 is confirmed. QED.

A dramatic and simple redemonstration for how free trade can hurt us is provided by the two-good case where, prior to the innovation, $a_1/a_1^* < a_2/a_2^*$, and we export good 1 in exchange for imports of good 2 from Japan. Now let innovation reduce a_2^* so much as to convert the inequality into an equality. This means that there are *no* exploitable differences in advantage: The free trade equilibrium becomes that of self-sufficient autarky; our terms of trade for exports in relation to imports P_1/P_2 have dropped all the way to a_1/a_2 (and a_1^*/a_2^*), robbing us of *all* of our consumer's surplus from trade; by the same token, Japan's terms of trade, P_2^*/P_1^*, have risen from somewhere in the old $(a_2^*/a_1^*, a_2/a_1)$ interval all the way to the top endpoint of a_2/a_1 – and at the same time the innovation gives Japan more of both goods to exchange at these improved terms. The dogmatic free trader who alleges that each and all *must* gain always is shown to be plain wrong.

The n-good case is, not surprisingly, considerably more involved; its details are included in an appendix to this chapter.

Reacting to free-trade's harm

Let one region (say, Japan) always play the free-trade game, always acting as if it is a price taker too small to affect competitive prices. Let us, after the innovation, try to use our monopoly power to offset the harm it may have brought to us. Does the United States have such monopoly power?

Yes. Even if each is a standardized good produced by many independent American and Japanese firms. As long as America has almost 25 percent of global product and Japan 10 percent, if our government acts in concert it should be able to move Japan on its competitive-reaction loci to a state of the system that improves American welfare. Usually a system of tariffs and quotas may not be the Pareto-efficient way for America to play the Mill–Edgeworth–Bickerdike game of "scientific protectionism." But it is one way.

Clearly, this ultrarational policy would never call for prohibitive tariffs and quotas that lead to U.S. self-sufficiency. Not-too-large tariffs are what is called for. Whether these are 10 percent or 50 percent tariffs must depend on the parameters of technology and of taste elasticities. Moreover, it is not clear whether the maximal gain achievable by this Machiavellian ploy is equal to a 1 percent increase in per capita U.S. living standards, or 5 percent, or a fraction of 1 percent.

Also, it is reasonably clear that Japan would not stand by and continue to adhere to the rules of the free-trade game if the United States is manifestly playing the role of what economists call the Stackelberg–Edgeworth one-sided duopolist. That tariff retaliation by Japan must presumably involve global deadweight loss, lowering what we can expect from maximally exploiting our monopoly power. Theoretically, *all* parties could end up worse than they would have done under doctrinaire free trade.

Whatever the merits of scientific protectionism, the current politics of would-be American protectionists is far removed from such abstractions. Old and stagnant industries, often with union-induced above-average wage scales, are the ones most likely to succeed in lobbying Congress for curbs on imports. Acceding to those desires can preserve some high-paying American jobs, but only at the cost of lowering the real wages elsewhere that clear the labor market and avoid self-imposed mass unemployment.

The story would be less simple if we postulated many corporations. Each produces goods at increasing returns, with marginal products rising with scale, $\partial^2 q/\partial L^2 \gg 1$. Laissez-faire leads under these conditions in America and Japan to multiple possibilities, in which each region might end with no predictable set of successful products.

Fair trade versus free trade

The economic theory of the seminar room and the learned treatises seems to be in another world from discussions in Congress and the newspapers. When imports from the Pacific Basin kill off American manufacturing jobs, that is assumed axiomatically to be an economic tragedy.

Most businessmen and politicians are ashamed not to pay lip service to free trade. Senator John C. Danforth of Missouri is a typical example, and was written up in the *Wall Street Journal* of December 2, 1986. He is upset when his constituents lose jobs in the shoe industry. He is not against really free trade. But he believes that the Japanese, while pretending to believe in free trade, in fact engage in unfair trade. They protect formally against imports of meat and citrus. Informally, they block bids by our telecommunications industries. They dump goods into our markets at below true costs. An elaborate system of reciprocity among Japanese corporations effectively excludes our exports from getting into the Japanese markets.

The net result is to make Danforth favor U.S. protectionism. Until the Japanese change their ways, as attested by a marked reduction in our bilateral trade deficit with Japan, people like Danforth would favor surcharges, tariffs, and quotas targeted against Japan and similar Pacific nations. Such protectionists also lend a friendly ear to proposals for "a new industrial policy."

My MIT colleagues Lester Thurow and Michael Piore, disturbed by what they see as a decimation of middle-class workers and sapping of vigor of the trade union movement, regretfully come out in favor of some interferences with free trade. The more liberal of our two parties, the Democrats, are at present more protectionist than conservative Republicans such as President Reagan.

There is some truth to the charge that Japan does impede some imports. It is a pity that naggings by friends like me get almost nowhere in persuading Japan to throw open her markets out of her own self interest. The Danforths would soon learn that the elimination of *all* unfair trade practices would still leave us with a large deficit on current account and trade.

Calling the bluff of protectionists would not convert them into free traders. The mayors of Pittsburgh and Detroit and the congressional delegations from those manufacturing regions would still want to protect their jobs from cost-cutting importers.

I must therefore rush on to discuss the basic economic causation of America's overvalued dollar and resulting trade deficit with Japan.

Basic trends

First, it is successful innovation and investment by Pacific Basin countries in bringing down costs of manufacturing that dictates a balance of payments problem for an advanced country like the United States with its reduced pace of productivity progress and its modest rate of private saving. Under floating exchange rates, the presumption would be for a declining dollar even if macroeconomic policy were optimal or tolerably good.

Second, United States macro policy in the Reagan years has been disastrous from the standpoint of the balance of trade. The single important factor raising real interest rates here and attracting demand for dollars on capital account is our colossal basic fiscal deficit. Rightist supply siders deny that "crowding out" of investment is possible. Neoclassical and post-Keynesian economics, however, recognize truth in the story that public fiscal thriftlessness compounds our low private thriftiness. Favorable tax incentives for investment – investment credits, fast depreciation, and so forth – reinforce the rise in market-clearing real interest rates. Financing the public debt competes with domestic investment needs for Americans' savings; eagerness of foreigners to cycle back their balance of payments surpluses perpetuates overvaluation of the dollar on current account as it alleviates the crowding out process here by having some of the crowding out of investment take place with respect to Asian and European domestic investments.

Robert Mundell long ago pointed out the therapy for such unbalance. America should raise taxes and cut expenditures to increase its overall saving and reduce its real interest rates; Japan and Germany should do the opposite, pursuing a looser fiscal policy and a tighter monetary policy.

Enlarged saving here and reduced saving there will call for less capital inflow into America. This means a downward floating dollar, and greater competitiveness in global production for American producers.

It is easy to diagnose these basics, but hard to implement the implied therapies.

Quantitative trends

Figures 5.1 to 5.4 provide a picture of U.S. international variables up through 1984. A glance at Figure 5.1 leads to a straightforward but superficial impression: During the 1980s the dollar floated upward, and at this same time our trade balance deteriorated drastically. This simple story accords with standard theories of international finance. Lerner–Marshall elasticities being orthodoxly favorable, appreciation of an exchange rate moves the balance of payments adversely.

An important corollary follows from this paradigm: To alleviate or reverse the deterioration of America's current account, somehow engineer a depreciation of the dollar and an appreciation of the yen and mark.

Other things being equal, one may agree with this thrust. Reality, however, is not so simple. Quantitatively, the "other things being equal" provisos of the elementary classroom have not been valid in the 1970–86 period. Irreversible accelerations in Pacific Basin productivities are an important part of the picture: Shifts of curves and not reversible movements along curves must be reckoned with. Therefore, it may well take a drop in the dollar exchange rate of more than its post-1978 rise of 40 percent to accommodate the greater pace of innovation ahead.

Figure 5.2 reminds us that we should be working with real exchange rates and not simply with nominal rates. Thus, H. S. Wainright, a Boston firm giving advice to Wall Street and one of the few practitioners of "rational expectationism" with a respectable forecasting performance, recently argued that the lire had depreciated more than the dollar and that the U.S. balance

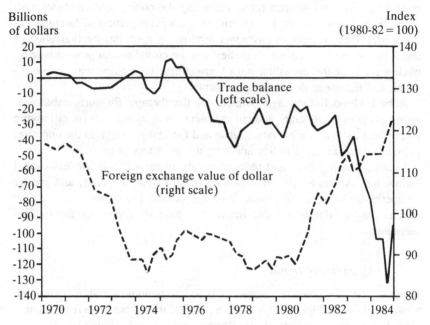

Figure 5.1   U.S. merchandise trade balance (seasonally adjusted annual rate) and weighted average real foreign exchange value of U.S. dollar (quarterly). *Source*: Data Resources Inc. and Morgan Guaranty Trust Co.

depreciated most. When the Italian price level rises faster than the American, experienced economists should know it is normal for a lire depreciation even when real exchange rates and real balances have not been changing at all.

Figure 5.2 reveals that in the crucial period of 1980–5, the real rise in the dollar averaged out to a bit less than its nominal rise, presumably because Japanese and German price levels were under slightly better control than our own.

Figure 5.3 confirms that interest rates in different countries tend to show common levels and common movements. During the first Reagan term, U.S. real interest rates did tend to move ahead of foreign rates, sucking in capital funds from abroad and suggesting to players in the futures markets that the dollar might be susceptible to a future fall in its relative level. Figure 5.3 could be augmented to show that the rise in U.S. real interest rates during the first half of the 1980s did help pull up real rates abroad.

Figure 5.4 both confirms and contradicts the thesis that expanding our rate of GNP growth tends to make the dollar depreciate. The Nixon–Burns boom of 1972 does cause the dollar to fall. The ensuing recession of 1974 does

Index
(1980-82 = 100)

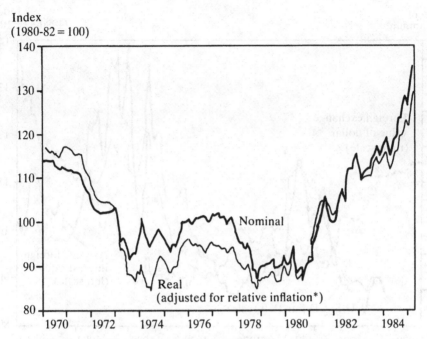

Figure 5.2   Weighted average foreign exchange value of U.S. dollar (in terms of 15 major currencies weighted according to bilateral manufactures trade, based on monthly averages of daily rates). *Source*: Morgan Guaranty Trust Co.
*Inflation measured in terms of wholesale prices of nonfood manufactures.

reverse its course. However, the rise of the dollar in the 1980s must be in answer to a different drumbeat since there was no concomitant oscillation in real GNP growth rates. Nor do we find in Figures 5.5 and 5.6 any extraordinary misbehaviors of price indexes or the money supply sufficient to account for the extraordinary rise of the dollar.

I must agree with Kazuo Ueda's analysis at the March 1986 conference in Tokyo sponsored by the National Bureau of Economic Research and Tokyo University. Among the long-term structural factors shaping our exchange rate are the differential saving tendencies of Americans and Japanese. The most notable change in these long-term tendencies was the drastic rise in the U.S. fiscal deficit between 1980 and 1982. This further lowered America's net saving and raised our market-clearing real interest rates.

The Reagan deficit, or if you will the Reagan–O'Neill deficit, did contribute to crowding out of investment here; and, by raising world interest rates, must also have been crowding out investment abroad as we absorbed on

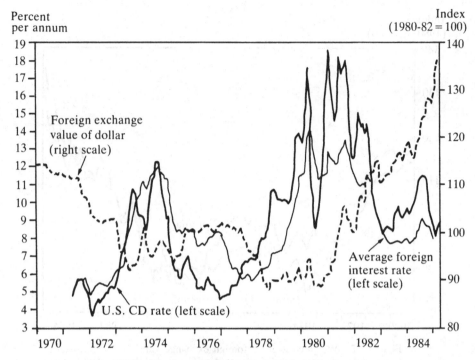

Percent
per annum

Index
(1980-82 = 100)

Figure 5.3   Three-month interest rates: United States and weighted average
for four foreign countries, and weighted average nominal foreign exchange
value of the U.S. dollar (monthly averages of daily figures). *Source*: Board
of Governors of the Federal Reserve System and Morgan Guaranty Trust Co.

capital account foreigners' limited savings, diverting some of this away from
financing capital formation abroad.

Current trends

The dollar has been floating downward relative to the yen and the mark ever
since February 1985. After September 22, 1985, when the Group of Five met
in New York to agree on official exchange-market interventions to help the
dollar depreciate further, good progress has been made in reducing the degree
of the dollar's overvaluation on current account.

Some economists dogmatically deny that a few tens of billions of dollars of
stabilization operations can have any perceptible effect on markets that involve hundreds of billions of dollars of gross transactions. Other economists,
like me, suspect that when the setting is right for the dollar to fall spon-

Index: 2nd qtr.
1973 = 100
(Ratio scale)

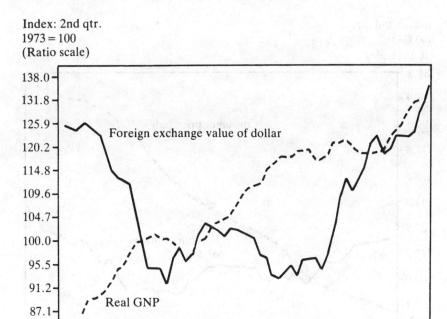

Figure 5.4   U.S. real GNP (seasonally adjusted) and weighted average real foreign exchange value of U.S. dollar (quarterly). *Source*: Data Resources Inc. and Morgan Guaranty Trust Co.

taneously, at just such a time the authorities have a window of opportunity. Then their limited pushes can speed up and accentuate the depreciation that is in accordance with economic fundamentals.

Still, I must confess to being pleasantly surprised by the degree and persistence of dollar weakness in the year after February 1985. Much of the credit, one suspects, was due to determined Japanese cooperation.

The Bundesbank and the German government were less enthusiastically cooperative. In private, Chancellor Helmut Kohl and his colleagues are quite pleased with Germany's current economic pattern. They are unwilling to risk present stability just because the tiresome Americans keep urging them to fire up their locomotive.

West Germany and the Common Market have less to fear from American resentment than perhaps the Japanese do. American public and Congressional opinion is resentful of the flood of imports from the Pacific Basin. Most of us economists, both in the United States and in Japan, have been urging that the most effective tactic against nascent American protectionism would be de-

Index: 2nd qtr.
1973 = 100
(Ratio scale)

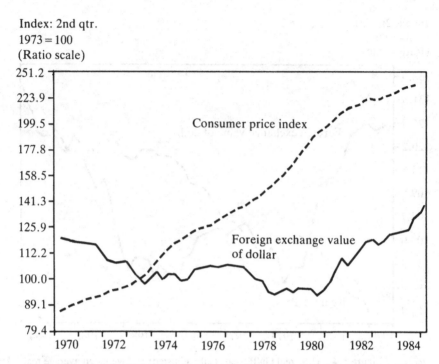

Figure 5.5   U.S. Consumer Price Index (seasonally adjusted) and weighted average nominal foreign exchange value of U.S. dollar (quarterly). *Source*: DRI and Morgan Guaranty Trust Co.

preciation of the dollar exchange rate. I believe the Japanese authorities have been persuaded to give this therapy a good hard try.

Repeatedly I have suggested that a powerful reinforcement to intervention operations would be informal capital controls designed to impede the automatic flow into dollar assets of the trade surpluses accruing to Japanese firms and investors.

I suspect that some of the 1985–6 success in raising the yen relative to the dollar has been due to strong moral suasion exercised by Japanese authorities on banks, insurance companies, corporations and institutional investors. I have no proof that this has been the modus operandi in the background. But it does seem plausible. In any case, some such forces need to be invoked to explain why relatively modest intervention operations were able to achieve such quantitative results.

If the goal of dollar depreciation has been so agreeably realized, cannot Japanese and American observers now breathe more easily? Hasn't protectionism been contained? Is it not reasonable to look ahead toward a substantial

Index: 2nd qtr.
1973 = 100
(Ratio scale)

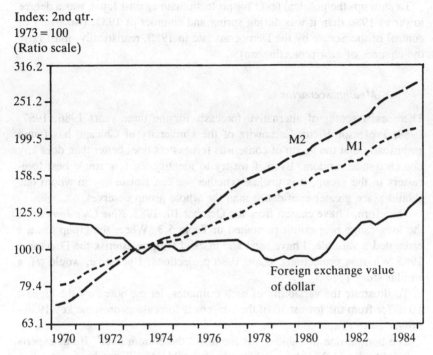

Figure 5.6   M1 and M2 (seasonally adjusted) and weighted average nominal foreign exchange value of U.S. dollar (quarterly). *Source*: Data Resources Inc. and Morgan Guaranty Trust Co.

reduction in the U.S.-Japanese bilateral trade deficit? Reckoning up the costs
of the stabilization interventions, can't we conclude now that they are behind
us that the game was well worth its costs?

I have to warn against comfortable affirmative answers to these questions.
The victory is not won. The game is not over.

Those Japanese investors who have been deterred from buying dollars by
fear that the yen would fall further, once they are confident that the yen has
reached a plateau around 160 to the dollar, may regain the courage to invest in
Wall Street securities. Successful intervention to keep the yen's value high
may have to be more than a one-time once-and-for-all operation.

The Nakasone government's engineered rise in Tokyo interest rates definitely did help the yen to appreciate in 1985. Against this must be reckoned
Washington's disappointment that Prime Minister Nakasone stalwartly re-
fused to embark on vigorous fiscal policy stimulus. Surely Japanese ec-
nomists understand the important logic of Columbia University's Robert
Mundell that I already mentioned.

To sum up, the political fever for protectionism against Japan was a degree lower in 1986 than it was during spring and summer of 1985. (Recovery of control of the Senate by the Democrats late in 1986, realistically, must raise the chances of new protectionism).

Median scenarios

There exist scores of alternative forecasts for the three years 1986, 1987, 1988. Professor Victor Zarnowitz of the University of Chicago has found empirically that the group of consensus forecasters does better than does any one chosen at random. Even if we try to identify the few single best forecasters in the group, it is unclear whether we can isolate any in whom one should place greater confidence than the whole group deserves.

Therefore, I have chosen from the October 10, 1985, *Blue Chip Indicators* the long-range projections presented in Table 5.3. Where the group has not estimated a variable, I have used and marked with an asterisk the December 1985 Wharton projections. (Late 1986 projections, I perceive, would tell a similar story.)

To illustrate the variability of such estimates, let me note how the highest 10 differ from the lowest 10 of the consensus forecasters on some key 1986–90 variables (Table 5.4).

The bottom line in Table 5.3 is literally "the bottom line." If our experts are right, the U.S. balance of payments problem will not be cured when President Reagan leaves the White House in January 1989. Nor will it be in sight of being solved, or even be on its way to being solved. And yet these experts are somewhat sanguine that

1. Some progress will be made in reducing our fiscal deficit.
2. Inflation will remain under good control.
3. The dollar will be floating downward in 1986–8.
4. No bad explosion of protectionism will have taken place.

A realistic outlook

I agree, in substance. A downward overshoot of the dollar will, I fear, be needed for several years if the dynamics of Pacific Basin innovation is to be fully offset. A drastic reduction in America's basic fiscal deficit will be required. The Federal Reserve will need to offset a new fiscal tightness fully and militantly.

Perhaps we face here one more case of economists' elasticity pessimism? However, going by the evidence and making eclectic use of prudent modern economic theory, we must face up to a continuing long-run problem with the

Table 5.3. Long-term U.S. projections

	1980	1981	1982	1983	1984	1985	1986	1987	1988
Real GNP, ann.gr.rate(%)	-0.3	2.5	-2.1	3.7	6.8	2.5	3.1	2.7	3.2
Inflation rate, CPI-all urban (%)	13.5	10.4	6.2	3.2	4.3	3.4	4.0	4.6	4.7
Unemployment, civ.rate(%)	7.2	7.6	9.7	9.6	7.5	7.2	7.1	7.1	7.0
Personal saving rate(%)	6.0	6.7	6.2	5.0	6.1	3.9	4.8	5.2	5.6
$ exchange rate (FRB:1973 = 100)	87.4	103.3	116.6	125.3	138.3	143.6	124.1	118.8	112
Auto sales (mi, with imports)	9.0	8.5	8.0	9.2	10.4	10.9	10.5	10.6	10.6
Housing starts (mi)	1.3	1.1	1.1	1.7	1.8	1.8	1.8	1.7	1.7
Federal surplus (NIA, Bil$)	-61.3	-64.3	-148.1	-178.6	-175.8	-190.7	-172.5	-142.8	-128
3-month Treasury rate(%)	11.4	14.0	10.6	8.6	9.5	7.5	7.6	8.0	8.1
AAA bonds (%)	11.9	14.2	13.8	12.0	12.7	11.4	11.2	11.1	10.8
Current account balance (Bil$)	1.9	6.3	-8.1	-40.8	-101.5	-134.8	-139.5	-127.1	-100

Source: From Blue Chip Indicators, October 10, 1985, p. 8; $ exchange rate and federal surplus are from Wharton Quarterly Model Outlook, vol. 4, no. 12 (December 1985), Table 1.1; 1988 estimates by Paul A. Samuelson.

Table 5.4. *1986–90 mean projections*

	Group average	High 10	Low 10
Real GNP growth	3.1	3.7	2.7
Price inflation	4.5	5.3	3.5
Unemployment	6.9	7.4	6.5

American balance of payments and with harmonious Japan–U.S. economic relations.

As I appraise the econometrics of the 1985–90 outlook for the United States and its trading partners, the U.S. deficit on current account will not heal itself by 1990. Even with a proper mix of macro policies here and abroad, improvements will be slow in coming. As a result, the rational odds of a protectionist blowoff in America must be put at no less than 1 in 2. Such an eventuality would be an economic tragedy – a tragedy for Japan and Asia, but also a tragedy for America's own well-being.

Appendix

n-good equilibrium

There are many goods in the world of reality. What is the minimal general equilibrium model that can justify the many Rules upon which our diagnosis and policy prescriptions are based?

The most manageable model is the two-region Ricardian one with tastes uniformly homothetic for all persons everywhere. These tastes can be summarized by the following "regular" first-degree-homogeneous utility function, $u[C] = u[C_1, \ldots , C_n]$, whose indifference contours are *strictly convex* and *smoothly differentiable*, are *insatiable*, and where something of every good is indispensable:

$$u[mC] = mu[C], \ m > 0 : \text{homotheticity} \tag{i}$$

$$u[A] = u[B] \text{ and } A \neq B \text{ implies}$$

$$u[\tfrac{1}{2}A + \tfrac{1}{2}B] > u[A] : \text{strict quasi-concavity} \tag{ii}$$

$$(\partial u[C_1, \ldots , C_n]/\partial C_j) = (u_j[C]) > 0 \tag{iii}$$

$$\text{for } C > 0 : \text{insatiability}$$

$$\text{For } A \gg 0 \text{ and } B > 0 , \ u[B] > u[A]: \text{indispensability.} \tag{iv}$$

We are given positive vectors of regions' labor costs and labor supplies: (a_j), (a_j^*), (L,L^*). With transport costs zero and trade free of quotas and other impediments, the geographical pattern of production is determined by competition (save for inessential indifferences at various singular specifications of the above parameters). Competition also determines a unique vector of the world totals of production $(O_j + O_j^*)$ and, what is the same thing, the world totals of consumption $(C_j + C_j^*)$. Also uniquely determined are real price ratios (P_j/P_1) and equivalent (P_j^*/P_1^*) and the real wage ratio W^*/W, along with (P_j/W) and (P_j^*/W^*). The regional breakdown of $(C_j + C_j^*)$ into unique fractional shares $s(C_j + C_j^*)$ and $(1 - s)(C_j + C_j^*)$ is also uniquely determinate in the present model, which has balanced income effects that preclude multiplicity of equilibria.

The present model is simple because the world totals can be generated as a solution to the following maximum problem:

Subject to

$$\sum_1^n a_j Q_j = L, \quad \sum_1^n a_j^* Q_j^* = L^*; \ Q_j \geq 0, \ Q_j^* \geq 0 \qquad \text{(v)}$$

$$\text{Max } u[Q_1 + Q_1^*, \ldots, Q_n + Q_n^*]$$
$$Q_j, Q_j^*$$

$$= u[L, L^*; a_j, a_j^*] = u[L, L^*] \text{ for short.}$$

It can be shown that $u[L,L^*]$ is first-degree-homogeneous and concave, with positive partial derivatives that measure each region's real wage (expressed in the numeraire of u itself, $P_u = 1 = P_u^*$):

$$\partial u[L,L^*]/\partial L = W/P_u = w > 0 \qquad \text{(v')}$$

$$\partial u[L,L^*]/\partial L^* = W^*/P_u^* = w^*.$$

The Kuhn–Tucker conditions for (v)'s maximum, expressed to take advantage of the goods' indispensabilities, yield the following first-order necessary-and-sufficient conditions for the competitive real prices and wages $(P_j/P_u = p_j = P_j^*/P_u^* = p_j^*; w, w^*)$:

$$u_i[Q + Q^*] = \text{Min}[wa_i, w^*a_i^*], \quad i = 1, \ldots, n \qquad \text{(vi)}$$

$$= p_i = p_i^* > 0$$

$$Q_i \, (\text{Min}[wa_i, w_i^* a_i^*] - wa_i) = 0 \qquad \text{(vii)}$$

$$Q_i^*(\text{Min}[wa_i, w_i^* a_i^*] - w^* a_i^*) = 0.$$

Conditions (v), (vi), and (vii) are sufficient to determine at least one positive solution for the unknowns $(Q_j, Q_j^*, p_j, p_j^*, w, w^*)$. A unique solution obtains for the variables $(Q_j+Q_j^*, p_j = p_j^*, w, w^*, \Sigma_1^n p_j Q_j, \Sigma_1^n p_j^* Q_j^*)$. For particular values of the parameters, as when $n = 2$ and $a_2/a_1 = a_2^*/a_1^*$, or for L^*/L ratios that entail $wa_3/w^*a_3^* = wa_4/w^*a_4^*$, there can be an infinity of breakdowns of the $(Q_j + Q_j^*)$ vector into (Q_j) and (Q_j^*) specialization patterns that are inessentially different.

Once we know the equilibrium p's and Q's we can deduce the equilibrium values for the regional consumption vectors, (C_j) and (C_j^*), from the balance of trade relations:

$$(C_j + C_j^*) = (Q_j + Q_j^*) \tag{viii}$$

$$(C_j) = [wL/(wL + w^*L^*)](Q_j + Q_j^*), \quad j = 1, \dots, n \tag{ix}$$

$$(C_j^*) = [w^*L^*/(wL + w^*L^*)](Q_j + Q_j^*).$$

Allowing capital movements will of course suspend (ix)'s balance of trade equality. But a model without transport impediments and tariffs is not one well designed to illustrate the deterioration of Japanese terms of trade that will be generated *endogenously* by Japan's running a chronic surplus on current account with America.

Remarks: Suppose that along with these n *freely* tradable goods, there were m nontradable goods $(y_1, \dots, y_m)$ and $(y_1^*, \dots, y_m^*)$. Then the device of a one-person maximizer would not work to generate the competitive general equilibrium. The same sacrifice in analytical simplicity would be introduced if some or all of these goods could be shipped in trade but at positive transportation costs. Thus, we might work with the 1954 Samuelson "iceberg" model in which export by us of y_j of good $n + j$ shrinks to $g_j y_j$ as $(1 - g_j)y_j$ "evaporates in transport" as the technical cost of shipment – where g_j is a fraction, $0 \leq g_j \leq 1$; and in which $g_j^* y_j^*$ of *Japan's export of g_j^* reaches our shore. For some $(1 - g_j)$'s being positive, the one-maximizer trick would need elaboration.

The present general equilibrium can be tested for its comparative statical properties. Thus, a balanced halving in all Japan's (a_j^*) coefficients would be equivalent to doubling its L^*: That must increase *world* potential well being since

$$u[L, 2L^*] > u[L, L^*].$$

And, save in the singular case where a^* is proportional to a and there are no operative comparative advantages, such balanced innovations must raise U.S. per capita real income in the form of w or $\partial u/\partial L$ – for the reason that $\partial^2 u/\partial L \, \partial L^*$ is generally positive.

The two-good instance is easy to diagram. Figure 5.7 depicts the three possible cases: (a) where we and they are enough balanced in labor supplies

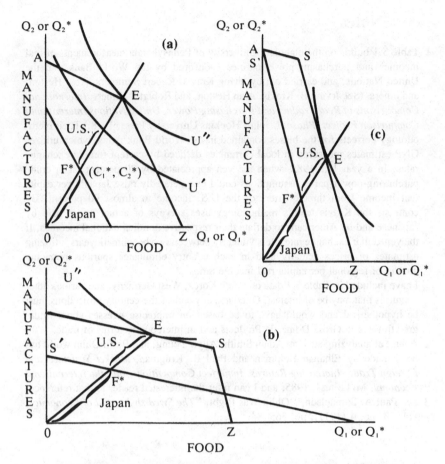

Figure 5.7 In (a) the United States specializes in food and Japan in manufactures, at E where the indifference slope is between the production cost slopes of regions. Japan's share of global E is at F^*, with U.S. share of F^*E. In (b), the United States produces both goods and its a_2/a_1 gives a price ratio equal to AS slope. In (c), Japan produces both goods and its a_2^*/a_1^* gives price ratio. Competition determines endogenously which one of (a), (b), or (c) obtains.

for each region to be producing only one good; (b) where Japan is so small as to require us to produce both goods; and (c) where it is the United States that is "small."

The three-good case requires three-dimensional geometry and can be left to motivated readers.

Notes

1 Table 5.1 builds on the elaborate University of Pennsylvania measurements of real incomes and purchasing-power-parities sponsored by the World Bank and the United Nations, and carried out by Irving Kravis, Robert Summers, Alan Heston, and others. (See Irving B. Kravis, Alan Heston, and Robert Summers, *International Comparisons of Real Product and Purchasing Power, United Nations International Comparison Project: Phase II*, Johns Hopkins University Press, 1978.) Their methodology corrects for the biases contained in the World Bank Atlas, which utilizes GNP estimates measured in local currencies deflated by current foreign exchange rates. In a year like 1985, when the yen appreciated by 20 percent, such crude purchasing-power-parity assumptions could exaggeratedly raise Japan's per capita real income from three-quarters of the U.S. income to almost 90 percent. By contrast, the Kravis team's methodology uses surveys of actual prices paid by Japanese and by Americans to deflate their respective nominal national incomes. If the yen/dollar exchange rate alters violently between two benchmark years, utilizing estimates of prices actually paid in each country eliminates spurious bouncing around of regional per capita real income ratios.

  I have included in Table 5.1 data on South Korea, West Germany, and various other countries that may be of interest. Of course any end-of-the-century projections must be hypothetical and would have to be based on imprecise guesses about future growth rates in Gross Domestic Products and in intercountry terms of trade.

2 A start at analyzing such an Adam Smith, Allyn Young, and Bertil Ohlin world has been made by Elhanan Helpman and Paul R. Krugman, *Market Structure and Foreign Trade: Increasing Returns, Imperfect Competitions, and the International Economy*, MIT Press, 1985, and I can refer the interested reader to that reference.

3 See Paul A. Samuelson, "Ohlin Was Right," *The Swedish Journal of Economics*, vol. 73, no. 4 (1971), pp. 365–84.

CHAPTER 6

Major microeconomic adjustments ahead

LESTER C. THUROW

The issue of trade imbalances can be viewed from a number of perspectives, but each of these perspectives reaches a similar conclusion. The changes that would have to be made to solve the imbalances are not marginal changes but major microeconomic structural changes. They are in fact so major that one can reasonably argue that what is required is economically or politically impossible. Yet they have to be made. They either will be made as a matter of public policy or they will be forced by the market. However, if forced by the market, the changes will have to be made in the midst of an economic crisis, the only unknown of which is its timing.

This unfortunate conclusion flows from the fact that the imbalances in today's trading systems are not minor but major. More important, these imbalances are such that they become larger and harder to correct the longer they are allowed to exist. In this case, to postpone the problem is to have a much larger problem.

Current trading problems are also not going to be solved with macroeconomic tinkering. Changes in macroeconomic policies are necessary, but more fundamental microeconomic structural changes will be necessary to put the world's trading system back on an equilibrium path.

A black hole

The American trade deficit is rapidly becoming the economic equivalent of the astronomer's black hole. Everyone's economy is adjusting to it and the larger it becomes and the longer it lasts, the harder it is going to be for anyone to escape from it.

A small American trade deficit has little structural impact. Foreign firms use the excess capacity that they would normally hold to service the ups and downs of their domestic markets to service their temporarily higher American sales, and American firms temporarily mothball a minor amount of their production capacity. But when trade deficits get as large and long lasting as

137

those now occurring in the United States, the productive capacity that is required to service the American market is not temporarily idle capacity, but dedicated capacity that has been built expressly to service the American market. Foreign firms build up productive capacities that they could not possibly use in their domestic markets. Conversely, in the United States firms do not temporarily idle capacity, but permanently scrap facilities and permanently dismantle their labor forces. The longer and larger the American trade deficit becomes, the more it gets built into physical equipment both at home and abroad.

Viewed from the perspective of the rest of the world, the American trade deficit ($150 billion in 1985, running at an annual rate of $176 billion in the first quarter of 1986) is a market that generates at least 4 million jobs. Major large-scale industries are being built in the rest of the world to service that American market. If one looks at the pattern of bilateral trade with the United States, about one-third of those industries and the necessary facilities are being built in Japan, about one-third in Europe and Canada, and about one-third in the rest of the world.[1]

Since most of the rest of the world has had a very weak recovery in domestic demand in the aftermath of the 1981–2 recession, initially the American market was simply a market to use idle local production capacity that would hopefully be needed in the domestic market in the not too distant future. But the recovery in domestic demand that was expected in the rest of the world had not occurred and there is now little likelihood that it will occur without major changes in monetary and fiscal policies, and these are seen by industrialists to be politically unlikely or impossible, as discussed later in the chapter.

Over time, capacity that could have been rediverted to service local markets has become capacity especially designed and built to service the American market. This capacity has become so specialized and so overbuilt in particular industries that the loss of the American market would mean wrenching readjustments – if not bankruptcy.

Think of the auto, consumer electronics, or textile industries outside of the United States. Few nations could come even close to absorbing their current output without the American market. Cutbacks in production would have to be massive everywhere in the world. Sweden, Germany, France, the United Kingdom, Korea, Brazil, Mexico, Japan – the American auto market absorbs a very large fraction of the total output of all of these countries and, if local foreign estimates are correct, generates an even greater percentage of their profitability. Japan could not possibly watch the number of video recorders that it is now selling in the United States, just as Italy could not possibly drink the amount of wine that it is now selling in the United States.

If these foreign productive capacities were being built up and their American equivalents being phased down in accordance with the dictates of gradual shifts in comparative advantage, one could view the local inability to absorb domestic production benignly. There would be no foreseeable circumstances under which foreign countries would have to absorb that production locally.

However, these foreign industries are not being built up in the context of balanced trading relationships. They are being built up in the disequilibrium circumstances of huge unsustainable American balance of payments deficits. At some point those deficits have to stop, and at that point trading patterns will undergo a major shift. The dollar will fall, American imports will decline, and much of the capacity dedicated to the American market will become redundant.

What will have to be done abroad tomorrow can be seen today in America's wheat-growing industry. Traditionally, American wheat growers have exported 60 percent of their output. America cannot possibly eat what it grows. At today's value of the dollar, little of that can be sold in world markets. Some wheat is still being shipped abroad but it was sold in the past under long-term contracts that will eventually run out and not be renewed. The rest of the world is rapidly expanding its wheat production capabilities to fill the American gap, but within the United States 60 percent of America's wheat farmers must be driven out of business and 60 percent of the land growing wheat must be taken out of production and made idle. Land cannot be diverted to alternative production since most of American agriculture is heavily dependent upon exports and subject to the same pressures for cutbacks faced by the wheat farmer. There are no economic alternative uses. Land that used to have economic value now has no economic value. This means wrenching structural changes. Farmers and their bankers must go broke and whole local communities must disappear.

What is happening in the United States today will have to happen in the rest of the world tomorrow, for it is simply impossible for any country to run a perpetual massive deficit in its balance of payments. What is unsustainable will not be sustained. The only question is how will the unsustainability make itself felt.

Three things are known with certainty when it comes to America's trade deficit. First, massive trade deficits cannot go on forever. Second, no one can predict the exact timing when market forces will bring those trade deficits to an end. Third, the longer the deficits last, the bigger the adjustments that will ultimately have to be made to correct them.

At the end of 1982 America had net foreign assets of $147 billion. On or about May 1, 1985, America shifted from being a net creditor nation to being a net debtor nation for the first time in almost three-quarters of a century. Early in 1986 the United States passed Brazil to become the world's largest net debtor nation.

Table 6.1. *International Indebtedness (billions of U.S. dollars)*

Year	Borrowing to finance trade surplus (+) or deficit (−)	Borrowing to pay interest	Total indebtedness
1	−150	0	150
2	−130	12	292
3	−110	23	425
4	−90	34	549
5	−70	44	663
6	−50	53	766
7	−30	61	857
8	−10	69	936
9	+10	75	1,001
10	+30	80	1,051
11	+50	84	1,085
12	+70	87	1,102
13	+90	88	1,100

In the past, the United States could run a substantial sustainable trade deficit financed by its earnings on net foreign investments. But that is no longer possible since the United States has liquidated those net foreign assets and no longer has earnings on its investments that can be used to finance a trade deficit. As the United States moves into the debtor class, it will have to borrow abroad both to finance its current trade deficit and to pay interest on its previous borrowings. Where current account deficits have been smaller than trade deficits in the past, they will start to become larger since the amount that the United States will need to borrow to pay interest on its debts rises very rapidly in the years ahead.

The problem can be seen easily with a simple numerical example set out in Table 6.1. Suppose that the American trade deficit falls at the rate of $20 billion per year (a sum that would remove 500,000 jobs per year from the rest of the world) and that the United States must pay an 8 percent interest rate on its international debts. The amount that has to be borrowed each year declines, but very slowly, from $150 billion in the first year to $79 billion in the eighth year. Before it reaches equilibrium 13 years hence, the United States has accumulated a net international debt of $1,100 billion and must have a trade surplus of $90 billion to counterbalance its interest payments of $88 billion.

This means that the rest of the world has to swing from a trade surplus of $150 billion in 1985 to a trade deficit of $90 billion in 1998. In other words, industries employing 6 million people have to be transferred from the rest of the world to the United States.

To look at the balance of payments deficit from a financial perspective and argue that the current value of the dollar is an equilibrium value, given higher interest rates in the United States, is a mistake. Even if American interest rates were never to come down, there has to be a point where the amount America must borrow to meet its obligations exceeds what the rest of the world is willing to lend.

When the lending stops, the dollar will fall and the real microeconomic adjustments that have been outlined above will commence. If the fall is brought about by market forces, it is apt to be very rapid. Every private lender decides not to lend at approximately the same time, since no one wants to be the lender left facing large foreign exchange losses. When the lending stops, there will also be pressures to get out of dollar assets, since large declines in the value of the dollar are to be expected. As a consequence, the financial pressures are apt to be much greater than those that would occur if only new lending were to stop.

Moreover, whatever fall in the value of the dollar is necessary to restore equilibrium, the market is apt to overshoot and produce a decline bigger than that warranted by a return to long-run equilibrium conditions. Overshooting occurs partly because of the herd nature of financial markets (everyone panics together) and partly because of the time lags in the trading system. If a 40 percent fall in the value of the dollar is needed to bring exports and imports into balance 24 months from now, a much bigger fall is necessary to balance exports and imports 1 month from now. When the world's financial markets decide that the United States has borrowed too much, they are not likely to then give it another 13 years of borrowing to solve its problems gradually. Thus the decline in the value of the dollar is apt to be much larger than that required to bring the system into long-run equilibrium. This of course means that the adjustments required in the real industrial economy are apt to be even bigger than those required by any calculations showing what must be done to return to long-run equilibrium.

Although some elementary debt calculations prove that America cannot continue to run its current trade deficits and that therefore the dollar must fall substantially at some point in the future, it must be emphasized that no one knows, or can know, the precise timing when the world's financial markets will collapse under the weight of rising American debt and force the dollar down. Different calculations can lead to very different predictions as to the timing, and truth is to be found only in the realization that fundamental uncertainties are involved.

The argument is often heard that it is unnecessary to worry about a rush from the dollar since those who have invested in dollars will have to stay in dollars as the sums are so large that they have nowhere else to go. This argument is both irrelevant and wrong. Structural changes are required not when foreigners wish to withdraw their money from the United States, but when they choose not to lend any more of their money to the United States. To finance its trade deficit the United States needs willing new lenders, not just satisfied old lenders. Furthermore, history shows that the argument is wrong. Just seven years ago, in 1979, no one in the world's financial community wanted to hold dollars. If the rest of the world found some satisfactory place to park its money outside of the United States in 1979, it can equally well find a satisfactory place in the 1980s.

Although America is much wealthier and more creditworthy than Mexico, the world's reaction to Mexico on August 13, 1982, still has some interesting lessons to teach about what should be expected in the future. First, the financial markets gave no hint that they were about to slam the doors shut on Mexican lending. In the week before August 13, a group of Texas banks lent Mexico over $1 billion. Second, when the lending doors did slam shut, they shut with a bang and no one was willing to lend Mexico money at any rate of interest.

Eventually it was learned that Mexico borrowed $85 billion dollars before the lending stopped, but at the time that Mexico went broke the world thought that it had lent Mexico about $45 billion. This amounted to about 13 percent of the Mexican GNP.[2] If you believe that the United States could borrow a similar fraction of its GNP before the lending stops, then one should start to worry about the world's willingness to lend only when accumulated U.S. debt topped $500 billion. This calculation is little cause for relief, however, since our numerical example above suggests that U.S. debt will reach this level in four years.

Some argue that, since most of the U.S. debt is dominated in dollars, foreigners have less to fear in terms of default. The United States can always print dollars to pay its bills and as a result default risks are minimal. Therefore the rest of the world will be willing to lend the United States much more relative to its GNP than it was willing to lend Mexico relative to its GNP.

Perhaps. But an argument can equally well be made that the world will in fact be less willing to lend the United States money than it was to lend Mexico money. This possibility arises because the U.S. dollar is the world's reserve currency. Billions of dollars are held not because people want dollars to use in some business transaction, but because they want a save secure place to hold some of their wealth. These holdings are intrinsically hot money. Although holders of these dollars may regard them as safe from default since most U.S. debt is demoninated in dollars, they are not regarded as safe in terms of purchasing power. If the dollar falls 50 percent, they lose 50 percent of their dollar-denominated wealth. Few would view such a prospect with equanimity. This makes such holders of dollars very nervous investors who may choose to jump out of dollars much faster than the world's more sophisticated major banks wanted to jump out of Mexico.

Although different arguments can be made, it is important to realize that the world is financially exploring new territory that has never before been explored. The world has never seen debts as large or rising as fast as those now being generated by the United States. The world has never seen the world's wealthiest country as the world's largest net debtor. The world has never seen a reserve currency backed by the world's largest net debtor nation. Reserve currencies have always come from net creditor nations since the holders of the reserve currency want to think that there are some international assets backing the reserve currency that they are holding. This is their assurance that the value of the reserve currency is unlikely to fall rapidly.

Anyone who tries to predict the exact timing of how the financial markets will react to this constellation of new circumstances is predicting something that is in principle unpredictable. But being unpredictable does not mean, however, that it won't happen. It will happen. At some point the lending will stop; and if history is any guide, it will stop abruptly and not gradually.

Finally, the longer the system is allowed to run on its present course the bigger the real corrections that will have to be made when the lending stops. In the 1970s the United States could finance 14 percent of its imports with earnings on its investments.[3] This of course meant that the United States could run a sustainable trade deficit of this magnitude and, conversely, that the rest of the world could run a sustainable trade surplus. However, this historical relationship must be turned on its head when the United States becomes a debtor nation. As the United States becomes a net debtor nation, it must run a trade surplus and the rest of the world must run a trade deficit.

As the United States builds up its position of net indebtedness, the changes that will be forced on the world (and the United States) grow larger and larger. Even being conservative and assuming that no one demands any repayment of principle, under the assumptions of the numerical example considered above America's interest payments will reach $88 billion before equilibrium is restored. This means that both the United States and the rest of the world will have to restructure themselves industrially so that the United States can run a perpetual trade surplus of $88 billion per year to make its required interest payments. This of course means that the rest of the world will have to restructure their industries so that they are consistent with a perpetual trade deficit of $88 billion per year.

It might also be pointed out that when the phrase ''the rest of the world'' is used, it does not mean the rest of the world in any proportional sense. The deficits have to be run by precisely those countries that have accumulated the net credits during the period when the United States runs into debt, since only they have the investment earnings necessary to finance the necessary trade deficits. If Japan, for example, rapidly becomes a net creditor nation and accumulates half of the American debt, then half of the trade surplus that the United States will have to run to make its interest payments will effectively have to be with Japan. This means that the value of the yen has to rise relative to that of the dollar not just enough to bring the bilateral trade deficit back to more reasonable levels, not just enough to bring bilateral trade into balance, but enough to generate a big bilateral American surplus in the trade between the United States and Japan. If Japan accumulates $100 billion in net American assets with a 8 percent interest rate, its economy will have to be restructured so that it shifts from the current trade surplus (expected to approach $80 billion in 1986) to a trade deficit of $8 billion per year. If Japan accumulates $200 billion in net foreign assets, it will have to run a $16 billion trade deficit.

How much the yen has to rise depends, of course, upon the size of the ultimate American indebtedness and the size of the credits that Japan accumulates. The changes will, however, have to be very much larger than those now being contemplated by either the government or private officials in Japan. Econometric equations are of very little use in predicting just how much the yen would have to rise to push American exports to Japan to the appropriate levels, since both countries would be operating well outside the range of historical experience. But to know the size of the changes that would be required in exports and imports is to know that the changes in the value of the yen relative to the dollar would have to be very large. The required changes in the value of the yen and trading patterns would be so large that major Japanese industries would effectively have to go out of business. They would have to lose all of their export market in the United States, and American firms would have to capture major portions of the local Japanese market to bring about the necessary changes in the bilateral balance of payments.

Although the industrial restructuring that would be required to bring about the necessary surpluses in the U.S. balance of trade cannot be avoided given what has already happened, the severity can be minimized. The sooner trading patterns shift to eliminate U.S. borrowing, the smaller the real industrial changes that will eventually have to be made. In this case, the creditor nations probably have as much interest in a rapid restructuring of trading patterns as the debtor nations.

In the elimination of trade deficits, debtor nations lose in the short run in that they are unable to enjoy a standard of living above that determined by their local productivity, but gain in the long run in that they minimize future debt repayments and future claims on their standards of living. Creditor nations lose in the short run in that they do not get to enjoy trade surpluses and the jobs that go with them, but gain in the long run since they minimize the size of the future structural changes that they will otherwise have to make.

From the historian's perspective, an interesting experiment is now under way. Can democratic governments act to avoid a problem that is clearly on the horizon, but not yet impinging upon them, or must they wait for a visible crisis to occur?

If they must wait for a crisis before they can act, contingency planning is necessary. When the private lending doors slam shut for the United States, foreign governments must be willing to lend massive amounts of money to the United States if they want to spread the real industrial adjustments that will have to be made over some reasonable period of time and do not want to see the value of the dollar overshoot to become grossly undervalued. Depending on how long the private lending lasts, one can work out how much will have to be lent by governments to spread the problem out over different lengths of time.

If private lending were to stop while the United States was borrowing $150 billion per year and foreign governments wanted to spread the employment shock over three years so that the trade deficit declined from $150 billion, to $100 billion, to $50 billion, and finally to $0 billion rather than from $150 billion to $0 billion instantaneously, they would have to be prepared to lend the United States $150 billion in the first year, $100 billion in the second year, and $50 billion in the third year to allow America to finance its trade deficits. Those sums represent very large expansions of domestic money supplies that few governments would want to generate, but foreign governments will be faced with an unattractive choice: Either lend the money or face instant massive shutdowns when local producers are cut off from their American markets since America can no longer borrow the money necessary to pay these producers.

Just to give some idea of the magnitude and worldwide distribution of the changes that would be required to bring world trading patterns back into balance, look at what would have been necessary if the changes had been made in the second quarter of 1985 – the quarter in which America shifted from being a creditor to a debtor nation (Table 6.2). At that time sustainability could have been obtained if the United States had balanced its current account. It did not need a surplus to make interest payments – as it did by the fourth quarter of 1985.

In the second quarter of 1985 the United States had a current account deficit of $128 billion. If this deficit had been eliminated through an expansion of American exports, exports would have to have risen by 60 percent. The first two columns of Table 6.2 show how American exports would have to have risen in different regions of the world assuming that every region of the world absorbed 60 percent more exports than it had been absorbing. Thus American exports to Europe would have to have expanded from $53.6 billion to $86.0 billion, those to Japan from $58.4 billion to $93.9 billion.

Table 6.2. *Changes in trade patterns necessary to restore balance, second quarter 1985 (billions of U.S. dolars)*

	Exports		Imports	
Country	1985 II	Needed	1985 II	Needed
Western Europe	$53.6	$86.0	$79.3	$49.9
Japan	58.4	93.9	74.1	46.6
Canada	20.8	33.2	68.5	43.1
Hong Kong, Korea, Singapore, Taiwan	16.6	26.5	36.9	23.2
Australia, New Zealand, South Afria	6.4	10.3	5.7	3.6
Rest of world	9.4	15.0	80.5	50.6

Source: U.S. Department of Commerce, *Survey of Current Business,* 1985.

The third and fourth columns of Table 6.2 show how American imports would have to have gone down if the current account deficit were to be solved with a proportional across-the-board cutback in imports. On the average, this would have required a 37 percent cutback in imports, Western Europe's exports to the United States would have to have fallen from $79.3 billion to $49.9 billion, and those from Japan from $74.1 billion to $46.6 billion.

These numerical calculations illustrate what might be called an impossibility theorem. It is impossible for the world to grow its way out of the U.S. trade deficit. If one asks how fast the world would have to grow to absorb 60 percent more American exports, the world would have to grow much faster than it can grow even if foreign fiscal and monetary policies were to be much more expansionary than those now in place. Therefore, the ultimately inevitable expansion in American exports is to some extent going to replace local production. This is going to put some strong downward (recessionary) pressures on the economies of the rest of the world and make it difficult for them to avoid a recession.

If America follows an import reduction strategy, the recessionary pressures will be much more intense. An examination of the import cuts that would be necessary to balance America's current account reveals that they are large relative to the economies of most of the world and would constitute a substantial negative macroeconomic shock even if one were to forget their localized microeconomic effects on individual industries.

A recession in the rest of the world, however, will make it that much harder for the United States to obtain the balance of payments surpluses necessary to make the system sustainable.

For the developing world, the third and fourth columns of Table 6.2 underestimate the burdens that they would have to bear since it is clearly impossible for countries of the developing world to sustain the share of the cutbacks that they have been allocated in these calculations. Exports from these countries to the United States cannot fall from $80.5 billion to $50.6 billion without their going broke and falling into a severe deflation. As a result, the developed world will have to be allocated the $29.9 billions of cutbacks that has been allocated to the developing in Table 6.1. If this were done proportionally, Japan's exports to the United States would have to fall not by $27.5 billion, but by $35.9 billion. By anyone's calculations, this constitutes a significant negative macroeconomic shock.

The macroeconomic controls

To say that macroeconomic policies caused a problem is not to say that macroeconomic policies by themselves can cure the same problem. The sequence of macroeconomic policies that created today's rapidly expanding black hole is clear, but the sequence of macroeconomic policies that lets the world avoid the black hole being created by America's trade deficit is not so clear.

The problems certainly began when the United States decided to dramatically cut taxes (supply side economics) and expand public spending (the defense buildup) in early 1981 and simultaneously fight inflation with high interest rates and tight money. Viewed narrowly, the policies were a great success. High interest rates and tight money produced a recession and essentially stopped inflation. As these monetary policies were being relaxed in the aftermath of the Mexican problems in 1982, the expansionary fiscal policies came into force and pushed the economy into a major expansion – essentially bringing unemployment back to where it was (about 7 percent) at the beginning of the process in late 1980.

Viewed globally, the policies were simultaneously a great success and a great failure. With a rapidly expanding economy and a rapidly expanding market for imports, they rescued the rest of the world from sinking even further into the 1981–2 worldwide recession. At the same time, they created the current American trade deficit that threatens to suck everyone into its black hole.

The problems arise from the fact that the macro controls in Japan and Germany (the second and third largest democratic industrial countries) were set in very different ways. Interest rates were far below those in the United States and fiscal policies were set to produce a Keynesian contraction rather than a Keynesian expansion. Thus, more than 100 percent of the net expansionary impulse had to come from the United States.[4] This in fact occurred since America's higher interest rates led foreign funds to flow into the United States, raising the value of the dollar and creating the export markets that foreign producers needed to get out of their recession.

None of this means, however, that a reversal of these policies will cure the problem. Unbalanced growth at one point in time (1982–5) may extract an unavoidable price at another (future) point in time.

Consider the standard macroeconomic remedy that calls for the United States to tighten its fiscal policies and lower its interest rates while Japan and Germany simultaneously loosen their fiscal policies. I would argue that such a shift in policies will not guarantee the "soft landing" that those who support such a shift believe possible. If the United States slowly eliminates its federal budget deficit (1992 is the target year for a balanced budget under the Gramm–Rudman bill), it will by 1992 have accumulated a huge international debt and the microeconomic structural changes that will have to be made in the rest of the world to accommodate the large American trade surplus that must go with such a debtor position will be enormous. Furthermore, there is every reason to believe that the international lending window may well slam shut long before 1992.

From an international perspective, a quicker shift in fiscal policies is called for than those mandated under Gramm–Rudman, but even Gramm–Rudman runs the risk of creating a Keynesian recession within the United States. Lower interest rates can stimulate some domestic demand, but there is little reason to believe that the demand-stimulating effects of interest rates can offset the demand-depressing effects of tighter fiscal policies. Monetary policies have not been able to do so in the past, and the fiscal restraint is being introduced into an economy that is only slowly growing with fiscal stimulus.

Although it is an exaggeration to argue that monetary policies are like a string – one can pull on it to tighten demand but cannot push on it to stimulate demand – there is a large element of truth in the analogy. This is especially true in the current circumstances when American consumers have already leveraged themselves to record levels and have little room to borrow regardless of what happens to interest rates.

Leverage buyouts and the merger movement have similarly led American business to take on record amounts of debt. But business also has little interest in expanding America's productive capacity until it is clear that the dollar is really down. Having been burned on the high-valued dollar, they are not going to invest until it is very clear that a low-valued dollar is here to stay.

As a result, there is little reason to believe that falling interest rates can fully offset tightening fiscal policies within the U.S. economy. If the United States is not to slip into a recession, falling domestic demands for U.S. products must be matched by rising international demands for U.S. products. Since the cut in American fiscal stimulus is going to be large ($200 billion), however, the rise in international demand for U.S. products must be equally large. To offset the negative Keynesian effects that will flow from America's strategy reducing the budget deficit, foreign monetary and fiscal policies must move not from slightly depressive to slightly stimulative, but from slightly depressive to massively expansionary. Basically, if world aggregate demand is not to fall for every dollar cut from the American fiscal deficit, a dollar must be added to world aggregate demand for every dollar subtracted in the United States.

As a result, the shifts in Keynesian policies that will be required in the rest of the world will be equal in magnitude and opposite in sign to those that are required in the United States. Such changes are so large that they are unlikely to be made, and thus the world is very likely to slip into a recession as the United States cuts its budget deficit.

Here again, however, the issue is one of timing. Since late 1982 American macroeconomic policies can probably best be viewed as constant fiscal stimulus with monetary policies swinging back and forth to stabilize the results. In late 1982 and early 1983, monetary policies were strongly stimulative to bring the 1981–2 recession to a halt. In late 1983 and 1984, it looked as though the fiscal stimulus was pumping up the American economy too much, and monetary policies swung over to those of restraint to keep the Keynesian pump of the federal budget deficit from overwhelming the system. By early 1985, the trade deficit was threatening to siphon too much aggregate demand out of the system, however, and the Federal Reserve Board swung back to stimulating the economy to prevent the trade deficit from causing a recession.

Such a policy continued throughout 1986. The dollar fell from its peak levels of March 1985, but only enough to slow down the rate of growth of the trade deficit – not by enough to cause a surge of international demand for U.S. products and a smaller deficit. No inflation is on the horizon and with Gramm–Rudman passed and budget reductions under way, the American economy will need all of the monetary stimulus it can get if it is not to slip to growth rates so low that unemployment begins to rise.

Such monetary policies prevented any recession from occurring in 1986. With the trade deficit growing only slowly in 1986, there was enough momentum in domestic demand to get the economy through 1986. Given time lags, the negative macroeconomic effects of 1986 cutbacks in expenditures or increases in taxes were felt mainly in 1987. Starting in 1987, however, there were problems in sustaining worldwide aggregate demand as America's contribution to worldwide aggregate demand swings from stimulative to contractive.

Better macroeconomic policies cannot cure the microeconomic structural problems that they have created. At some point in the not too distant future, major changes in the industrial mix produced of different countries will be required. The United States will have to shift from having a large trade deficit to having a substantial trade surplus. No macroeconomic policies can reverse this shift. It can only be reversed if the United States once again becomes a net creditor nation, and this requires the United States to run large trade surpluses for some substantial period of time.

But it is also doubtful that macroeconomic policies can cure the macroeconomic problems that they have created. Avoiding the recession that has been built into the system by past imbalances in the macroeconomic policies of the world's major countries will require very large, carefully timed, future imbalances (West Germany and Japan will have to massively stimulate their economies as the United States stages massive cutbacks in its fiscal stimulus) that are unlikely to occur.

An ignored fundamental problem

Although macroeconomic policies have enlarged the dimensions of the current microeconomic problem (the United States did not need to become a debtor nation), in some fundamental sense they did not cause it. The real long-run causes of the microeconomic adjustments that must be made are to be found in the productivity growth gap between the United States and either Japan or Western Europe. This gap played a positive role in the world economy as long as the rest of the industrial world was essentially catching up with American levels of productivity, since the rest of the world needed higher productivity growth rates if it was to eventually enjoy an equal standard of living.

The productivity growth gap plays a negative role, however, when the rest of the world reaches the point where its productivity begins to exceed that of the United States and continues to grow much more rapidly. The United States will see its industries lagging behind and being beaten in international competition and will likely resort to protectionist measures.

What macroeconomic policies have essentially done, however, is to bunch together industrial changes that otherwise would have been spread out over some substantial period of time. Instead of falling 4 percent per year for 10 years, the dollar falls 40 percent in 1 year. This makes the adjustment process much harder, but does not necessarily require different adjustments than those that would in the long run have been required given different rates of productivity growth.

Complementary macroeconomic policies in the United States, Germany, and Japan can still spread those changes out over time but, because of the U.S. debtor position, only at the cost of making the ultimate adjustments much larger than they would have to be if the adjustments are made quickly.

Since no one wishes to lower the rate of productivity growth elsewhere in the world, this is a problem that must be solved in the United States. Solving this problem is beyond the scope of this chapter, but it should not be forgotten as a source of long-run disequilibrium in the world trading system.[5] Over and above its immediate problems, the world trading system will need some fundamental readjustments if U.S. productivity levels do sag substantially below those in Europe or Japan.

Some of the changes are economic. It is difficult to believe that the world will wish to use dollars as its reserve currency if the dollar is not backed by a strong economy. If investors want to shift from dollars to some other currency, there is no easy way to do so unless the United States is at the time running a trade surplus to repay those debts that were incurred when foreigners decided to hold some of their assets as dollar reserves. To run a trade surplus while one's productivity is growing slower than that of one's trading partners requires a substantial annual depreciation in the value of the dollar (see the next section). This of course means that those holding dollar reserve assets are losing some fraction of their wealth every year and are even more anxious to escape from the dollar. However, the more that they try to escape, the more difficult escape becomes. Slow productivity growth is a problem that Americans will have to solve, but their ability or inability to solve it is going to have consequences for their industrial neighbors.

The net flow of savings

Economists often point out that consistent macroeconomic policies must be followed if the world economy is to work. If American interest rates are well above those in Germany or Japan, they create capital flows that destabilize the system. If interest rates are to be roughly equal, fiscal policies must be consistent, and this means that the United States must cure its federal budget deficit.

All of that is correct, but it is equally true that microeconomic performances must be consistent if the world economy is to work politically and economically. This is true when it comes to the productivity growth rates that have just been discussed, but it is equally true with respect to other microeconomic parameters. Consider the differences in savings rates that are found from country to country. In a world of isolated national economies, different savings rates would simply be one of the factors leading a country to grow more rapidly than its neighbors. In an integrated world economy, large differences in national savings rates create problems.

In a world where goods flow freely between countries but capital does not, different savings rates contribute to different productivity growth rates and the imbalances already discussed. The country with the lower rate of productivity growth sees itself systematically being squeezed out of what it considers its best industries and reacts with defensive measures that stop the free flow of goods.

If capital also flows freely around the world, national savings rates cease to have any significance when it comes to productivity growth rates. Those living in economies with low savings rates simply borrow investment funds from those living in countries with high savings rates. Those who save essentially become the world's capitalists, providing the equity or loans that the low savers need. Small differences in savings rates present no problem for a smoothly functioning world economy, but large differences present major problems. These come about because the world's economy does not use a single currency, but many currencies.

If capital must flow from an economy with a high savings rate to an economy with a low savings rate, the economy with the high savings rate must run a permanent trade surplus to effectuate the real transfer of resources. Conversely, the recipient economies of those who save little must run permanent trade deficits. No one worries about, or keeps track of, whether New Jersey is a net debtor state and New York is a net creditor state since both states use dollars and the net debtor or creditor status of any state has no impact on the value of dollar assets. People do, however, worry about, and keep track of, the net debtor or creditor status of countries. They do so since debtor or creditor status affects the value of any currency and hence the value of assets as seen from countries using other currencies. Lenders do not rush out of dollar assets if the people and institutions of New Jersey have borrowed what the lenders see as too much; lenders do, however, attempt to run out of peso assets if the people and institutions of Mexico are seen to have borrowed too much. Thus what is possible within a single-currency country – perpetual flows of savings from one region to another – becomes impossible in a multicurrency world economy.

There is also a political problem that exists with such flows of savings across countries that does not exist when the flows of savings are within countries. If there are no creditworthy borrowers in the low-savings regions to which savings should flow from the high-savings regions, the savers in the high-savings regions simply become owners and equity investors in the low-savings regions. With current world trade parameters, at some point today's loans to the United States will have to become equity investments in the United States if the savings flows are to continue. Some foreign equity investments naturally occur, but if one looks at the numerical example that was given earlier and the size of the American current account deficits that are looming ahead, the equity investments have to become very large. Within a relatively short period of time, foreigners would end up owning essentially all of the physical assets in the United States. One can ask whether foreigners will really want to become American equity owners to the extent that will be required. One knows that Americans will not politically tolerate the degree of foreign ownership of the American assets that is implicit in the idea that such savings flows can go on forever.

However, to reverse such flows requires a change in microeconomic behavior patterns. Correcting the American fiscal deficit would be a step in the right direction toward equalizing net savings flows, but it would not solve the problem. The balance between consumer and corporate borrowing and consumer and corporate savings would still show the United States needing a net inflow of savings from abroad.

Within a country, differences in savings behavior are to some extent economically tolerable and to a great extent self-correcting. Those who save become richer than those who do not save, and within limits, every country is willing to tolerate some differences in wealth. The self-correcting nature of the system comes about since every individual is thought to save to provide future consumption benefits for oneself or one's family. As a result, there comes a time when every individual shifts from saver to dissaver, and this limits differences in the accumulation of wealth among citizens of the same country.

However, across countries there is no automatic self-correcting mechanism. Individuals know that they are going to die and the time to commence dissaving has to begin at some point. Countries do not die, however, and never reach the point where they collectively must shift from saving to consumption.

Even with individual countries there are limits to how large differences in wealth can become before they are politically intolerable. Every country adopts policies to prevent the differences from becoming too large. Progressive taxes reduce the saving ability of high-income groups and compulsory savings systems (Social Security payroll taxes to finance old age pensions with the United States is one example) force low savers to save. To make a world economy work, public policies designed to limit differences in saving behavior (and hence wealth) among trading partners are just as necessary as they are within countries, but there is no international mechanism for bringing them about.

To correct the problem requires a restructuring of savings behavior to raise savings rates in the United States or to lower them in the rest of the industrial world. Since a world with high savings rates grows faster than a world with low savings rates, high savings rates would seem to be preferable, so that the United States should restructure itself to raise its savings rates rather than urging countries such as Japan to lower their savings rates.

What to do to raise savings rates is not hard to specify economically. How to do it politically, however, is virtually impossible to specify. Since most individuals save to finance future consumption purchases, individual propensities to save are most easily raised by limiting consumer credit in terms of less availability, larger down payments, faster repayment periods, and no tax deductibility of interest payments. To an economist, the fact that the country with the world's most generous provisions for consumer credit has the lowest saving rate among industrialized nations comes as no surprise.

To make the shift, however, the average American voter would have to be willing to politically support a restructuring of the economy that would in all likelihood lower the consumption standard of living for a period of years during the transition from today's society, with its much less generous provisions for consumer credit. For a time, the average consumer would still be making repayments on old loans and have to accumulate the savings necessary to begin making larger consumer purchases in a world with less consumer credit. In microeconomic terms this would mean a temporary reduction in standards of living, and in macroeconomic terms it would be a deflationary transition. Neither mean that the shift is impossible or undesirable, but they do point to the difficulty of the transition that would be necessary to make microeconomic parameters compatible.

If one looks at the world capital market as an allocator of savings flows from high- to low-savings regions of the globe, there is a problem. Savings should flow to equalize interest rates from region to region. Within a single currency region, they do. Within multiple currency regions, interest rates should equalize except for expected changes in exchange rates. If one is looking at three-month bills and the interest rate is 7.9 percent in the United States and 6.3 percent in Japan, the market is expecting a 1.6 percent fall in the value of the dollar within the next three months. Only such a fall will make the two interest rates equivalent and make the market into an equilibrium financial market.

Problems emerge, however, if one looks at three-month bill rates from 1980 through March of 1985. American interest rates were higher, often much higher, despite an appreciation of the value of the dollar. Ex-post returns on dollar treasury bills have been far above those in the rest of the world. That should not have happened if one believes in the efficient market hypothesis. One can explain this empirical observation in a number of ways, but all of them leave a problem.

One explanation is that we don't really have a world capital market in which capital flows equalize returns. The market either never gets to equilibrium or the time lags are very long. Given the speed and magnitude of the flow of funds through the world's capital markets, this is a difficult hypothesis to maintain.

Another hypothesis is that the market has been consistently wrong about an expected depreciation of the dollar for almost five years. If markets can be consistently wrong for five years on one issue, they can be consistently wrong on other issues. If this hypothesis is believed, the mistakes of the world's financial markets are being built into the structure of the world's economy.

The standard explanation for the rise in the value of the dollar in the early 1980s is that capital flows now dominate trade flows when it comes to determining the value of the dollar. The magnitude of the world's capital flows are simply much larger than the magnitude of the world's trade flows.

Let me suggest that this is what Americans believed about futures markets for commodities in the 1920s. The volume of futures contracts being traded for wheat were much larger than the volume of wheat actually being grown and consumed and therefore people believed in the 1920s that wheat prices were determined in the futures markets and not in the real markets for wheat. They learned in the collapses of the late 1920s that they were wrong. In the long run, the price of wheat is determined by the demands and supplies of wheat regardless of the volume of future contracts traded.

This may be a lesson that the world's currency traders are going to have to learn. In the long run, trading flows are going to determine currency values, and capital flows are market noise that has to be discounted in determining long-run currency values.

The belief that financial markets can make no major fundamental mistakes (a widespread current belief) is exactly the belief that brought real economies to ruin in the late 1920s.

Whatever you believe about the likelihood of a sudden crisis, however, the restructuring of parameters has to go far beyond macroeconomic parameters if the world economy is to work successfully in the long run. The imbalances in the system are not simply imbalances put there by inconsistent macroeconomic policies or imbalances removable by the adoption of consistent macroeconomic policies.

U.S. financial markets

Much as in the late 1920s, there are some fundamental stresses and strains arising within the U.S. financial markets. Some of these stresses and strains flow from the world economy, but all of them will have an impact on the world economy.

Everyone is familiar with the debt problem of the developing world, but everyone also wants to be an ostrich about solving them. In the past four years the fundamental problems have been papered over with austerity policies in the developing world and additional lending to allow those countries to pay interest to the developed world. Neither can continue. Austerity is not a policy. It simply buys time to find a workable policy. Lending to pay oneself interest is likewise not a policy. It simply buys time to find a workable policy.

The Baker initiative is not such a policy. It requires further lending to pay interest, and there is no policy for causing growth in the developing world that is consistent with a large transfer of resources from the developing world to the developed world to meet even part of their interest bill.[6] To grow, the developing world would have to stop exporting capital and return to importing capital.

In the end, what I call "loss allocation" will have to occur. Eventually realistic estimates must be made of what developing world debtors can reasonably be expected to pay, and debts in excess of this amount are going to have to be written off. The only question will involve how to split the losses between the bank shareholders and taxpayers. But before the taxpayer pays, the shareholder is going to take a major part of the losses.

If the lending problems of developing countries existed in isolation, they would not be a cause for serious concern. Unfortunately, however, they exist in the context of similar problems in domestic U.S. lending. Because of the value of the dollar and the loss of export markets, farm loans are probably at greater risk than those in South America. Land values are down 50 percent in much of the Midwest, and real land values are down even more since the banks are not selling foreclosed properties for fear of driving the reported values still further down and thus forcing them to write off even more farm loans. At some point, America's farmers will realize that their smartest financial move is to give their farm back to their banker, walk away from it, and start over. This occurs when the outstanding value of their mortgage exceeds the current market value of their farm.

The debt of the developing world involves the juggling of 5 big debtors and 12 big banks. The farm debt involves the juggling of hundreds of thousands of farmers and tens of thousands of banks. Individual farmers will be defaulted, however, and if enough of them are defaulted, the result will be equivalent to that of a default for Brazil.

Energy debts are rapidly coming to resemble farm lending as a source of concern in the financial headlines. Falling oil prices are the equivalent of falling farmland prices. All energy loans have been based on some estimate of future energy prices. As energy prices fall, they convert what had been good loans into bad loans. If they fall far enough, they force energy investors to walk away from what are, at the new lower prices of energy, worthless investments – the interest and principal payments owed upon them exceed their market resale value.

Adding to the problems created by the weak developing world, farm, and energy loans is the fact that American consumers and corporations have both decided to leverage themselves to record levels. Whereas disposable personal income rose 4.1 percent from the third quarter of 1984 to the third quarter of 1985, consumer installment credit rose 19.1 percent, or almost five times as fast.[7] Debt relative to income and interest payments relative to income are both at record levels. Consumers are simply consuming more than they earn.

Similarly, American corporations are borrowing at record rates. Most of this borrowing is not to finance new investments but to alter debt-to-equity ratios. The need or desire to do so arises from the leveraged buyout and merger wars that are now sweeping American industry. In either a leveraged buyout or a successful merger, those taking over the firm seek to mortgage the firm's assets to a maximum degree to pay down the loans they took out to finance the takeover. The idea is to finance the takeover with the assets of the firm being taken over, but this means buying out the equity shareholders with debt. A firm wishing to avoid a takeover also converts equity to debt since a firm that is fully leveraged is not an attractive takeover candidate because those taking it over cannot repay any of their loans by taking out additional loans on the firm's assets. Thus, regardless of whether the merger wars are won or lost, the net result is more corporate debt and less equity. Everyone goes to the margin where the financial markets are not willing to lend them anything more. This creates a very brittle financial structure for both consumers and the corporations, for, should a recession occur and an unexpected decline in incomes arise, neither the consumer nor the corporation could meet their interest payment obligations.

What has been created is a financial structure that is now much less robust with respect to recessions than the one that previously existed. Precisely the groups that were able to weather recessions financially in the past will not be able to weather recessions in the future. Given the widespread nature of this change, the macroeconomic policy makers have lost their ability to create recessions to stop inflation and now have to make sure that they do not let recessions occur.

At this point, the pressures emanating from an overvalued dollar, a large trade deficit, and a rapidly expanding international debt intersect with those flowing from a weak banking system. If the dollar suddenly started to fall, the standard technique for reducing the rate of decline would be for the Federal Reserve Board to raise interest rates. But given the weak developing world, farm, and energy loans and the fully leveraged consumer and corporate sectors, raising interest rates would induce a massive wave of defaults. Thus, one of the principal weapons for dealing with a currency crisis has effectively been removed. A currency crisis would have to be managed without raising interest rates.

Another conflict arises between the need to reduce the federal deficit (a deflationary action) and the need to avoid recessions given the weakened financial structure of the United States. Any budget-balancing exercise would be likely to cause a recession, but the financial structure of the United States would be likely to crack if there were a recession.

The changing structure of American exports and imports

If one examines the econometric literature on America's exports and imports, the dollar would need to have fallen about 40 percent to balance exports and imports as of January 1985. Although all of the equations produce similar results, the problems can be best illustrated by analyzing a specific set of equations such as those estimated by Robert Lawrence of the Brookings Institution.[8] The Lawrence equations show that to regain a balance in manufactured goods the United States would have needed a 38 percent decline in the value of the dollar as of January 1, 1985. Since the dollar rose 6 percent from the first of January until its peak in early March and by May 1986 had fallen about 30 percent, these equations indicate that the dollar would need an additional 14 percent fall to restore balance between exports and imports.[9]

As the United States becomes a debtor nation, however, it needs to do more than restore a balance between exports and imports. The more it becomes a debtor nation, the bigger the surplus that it must run in its trade accounts. The Lawrence equations indicate that a 10 percent fall in the value of the dollar is necessary to produce a $30 billion improvement in the U.S. trade deficit. Thus if America's international debts rose to $200 billion at the end of 1986 and interest rates averaged 8 percent, an additional 5 percent fall in the value of the dollar would be necessary to produce the trade surplus necessary to make the $16 billion in interest payments that would be required.

To compensate for the lower rate of growth of productivity in the United States, the Lawrence equations also indicate that the dollar would have to forever fall by 0.4 percent per year to maintain stability in America's trading accounts.[10] This latter calculation, however, is made on the assumption that the U.S. GNP growth rate is one-third lower than that of the rest of the world. Such a difference in growth rates occurred between 1964 and 1980 and was necessary if the standards of living in other industrial countries were to catch up with those in the United States. Such differences are not functional, however, after the rest of the world has caught up. To make the world economy work, the United States has to grow as fast as the rest of the world. If it were to do so, the annual fall in the value of the dollar would have to be 1.8 percent per year according to the Lawrence equations.

Sooner or later the financial markets will come to realize that the fundamentals of interest repayment and low productivity growth call for a perpetual fall in the value of the dollar and will start to speculate against the future value of the dollar. This could easily lead to declines in the value of the dollar greater than those that are required by the fundamentals.

There is also reason to believe that the Lawrence equations are, if anything, on the optimistic side. Lawrence's equations indicate that there has been a substantial recent slippage in America's competitive position. For both imports and exports Lawrence estimates two equations – one with data from 1964 to 1980 and one with data from 1964 to mid-1983.[11] By comparing the parameters of the two equations it is possible to isolate the structural deteriorations that have occurred in the American position in the 1981–3 period.

Such a comparison reveals a systematic deterioration in America's competitive strength. After correcting for changes in the value of the dollar, foreigners over those three years were buying fewer (1 percent less) U.S. exports when their industrial production rose than they previously had, and they were becoming more sensitive to the price of U.S. exports, cutting their purchases back more (9 percent) than they previously did when American prices rose. On the import side, a given increase in the American GNP led to a bigger (14 percent more) rise in imports than it previously had, and a fall in foreign prices led to a bigger rise (6 percent more) in American imports than it previously had.[12]

Such shifts are the mark of a country whose exports are becoming less unique, less competitive, and must more and more be sold as simply cheaper rather than better. Conversely, foreign exports into the United States are becoming more unique, more competitive, and less and less have to be sold simply on the basis of lower prices. After correcting for the effects of a high-valued dollar, Americans want more foreign products relative to their incomes than they did in the past, whereas foreigners want fewer U.S. products relative to their incomes than they did in the past. Bigger and bigger American price reductions are needed to secure foreign markets, whereas foreigners can charge higher and higher prices without losing their American markets.

If the addition of three years of extra data to the Lawrence equations moves them consistently toward a more adverse American position, as it does, strong underlying adverse trends are running against the United States and will gradually enlarge the annual decline in the value of the dollar necessary to remain competitive. Extrapolating forward to the end of 1984, the Lawrence equations predicted a rise in the deficit in manufacturing trade, but the actual rise in the deficit was twice as large as that predicted.[13]

There is also every reason to believe that the Lawrence equations underestimate the magnitude of the adverse shift against the United States. The extra three years of data were added to the context of a rapid military buildup. Military spending is a captive market for American manufacturing. Americans don't ask for competitive foreign bids on military equipment. If they did, all of our naval ships would be made in Japan. However, this means total manufacturing looks much stronger than civilian manufacturing would look if separated out from the totals.

In addition, the period has been one of protection. The percentage of U.S.-manufactured goods protected by nontariff restrictions has risen from 20 percent in 1980 to 35 percent in 1983. If such protection had not occurred, the adverse shift against the United States would have been much larger than that estimated by Lawrence, for protection prevented Americans from buying all of the foreign products that they would have liked to buy.[14]

Whereas America was running a trade surplus in high-technology products in the 1970s, in the 1980s it has been moving rapidly toward a trade deficit.[15] It already has a large bilateral deficit in high-tech products vis-à-vis Japan and is just barely holding its own vis-à-vis Germany.[16] Since countries lose their home markets last for the things that they do best, an inability to compete against Japan and West Germany on high-tech products such as semiconductor chips or machine tools in home American markets has to be taken very seriously

As a result, the econometric estimates of how much the dollar would have to fall to restore sustainability to the American balance of payments is apt to be much larger than the estimates that are commonly used. A one-time 44 percent fall in the value of the dollar from its March 1985 levels is very unlikely to be enough to restore sustainability. And each year the decline that will be necessary to reach sustainability rises at an exponential rate because of the exponential increase in the interest repayments that the United States will owe to the rest of the world. The necessary changes are not marginal changes and will require major adjustments in the macro and micro structures of most of the world's economies.

Notes

1 U.S. Department of Commerce, *Survey of Current Business*, Government Printing Office, September, 1985, p. 36.
2 International Monetary Fund, *International Financial Statistics*, Yearbook 1983, p. 367.
3 Council of Economic Advisers, *Economic Report of the President 1985*, GPO, 1985, p. 344.
4 Morgan Guaranty Trust, "Countering World Deflation" *World Financial Markets*, December 1985.
5 For an analysis of the causes and cures of the U.S. Productivity problem see Lester C. Thurow, *The Zero-Sum Solution: Building A World-Class American Economy*, Simon and Shuster, 1985.
6 Carol J. Loomis, "Why Baker's Debt Plan Won't Work," *Fortune*, December 20, 1985, p. 98.
7 Council of Economic Advisers, *Economic Indicators*, October 1985, pp. 6, 28.
8 Robert A. Lawrence, *Can America Compete?*, Brookings Institution, 1984, p. 46.
9 Morgan Guaranty Trust, *World Financial Markets*, February 1985 and March/April 1985.
10 Lawrence, *Can America Compete?* p. 47.
11 Ibid., p. 46.

12 These percentages are calculated by comparing the income and price elasticities of demand for the two periods of time.
13 Lawrence, *Can America Compete?* p. 49.
14 Ibid., p. 121.
15 Charles Schultze, "Industrial Policy: A Dissent," *Brookings Review*, Fall 1983, p. 5.
16 National Science Board, *Science Indicators*, 1982, p. 22.

PART III

Japan's response

The U.S.–Japan trade imbalance: causes and consequences from the Japanese perspective

RYUZO SATO and JOHN A. RIZZO

Introduction

Japan's success in coping with two rounds of skyrocketing oil prices in the 1970s has dramatically changed both its economic structure and competitiveness in the world market. The oil shocks of the 1970s were regarded in Japan as a national emergency to a country poor in raw materials and arable land. As a result, the government and the business community worked rigorously to maintain the competitiveness of Japanese industry through research and development to reduce energy costs and industrial restructuring efforts.

By the end of the 1970s, these objectives had been largely achieved. Japan had invested almost twice as much as the United States in research and development to reduce energy costs and to create newer and younger vintages of capital stock in Japan. Overall investment in Japan has grown much faster than overall investment in other advanced countries. For instance, capital per unit of employment between 1973 and 1979 increased at an average annual rate of 6.1 percent in Japan, whereas in the United States it grew at an average annual rate of only 0.9 percent.[1] Japanese imports and exports roughly balanced at the rate of 16 percent of GNP in 1981 and the excess of savings over domestic investment exactly matched the government's budget deficit, leaving domestic effective demand and supply in equilibrium.

In the early 1980s there was a growing concern among government officials and business groups, notably the Keidanren (the most powerful federation of business organizations in Japan), that the large government deficit would eventually cripple the economy and that the size of the government was becoming too large. This was the period in which Mr. Inayama's *Gaman-no-Tetsugaku* (philosophy of perseverance) became the national motto. As Chairman of the Keidanren, Mr. Inayama advocated *Gaman-no-Tetsugaku* and government austerity accompanied by further individual sacrifice to prepare for future challenges to Japan.

The anticipated challenges never arrived. Instead, both falling oil prices and extremely brisk foreign demand for Japanese products, accompanied by large deficits in the U.S. government budget and the resulting high U.S. interest rates, brought unexpected windfalls to Japan. By the end of 1986, the proportion of Japan's imports declined to 13 percent of GNP, noticeably down from its high of 16 percent in 1981, whereas exports continued to grow at a higher rate than during the pre-Reagan era. The upshot is that Japan has now generated the largest trade surplus of any nation in history.

The expression *Gaiteki Fukinko* (external imbalance) started appearing in several Japanese newspapers around the end of 1983. There were fierce arguments as to whether Japan's balance of payments surplus was cyclical or structural. But by 1985 it was generally conceded that the export-prone structure of the Japanese economy was largely responsible for the persistent external surplus.

On October 31, 1985, the Mayekawa Commission was organized to study "economic structural adjustments for the promotion of international harmony," in order to correct "the external imbalance of the Japanese economy." The commission issued its report on April 7, 1986, which, for the first time in the postwar period, recommended that the Japanese economy be transformed from a savings-export orientation to a consumption-import orientation.

Despite such efforts as the Mayekawa Commission report, problems of trade imbalance and trade friction between Japan and the United States have continued to mount. The U.S.–Japan trade conflict approached a critical point when in April 1987 the Reagan administration imposed 100 percent tariffs on certain Japanese products containing semiconductor chips.

These issues often lend themselves to emotional and even heated debate, but they can only be resolved through cool observation and analysis. The preceding chapters of this volume have done an outstanding job of analyzing the trade imbalance from a U.S. perspective. In this chapter, we wish to provide a sense of balance to the discussion by focusing on Japan's perspective and the features of Japan's economy that have played important roles in the trade imbalance and noting the implications for future trade relations between Japan and the United States.

Components of the trade imbalance

Trade among various countries is determined by several factors, which include domestic and foreign demands, changes in relative prices and exchange rates, and tariffs and nontariff barriers. Between 1983 and 1985, Japan's overall trade surplus increased by almost $40 billion, whereas the U.S. overall trade balance deteriorated by more than $100 billion. Higher interest rates in the United States – resulting from a large federal budget deficit, a stronger

Table 7.1. *Factor analysis of the rise of the U.S.–Japan trade imbalance, 1982–5 (percent)*

Component	Japan, surplus	United States, deficit
Due to growth effects	41	41
Due to elasticity differences	32	23
Due to exchange rates	30	17
Due to relative prices	−15[a]	12

Note: The sum of the factors shown here does not add to 100 percent because of the omission of other "unexplained" factors.

[a]The negative sign indicates that changes in relative prices served to decrease Japan's trade surplus by 15 percent below what it otherwise would have been in the absence of such price changes.

Sources: Calculated from Economic Planning Agency's White Paper (1986).

dollar, and a higher growth rate of U.S. GNP – are alleged to have contributed to this pattern. Many also blame Japan for restricting access to its domestic markets.

Scientific studies to determine the exact sources of the trade imbalance are hard to come by, but a 1986 study by Japan's Economic Planning Agency (EPA) provides a rough breakdown of the sources contributing to the Japan–U.S. trade imbalance. Using regression and factor analysis, the EPA study demonstrated that trends in demand growth, import and export elasticities, exchange rate changes, and relative price fluctuations have each played an important role in shaping Japan's trade surplus and the U.S. trade deficit (see Table 7.1).[2]

This section highlights these four major components of the Japan–U.S. trade imbalance. Subsequent sections explore the economic, political, and social factors responsible for these differential demand growths, exchange rate changes, and other components of the trade imbalance.

Demand and growth

Figures 7.1a and 7.1b show how divergences in the growth rates of domestic and foreign demands in both the United States and Japan have contributed to the drastic increase in the bilateral trade imbalance. Total domestic demand in Japan grew steadily at an annual rate of 4 percent during 1982–5, which is approximately the same rate as the average expected rate of growth calculated from the trend line for the 1978–85 period (the shadowed portion). On the

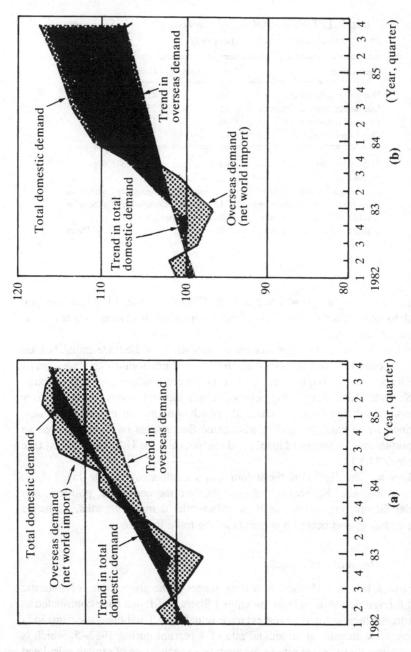

Figure 7.1 Growth gaps in (a) Japan and (b) the United States. *Source:* IMF statistics and Economic Planning Agency's regression analysis (1986).

Table 7.2. *Elasticity comparisons*

	Export elasticity with respect to Income (A)	Import elasticity with respect to Income (B)	Imbalance factor (A/B)
Japan	2.210	0.725	3.05
U.S.A.	1.133	1.687	0.67
W. Germany	0.976	0.803	1.22
S. Korea	4.207	0.746	5.64

Source: Calculated from EPA's White Paper (1986).

other hand, foreign demand for Japanese products grew much faster than the trend line (2.6 percent).

A substantial increase in the foreign demand for Japanese goods came from the United States. While U.S. exports moved along the trend line of 2.4 percent, overall domestic demand in the United States exceeded its trend line of 2.2 percent by a substantial margin. Given the fixed nature of the propensity to import, this unprecedented rise in the U.S. domestic demand provided the basis for a sharp increase in imports, especially from Japan. It was the much higher growth rate in U.S. domestic demand more than Japan's efforts to raise exports that fueled the fire for ensuing trade friction.

Elasticity differences

Table 7.2 compares the elasticities of imports and exports in various countries. We find that the import elasticity with respect to income is the lowest (0.725) in Japan and the highest (1.687) in the United States. However, the export elasticity with respect to income is the highest (4.207) in South Korea, not in Japan (2.210). In passing, note that West Germany is relatively balanced between exports and imports as their elasticities have a relatively small deviation.

Among the four countries compared, the United States is the only one whose imbalance factor is less than one (0.67), which implies that the United States tends to import more than it can afford. By contrast, South Korea and Japan depend too much on exports for income generation.

Exchange rates – expensive dollar and cheap yen

Another major factor responsible for the trade imbalance between Japan and the United States in the first half of the 1980s was the overvalued dollar.

According to the factor analysis presented in Table 7.1, 30 percent of the increase in Japan's surplus is due to this factor, as is 17 percent of the U.S. deterioration of the trade balance. The high valuation of the U.S. dollar was sustained by high interest rates reflecting the huge U.S. fiscal deficits.

Price effects

The declining prices of crude oil and other primary products contributed to improvements in the trade balances in both Japan and the United States. But the overall effects of changes in the relative prices of both export and import goods worked against both countries. The export and import functions that the Economic Planning Agency estimated for this period in 1986 seem to verify this assertion.

Causes of the trade imbalance

The causes of the bilateral trade imbalance cannot be fully understood without some knowledge of the economic structure and policy of both Japan and the United States. Other chapters in this volume have ably covered the U.S. economy. In this section, we concentrate on four factors specific to Japan that have played important roles in the trade imbalance: (1) Japan's macroeconomic structure and policy, (2) its industrial structure and policy, (3) its trade barriers, and (4) its capital markets.

Macroeconomic structure and policy

Japan's economy differs in important respects from that of the United States. Factors such as Japan's high savings rate and weak domestic demand have served to promote a Japanese trade surplus vis-à-vis the United States. The high rate of saving and weak domestic demand reflect in part the high cost of housing and education relative to income.[3] Therefore, this pattern of saving and domestic demand is likely to persist unless the Japanese government takes active steps to induce structural change. However, to the extent that saving reflects cultural factors,[4] expansionary government initiatives may be less effective and less appreciated than they would be in a more consumption-oriented society.

On the surface, Japan's tax structure does not appear to be responsible for its sluggish personal consumption. As Table 7.3 indicates, taxes on individual income account for a smaller percentage of tax receipts in Japan (36.1 percent) than in the United States (48.3 percent). This is rather surprising in view of the fact that the United States is by far the more consumption-oriented society. In the past, the damaging effect of Japan's tax structure on personal

Table 7.3. *Distribution of tax receipts by type of tax in Japan and the United States, 1983 (percent)*

	Individual[a]	Corporation[b]	Goods and services	Other
Japan	36.1	34.8	13.2	15.9
United States	48.3	22.3	15.6	13.8

Note: Taxes on goods and services are listed separately because both corporations and individuals pay these taxes. At any rate, the striking difference in tax incidence between Japan and the United States is found in the income and social security taxes.

[a]Includes individual income taxes and employee contributions for social security.

[b]Includes corporate income tax and employer's contributions for social security.

Source: Organization for Economic Cooperation and Development, *Revenue Statistics of OECD Member Countries* (Paris, annual).

consumption has come from what has not been taxed rather than from what has been taxed. In particular, the formerly tax-exempt status of private savings has raised saving relative to personal consumption. Recently, however, this exemption has been eliminated. This suggests that Japan's consumption may start to rise relative to saving.

Other factors are also important. Paltry increases in real earnings have kept consumption in check. As Table 7.4 indicates, real cash earnings in Japan rarely increased by more than two percent per annum over 1979–85, in spite of annual productivity gains that seldom increased by less than 2 percent (and that usually increased by substantially more). Other structural features, such as Japan's longer working hours, have also served to strengthen savings and dampen demand.

Nor are consumption increases driven by economic growth a likely outcome. Investment growth has been trending downward in Japan for years (see Figure 7.2a). This pattern is to be expected for a maturing economy. The alarming fact, however, is that in recent years, investment and savings have diverged. Figure 7.2b indicates that, from about 1983 onward, savings rose sharply as a percentage of GNP, whereas investment leveled off. This divergence, in turn, has induced a capital outflow that has resulted in a weaker yen and a larger trade surplus for Japan.

Private consumption has become an increasingly important component of domestic demand in Japan over the past 15 years. For instance, whereas business investment accounted for 21 percent of domestic demand in 1970,

Table 7.4. Wages, productivity, and unit labor costs. Percentage change from a year earlier

	Wage increases negotiated in spring rounds[a]	Regular wages[b] (A)	Overtime (B)	Contract[b] (C) (A) + (B)	Bonus payments, etc.[b] (D)	Total cash earnings[b] (C) + (D)	Total cash earnings[c] (real)	Compensation per employee	Productivity Total[d]	Productivity Mfg[e]	Unit labor costs Total[f]	Unit labor costs Mfg[g]	Memorandum: GNP deflator
Monthly average per worker[a]		209.445 (67.5)	21.149 (6.8)	230.594 (74.3)	79.869 (25.7)	310.463 (100)							
1979	5.8	5.1	12.1	5.8	6.4	6.0	(2.3)	6.0	3.9	2.7	2.7	−0.7	2.6
1980	6.7	5.6	0.9	5.7	8.2	6.3	(−1.6)	6.3	3.7	3.6	3.9	3.7	2.8
1981	7.7	5.3	4.1	5.2	5.6	5.3	(0.4)	6.4	3.2	0.0	4.0	5.6	2.7
1982	7.0	5.3	3.6	5.1	2.5	4.5	(1.7)	4.4	2.2	−0.5	2.7	5.4	1.7
1983	4.4	3.9	5.0	4.0	2.0	3.5	(1.6)	3.0	1.3	3.6	2.1	0.2	0.5
1984	4.5	3.6	9.6	4.2	5.1	4.5	(2.2)	4.1	5.1	9.6	−0.3	−4.5	0.6
1985	5.0	—	—	—	—	—	—	—	—	—	—	—	—

[a]For 1984: In Yen, the figures in parentheses are shares in total cash earnings.
[b]Established with more than 30 regular employees.
[c]Deflated by the consumer goods. Also established with more than 30 employees.
[d]GNP at constant prices divided by total employment.
[e]Industrial production divided by the number of regular employees.
[f]Compensation of employees divided by GNP at constant prices.
[g]Total cash earnings divided by manufacturing productivity.
Sources: Ministry of Labor, Monthly Labour Survey; MITI, Industrial Statistics Monthly; EPA, Annual Report on National Accounts.

(a)

percent per annum

(b)

percent of GNP

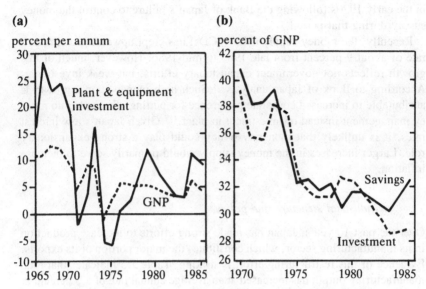

Figure 7.2   Japan: (a) real investment and output growth percent per annum, (b) domestic savings and investment percent of GNP. *Source*: *World Financial Markets* (New York: Morgan Guaranty Trust Co., November 1985).

more recently it has accounted for only 16 percent.[5] Although public sector spending increased substantially after the first oil shock, its share of domestic demand today is roughly the same as it was in 1970, about 17 percent. For this reason, sluggish private consumption is of particular concern today.

Japan's macroeconomic policies have tended to reinforce the effects of its macroeconomic structure on the trade imbalance. Where expansionary fiscal policy might have significantly increased domestic demand, redressing the need to expand exports, Japan has instead pursued a course of fiscal restraint over the past several years. Given current Japanese sentiment, it may be difficult to implement expansionary fiscal policy. In the business community, fiscal expansion is viewed as an avenue of last resort. For example, Eishiro Saito, chairman of the Japan Federation of Economic Organizations (Keidanren) has emphasized that the government should explore other possibilities before resorting to expansionary fiscal policy via a construction bond issue: "Some people argue that construction bonds to finance social infrastructure building are different from deficit-covering bonds, but in reality they share the same effect of leaving debts to future generations."[6]

Monetary growth has been moderate for the past decade or so. This pattern may have come in response to the unprecedented inflation Japan experienced in the early 1970s following the Bank of Japan's failure to control the money supply during that period.

Recently, the money supply (M2 + CDs) has crept upward, growing at a rate of about 9 percent from late 1985 to mid-1986. However, much of this growth reflects not government expansionary efforts, but weak investment. According to Bank of Japan analysts, "Such high money supply growth is attributable to increased corporate preference for putting idle funds into money management instead of investment in plant."[7] Given Japan's low interest rates, it is unlikely that monetary policy could play a strong expansionary role. Larger increases in the money supply would primarily serve to increase inflation.

Industrial structure and policy

Over the past 10 years, Japan has made strong efforts to increase production in its manufacturing sector, which constitutes the major portion of its exports. Evidence of this restructuring effort is striking. Table 7.5 indicates that total manufacturing output has increased at an average annual rate of 5.5 percent in Japan over 1975–84, which compares with 4 percent for the United States and is well in excess of other major industrial countries. These manufacturing increases have been concentrated in the more advanced industries, such as electric machinery and processing industries, rather than in heavy industries.

Japan's industrial structure today is the outcome of a concerted effort to become more energy efficient in response to the oil shocks of the 1970s. Besides increasing productive efficiency, Japanese industries have successfully advanced into those fields having a high income elasticity of demand, as Table 7.2 suggests.

Just as Japan's macroeconomic policies have complemented structural features of its macroeconomy, Japan's industrial policies have complemented its industrial structure. In response to the havoc wrought by the first oil crisis, Japanese industrial policy sought to promote investment in research and development in high-technology industries and to assist stagnant industries in downscaling operations.

It should be noted, however, that Japanese industry, more so than the Japanese government, was responsible for changes in industrial structure. To be sure, the government provided guidance and incentives, but it was industry that made the decisions altering Japan's industrial structure. Adherence to government directives was largely elective. Commenting on the relationship between government and industry during this period, Suzumura and Okuno-Fujiwara have remarked that "private firms did not have much reason to comply with administrative guidance unless such compliance was mandatory and/or doing so was consistent with the firm's private motives. Thus, the

Table 7.5. *International comparisons of structural change in manufacturing, annual average percentage changes, 1975–84*

	Japan	United States	Canada	France	Germany	Italy	United Kingdom	Belgium	Netherlands	Sweden
Industrial production										
Total manufacturing	5.5	4.0	2.0	1.4	1.7	2.2	-0.5	3.1	2.5	0.8
Electrical machinery	16.4	7.2	1.6	3.5	3.1	1.7	1.5	0.3	5.4	3.4
Other processing industries										
General machinery	5.9	4.1	3.0	0.4	2.1	2.1	5.3	1.1	-0.1	1.7
Transportation equipment	3.4	3.9	2.4	3.4	2.9	3.8	2.9	4.9	-2.1	1.0
Metal products	3.3	2.5	-0.4	1.8	0.7	-1.5	-0.5	-0.1	0.4	0.1
Heavy industries										
Chemicals	6.1	5.2	3.4	2.3	2.4	2.6	1.8	3.9	4.2	2.7
Basic metals	2.0	3.4	-0.7	0.1	0.5	1.8	1.8	-0.7	-0.5	-2.8
Iron and steel	2.5	-2.0	1.1	-1.4	-0.5	1.2	-4.1	0.1	—	-1.0
Nonferrous metals	3.9	2.5	3.0	4.0	2.0	2.1	-0.4	3.2	—	0.8
Labor industries										
Food	2.6	3.0	1.4	1.7	1.4	2.4	1.1	2.4	3.1	0.9
Textiles	0.5	0.8	0.6	-1.4	-1.9	1.7	-2.1	0.4	-3.2	5.5
Standard deviations	4.5	1.0	1.1	1.5	1.2	0.9	1.1	1.8	—	1.6

Source: OECD, *Indicators of Industrial Activity;* OECD Secretariat.

Table 7.6. *Comparison of management objectives in Japan and the United States*

Corporate Objectives	United States	Japan
Rate of return on investment (ROI)	2.43	1.24
Increase in stock prices	1.14	0.02
Increase in market share	0.73	1.43
Improving product portfolio	0.50	0.68
Rationalization of production and physical distribution systems	0.46	0.71
Net-worth ratio	0.38	0.59
Ratio of new products	0.21	1.06
Improving the social image of the company	0.05	0.20
Improving working conditions	0.04	0.09

Source: Tadao Kagono, *A Comparison of Management of Japanese and U.S. Companies (in Japanese).*

character of industrial policy became mostly passive, indicative and inter-mediary rather than active, interventionist and regulatory.''[8]

In large part, Japan's industrial policies have been shaped by managerial objectives. It is therefore instructive to examine managerial objectives in Japan and contrast these with the objectives of managers in the United States. Table 7.6 summarizes survey results of management objectives in Japan and the United States. In these surveys, representative groups of managers in both countries were asked to rank potential managerial objectives on a scale of 0 to 3, where a score of 0 means that the objective in question is viewed as unimportant, and a score of 3 indicates that the objective is considered very important. U.S. managers emphasize the rate of return and the profit rate as their primary objectives, whereas Japanese managers emphasize increasing market share more than any other objectives. Achieving high stock prices ranks as a top priority in the United States, but it is the least important objectives for the Japanese companies. A comon American perception of the typical Japanese corporation is that managers take care of workers' welfare. Interestingly, both American and Japanese managers apparently attach little importance to this problem.

Another revealing aspect of Table 7.6 is that it shows Japanese managers emphasize the introduction of new products more than their U.S. counterparts (1.06 vs. 0.21).

The comparison of managerial objectives suggests that Japanese managers are more concerned with attaining goals that are likely to guarantee the suc-cess of the firm over the long run (i.e., increasing market share), whereas

U.S. managers are more concerned with short-run objectives (high rates of return and high stock prices). Greater concern for long-run objectives is a policy that may have served Japan well in competing with the United States.

In addition to sound managerial policy, Japan's technological improvements have played a major role in its industrial success. Japan has already achieved a high state of technological efficiency in the basic materials industry and great flexibility in small- and medium-size subcontracting firms, and it has used general "process" innovations to improve existing production methods. Although Japan is still behind other advanced countries when it comes to general technology, in some areas it has surpassed them. The "technological power" of Japan is certainly responsible for Japan's high growth rate in export markets.

In the main, Japanese technology has developed by importing technology from abroad and then adding process innovation for quality improvements and cost reductions. Thus, Japan has been able in some cases to surpass Western technology through imitation and improvements. An important advantage for Japan has been the ready availability of basic technology developed by other advanced countries, notably the United States. Basic technology often results from noncommercial or defense-related research and development. Interestingly, Japan's surge in the export industry may be a temporary phenomenon that is the direct result of its present state of technological and industrial development.

Many firms that make up Japan's export sector have now reached the third stage of export growth in the so-called product cycle. According to product cycle theory, as a given industry develops it goes through a cycle of importing, import substitution, export growth, maturation, and reverse importing.

The Japanese export industry is now at the third stage, or export growth phase, where the growth of the domestic demand slows down but production increases and exports surge. The product cycle is usually associated with changes in quality, investment, and technology cycles. It is known that large export products such as steel, televisions, automobiles, and machine tools are already approaching the mature stage in Japan, whereas semiconductors and computers are still in the growth stage, and aircraft is in the beginning or importing stage. Apparel and furniture production are declining industries in Japan and are in the reverse importing stage. In the United States, the product cycle in these industries was ahead of the Japanese cycle, which may explain why Japan tends to export more than the United States.

Trade barriers

In terms of actual tariffs and quotas, it is difficult to argue that Japanese protectionism has contributed meaningfully to its trade surplus. The supporting evidence simply is not there. Table 7.7 indicates, for example, that

Table 7.7. *Nominal tariff levels (percentages weighted by own-country imports, excluding petroleum)*

	Japan	United States	Germany	France	United Kingdom	Italy	Canada	Benelux
All industries	2.9	4.3	6.3	6.0	5.2	5.4	5.2	5.9
Textile	3.3	9.2	7.4	7.3	6.7	5.6	16.7	7.2
Wearing apparel	13.8	22.7	13.4	13.2	13.3	13.2	24.2	13.4
Iron and steel	2.8	3.6	4.7	4.9	4.7	3.5	5.4	4.6
Nonelectrical machinery	4.4	3.3	4.5	4.4	4.2	4.5	4.5	4.3
Electrical machinery	4.3	4.4	8.3	7.7	8.1	8.0	5.8	7.4
Transport equipment	1.5	2.5	7.7	7.9	7.2	8.8	1.6	7.9

Note: This table shows Tokyo Round tariffs reached in 1987.
Source: Trade Policy in the 1980s, Institute for International Economics, 1987.

nominal tariff rates are low in Japan relative to other major industrialized nations.

Some complaints have been voiced, however, to the effect that unduly stringent and even discriminatory nontariff barriers, such as health and safety requirements, have effectively limited exports to Japan. Given the difficulties in obtaining reliable quantitative evidence on either side of this argument, available evidence is anecdotal in nature. Thus, this is likely to remain a controversial issue for some time. Since the Japan–U.S. trade imbalance occurred quite rapidly and is of relatively recent vintage, however, it is unlikely that this pattern was strongly driven by long-standing nontariff barriers. Nor do there appear to have been substantial recent changes in nontariff barriers that might have caused a large trade imbalance.

In fact, quite the opposite appears to be the case. Recent efforts in Japan to reduce both tariff and nontariff barriers suggest that Japanese markets are opening up. For example, in an effort to sidetrack the protectionist sentiment growing in the United States and to signal that progress was being made in opening up the Japanese marketplace to American goods and services, the Nakasone government announced The Action Program for Improved Market Access on July 30, 1985. As the Action Program is hard to summarize briefly because it is so comprehensive, we cite three examples in which progress has been made and improvements are forthcoming: telecommunications equipment, automobiles, and wine.

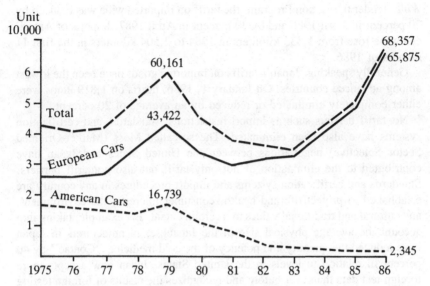

Figure 7.3   Japan: Initial registration of imported cars. *Source*: Japan automobile importer's association.

Telecommunications: The telecommunications market was liberalized in April 1985 when Nippon Telegraph and Telephone (NTT) was made a private corporation. The Action Program removed all tariffs on telecommunications equipment in January 1986. The number of technical standards for terminal equipment was reduced from 53 to 21. As a result, approvals for foreign terminal equipment jumped from 25 cases in 1984 to 103 cases in 1985. Japan Communications Satellite placed an order with Hughes Communications for two satellites and related ground facilities. In December 1985, NTT reached a contract with Northern Telecom Inc. for the purchase of a digital switching system – the first foreign purchase. Ford Aerospace Communications succeeded in the sale of communications satellites to Japan. These purchases alone increased Japan's imports by $800 million.

Automobiles: Tariffs on finished automobiles were completely eliminated in April 1978. Tariffs on automobile parts were virtually abolished by January 1986. The effect of the Action Program is seen by the doubling of import value in one year. Figure 7.3 shows a sharp increase of imported cars after the Action Program was implemented. But is it to be noted that imports of U.S. manufactured automobiles have remained virtually unchanged, whereas imports of European cars have increased sharply.

Wine: Under the Action Program, the tariff on imported wine was reduced by 20 percent in April 1986 and by 30 percent in April 1987. Imports of American wine rose from 1,333 kiloliters in 1984 to 2,504 kiloliters in the first 11 months of 1986.

Generally speaking, Japan's tariffs on imported goods have been the lowest among advanced countries. On January 1, 1986, tariffs on 1,819 items were either completely eliminated or reduced by an average of 20 percent.

Nontariff barriers such as import restrictions, standards, and certification systems have also been eliminated. The so-called Moss (Market-Oriented Sector Selective) negotiations between the United States and Japan have contributed to the elimination of not only tariff but also nontariff barriers. Standards and certification systems and import procedures in any country are established to protect life and health, consumer interests, the environment, and cultural and traditional values to a certain extent. For example, taking into account the average physical size of the Japanese, manufacturers in Japan have reduced the quantity and potency of the cold medicine "Contac" by 40 percent in relation to levels in the United States. Japan now accepts more foreign test data than ever before and recognizes the results of foreign testing organizations. Foreign companies also have easier access to the Japan Industrial Standards (JIS) ratings of manufactured goods.

Capital mobility and Japan's capital markets

For the past several years, the United States has been clamoring for increased liberalization of Japan's capital markets and increased capital mobility. This pressure culminated in the so-called Yen/Dollar Agreement reached at the summit meeting in Tokyo in November 1983. The intent of this agreement was to eliminate yen depreciation allegedly caused by a combination of low interest rates in Japan and restrictions on capital flows – restrictions that were particularly discouraging to capital inflows into Japan.

The actual importance of these factors for the yen/dollar exchange rate and, ultimately, the Japan–U.S. trade imbalance, is a matter of considerable dispute. Some have argued that in the past Japan has deliberately tried to depreciate the yen by keeping domestic interest rates artificially low. At first blush, there seems to be some evidence to support this claim. As Table 7.8 indicates, interest rates have tended to be substantially lower in Japan than in the United States. Furthermore, although interest rates for long-term government bonds declined in both Japan and the United States over 1982–5, the spread actually increased.

Predictably, Japan experienced a net capital outflow of $37 billion in 1984, $55 billion in 1985, and approximately $70 billion in 1986. The expanded outflow of Japanese capital went mainly to the United States in the form of the

Table 7.8. *Interest rates in Japan
and the United States yields on long-term
government bonds (percent)*

Year/month	Japan	United States
1982(December)	7.96	10.61
1983(December)	7.45	12.00
1984(December)	6.36	11.61
1985(December)	6.10	9.49

Source: World Financial Markets, Morgan Guaranty Trust, March 1986.

purchase of securities and other financial instruments. The bond investment in 1985 constituted a more than eightfold increase over 1984. To some observers, particularly to Japanese observers, these financial investments in the United States represented the positive aspect of the trade imbalance in goods and services, because they supplied much needed funds to the United States and prevented U.S. interest rates from rising even further. They not only provided a stimulus to the bond and stock markets in the United States, but also helped manufacturing and other nonfinancial institutions to invest in physical and real investments.

Furthermore, in terms of actual exchange rate outcomes, the claim that Japan has in the past deliberately tried to depreciate the yen is difficult to justify. Frankel demonstrates that, when currency values are measured in terms of a weighted average among trading partners, the effective exchange values of European currencies decreased over 1980–4, but the effective exchange value of the yen actually increased. Frankel therefore concludes that "the primary problem is with the strong appreciation of the dollar and the roots of that appreciation within U.S. economic policy, not with yen appreciation or Japanese economic policy."[9]

Although Japan's capital investments in the United States may well have benefited U.S. manufacturing and financial institutions, not only in terms of appreciating the yen, but also by promoting greater equity and efficiency, it has been noted that "domestic liberalization of (capital markets) might be considered the most likely (measure) to have a significant upward effect on the yen, and to have beneficial implications for the efficient and equitable working of the Japanese economy."[10] Recent efforts have been taken to liberalize Japan's financial and capital markets. The government began public offerings of Japanese Treasury Bills for the first time in 1986. The Action Program has given foreign financial institutions improved access to Japan's market. By the end of 1986, nine foreign banks had already received licenses to engage in trust banking and the Tokyo Stock Exchange admitted 10 new members, 6 of them foreign securities companies.

What will Japan do?

There is a genuine sentiment in Japan that the United States is largely responsible for the current trade deficit and is trying to "slough off" responsibility for it onto Japan. Expressing the Japanese view on this issue, Komiya states: "That the fundamental sources of the American current account deficit lie principally in the American economy and a correction of the (trade) deficit depends on improvement in macroeconomic policies of the United States itself, must be very clear to people who understand just a little economics."[11] To many Japanese, U.S. accusations of Japan's responsibility in the trade imbalance is little more than the irrational ravings of a bested competitor: "When a country falls into a difficulty, the domestic reaction is often to emphasize that it is caused by unreasonable and unfair actions of foreign countries. Criticism of Japan is partly to be understood in this context, and is thus not something which will drift away on its own accord."[12] To be sure, the official stance of the Japanese government on Japan's role in the trade imbalance is considerably more diplomatic. On numerous occasions, former Prime Minister Nakasone has declared that Japan should promote international harmony by cooperating to reduce the trade imbalance.

The official government position almost certainly results from Japan's concern over potential U.S. protectionism, not because Japan feels responsible for the trade imbalance. That Japan does not feel responsible for the trade imbalance and resents U.S. pressure to help alleviate it seems to suggest it will do little more than pay lip service to U.S. demands for active involvement in reducing the trade imbalance. Such a conclusion, however, is inaccurate. It is inaccurate for the simple reason that Japan has too much to lose by failing to cooperate with the United States. Strong protectionist measures by the United States would be disastrous for the Japanese economy, and Japan would much sooner cooperate, albeit grudgingly, than deal with U.S. protectionism. There are a variety of measures Japan might take to alleviate the trade imbalance, and we turn now to an examination of these possibilities.

Exchange rate realignment

Exchange rate realignment has already taken place on a grand scale, with the yen appreciating from a low of 240 yen/dollar in September 1985 to about 140 yen/dollar by May 1987. Although the conventional wisdom holds that yen appreciation alone will not resolve the U.S.–Japan trade imbalance, the United States must recognize that the yen appreciation that has already occurred has had a substantial and negative impact on the Japanese economy.

The high yen shock, called *Yen daka Shokku,* has wreaked havoc on Japan's economy. The Japan Institute for Social and Economic Affairs (the Keidanren's public relations and communications branch) describes how much Japan's economy has suffered from the yen appreciation:

While domestic demand has stayed firm the strengthening of the yen has caused Japan's export sector to contract. Real gross national product in the second and third quarters of 1986 was up less than 3% over 1985 levels.

A real growth rate of only 2.3% is the average forecast of 20 major private research organizations for fiscal 1986 (April 1986 to March 1987). This would be the lowest level since the 1971 slump induced by the first oil crisis – Japan has lost the ability to be a locomotive of growth for the world economy as other countries had hoped.[13]

The yen shock has had a devastating effect on employment. It is estimated that in 1986 the number of "surplus" employees reached about 100,000 just in the 457 manufacturing and shipping companies listed on the first section of the Tokyo Stock Exchange and about 900,000 in the manufacturing sector as a whole. If firms were to lay off all of those excess workers, the unemployment rate would jump from the present level of 3 percent to 5 percent. The Keidanren's survey shows that major steel and shipbuilding companies have already closed some plants and factories. The result has been a 20–40 percent reduction in employment.

Despite this effort and sacrifice, Japan's trade surplus has continued to rise to a level approaching $100 billion. What is happening here? Economists often attribute this to a phenomenon called the J-curve effect, whereby a trade surplus (deficit) actually increases for a period even after the country having the surplus (deficit) has appreciated (depreciated) its currency.[14]

The analysis contained in the EPA's White Paper (1986) of the J-curve effect, although admittedly tentative, gives some insights into how the huge surplus continues to exist for the Japanese economy.

Following the final quarter of 1985, when the G-5 meeting took place, the margin of surplus resulting from the combined quarterly effects expanded to approximately $3 billion in the second quarter of 1986 and reached some $4.1 billion in the fiscal year 1985. Although this is only 8 percent of the Japanese trade surplus in 1985, the continued appreciation (rather than a once-for-all appreciation of the yen) reflects various lags at work.

A certain period will be required before all the J-curve effects, or lags, are absorbed. How long it takes depends on the speed of contract renewals and other factors such as (1) adjustment of transportation and distribution systems, (2) inventory liquidation, and (3) changes in production plans.

Table 7.9. *International comparison of total annual actual working hours (production workers in manufacturing industry)*

Year	Japan	United States	United Kingdom	France	Federal Republic of Germany
1975	2,043	1,888	1,923	1,830	1,678
1978	2,137	1,924	1,955	1,772	1,719
1981	2,146	1,888	1,910	1,717	1,656
1982	2,136	1,841	1,915	1,683	1,616
1983	2,152	1,898	1,938	1,657	1,613
1984	2,180	1,934	1,941	1,649	1,652
Scale of more than 5 company workers	All workplaces	More than 10 workers	More than 10 workers	More than 10 workers

Note: figures up to 1983 are estimates of the Planning Section, Wages and Welfare Department, Ministry of Labor; Figures for 1984 are estimates worked out by the Leisure Development Center in accordance with the Ministry of Labor's method of calculaton.
Sources: Ministry of Labor "Monthly Labor Statistics Survey"; U.S. Labor Department "Monthly Labor Review"; "Employment and Earnings" (Statistics Bureau "Labor Cost in Industry"); International Labour Organisation, "Bulletin of Labor Statistics," and others.

Domestic demand expansion

This is the most potent and controversial measure Japan can take to alleviate the trade imbalance. In spite of its great promise, domestic demand expansion will proceed more slowly than did the realignment of the exchange rate. Japan is concerned about possible adverse effects of fiscal stimulus and is likely to implement substantial fiscal stimulus only if U.S. pressure to do so increases.

Japan's reluctance to implement domestic demand expansion results from several factors. First, there is the problem of the "graying" of Japan, the ever-increasing number of Japanese who must be supported by Social Security. To support their retirees "many in Japan deem vital the present buildup of foreign assets through the current account surplus."[15] Second, there is concern that fiscal stimulus will substantially increase government deficits. It is also feared that such deficits will limit policy makers' ability to set interest rates, and will ultimately be inflationary. Another concern is that, given Japan's low propensity to import, fiscal stimulus will have little effect on imports and will not substantially improve the trade imbalance.

Generally speaking, there is some agreement as to the value of domestic demand expansion in a broad, abstract sense. There are considerable differences, however, as to how such stimulus might best be implemented.

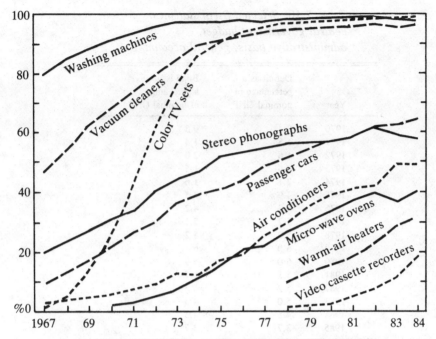

Figure 7.4   Household ownership of durable consumer goods (all households). *Source*: *Statistical Handbook of Japan 1985*.

Given Japan's high saving rate (which is largely due to high personal saving)
and low personal consumption, an ideal policy would be one directly aimed at
reducing saving and increasing personal consumption. The government has
helped to achieve this goal by removing the tax-exempt status of personal
saving and by reforming tax and finance policies to promote housing investment and demand.

Furthermore, there can be little doubt that shorter working hours would
significantly expand demand in the services industries. This is so because (1)
Japanese work much longer hours than do their counterparts in other industrialized nations (see Table 7.9) and (2) although many Japanese have already
acquired manufactured goods, there seems to be strong pent-up demand for
services.

Figure 7.4 shows the dramatic rise in Japan's consumption of durable
goods in the past 15–20 years. Today, nearly all households in Japan own
washing machines, vacuum cleaners, and color TV sets. Sizable proportions
own stereos and automobiles as well.

On the other hand, consumption of services seems to have lagged behind.

Table 7.10. *Selected fiscal statistics:*
central government budget,
administrative basis, general account

Year	Deficit as a percentage of nominal GNP	Bond issues as a percentage of nominal GNP
1970	0.4	0.5
1971	1.3	1.4
1972	1.6	2.0
1973	0.6	1.5
1974	2.1	1.6
1975	3.9	3.5
1976	4.2	4.2
1977	5.2	5.1
1978	5.0	5.2
1979	6.0	6.1
1980	6.0	5.9
1981	5.1	5.1
1982	5.2	5.3
1983	5.0	4.3
1984	4.5	4.3
1985	3.7	3.7

[a]Bond issues plus carryover from the previous fiscal
year.
Sources: Adapted from Ministry of Finance, *Financial Statistics,* and EPA, *Annual Report on National Accounts;* 1985 estimates are based on official forecasts.

This pattern does not, however, reflect consumer apathy toward services. Indeed, 1984 public opinion survey data indicate that the Japanese gave top priority to enjoying their leisure activities.[16] This rated ahead of housing, which had received top priority each time the public opinion survey had been conducted prior to 1984. By contrast: "'durable goods' and 'clothing' for which most families have already attained satisfaction [did] not play important roles in planning or wishes concerning future living."[17] It is also interesting to note that, from 1970 to 1984, the share of consumption expenditures devoted to reading and recreation activities actually decreased from 9.2 percent to 8.7 percent.[18] The overall impression is that potential demand in the services industry – particularly recreation-related services – is a major untapped source of economic growth.

It will not be easy to translate potential demand for services into actual demand, however. Major Japanese firms and their subcontractors have already suffered from yen appreciation, and they are hardly likely to respond to this setback by asking their employees to work shorter hours. Another unhappy result of Japan's sluggish industrial sector is that wage hikes should continue to be low, which will also hinder demand for services. In addition, substantial increases in the demand for services will require a shift in industrial structure from manufacturing industries to service industries. Some industries will surely suffer from such restructuring, and they will naturally resist.

Moreover, both the Japanese government and the business community have been obsessed with the idea that the government budget has to be balanced before measures for expansionary domestic demand are adopted. Mr. Inayama's *Gaman no Tetsugaku* was the philosophy often said to be responsible for this sentiment, as mentioned at the beginning of this chapter.

The government sought to close the gap of the budget deficit by implementing indirect taxes, specifically a European value-added tax system. The government proposal of this new tax, submitted in the fall of 1986, was soundly defeated, however, by the opposition parties. Nevertheless, the Japanese government and the Liberal Democratic Party (LDP) have devoted most of their political energy to the passage of the tax law, rather than to the passage of import-stimulating measures. This points to a clear difference in priorities between the United States and Japan. The U.S. priority was to see that Japan spends more effort on reducing the trade imbalance, rather than on instituting a new tax system that will in many cases reduce domestic effective demand. The Japanese priority was, however, to institute a new tax system that will balance the budget and enable the government to expand public expenditures at a later stage.

Japan has clearly been more inclined to expand domestic demand by increasing public, rather than private, expenditures. For example, the government is committed to implementing increases in construction bonds to finance improvements in Japan's infrastructure, although former Prime Minister Nakasone stressed that such increases should be kept to a minimum.[19] As Table 7.10 indicates, both government deficits and bond issues have been trending steadily downward relative to GNP since 1979. Thus, there appears to be a good deal of room for this type of domestic demand stimulus without inviting adverse consequences. Such expansion will indirectly reduce the trade surplus by reducing aggregate saving in Japan, thereby decreasing capital outflow and strengthening the yen.

Alternative possibilities

Aside from exchange rate realignment and domestic demand stimulus, there is the possibility of improving the bilateral trade deficit between Japan and the

Table 7.11. *Japan's exports to five major sources, 1984*
(in billions of dollars)

Country	Total	Machinery and chemicals	Nonmetal products	Metal products	Other
U.S.	59.9	47.9	1.2	4.8	6.0
	(100)	(80)	(2)	(8)	(10)
Korea	7.3	4.7	0.2	1.2	1.1
	(100)	(65)	(3)	(17)	(15)
China	7.1	3.6	—	1.2	0.7
	(100)	(50)	—	(40)	(12)
Federal Republic of Germany	6.6	5.8	—	—	0.8
Hong Kong	6.6	4.0	—	0.7	2.0
	(100)	(60)	—	(10)	(30)

Note: Percentage distribution by country in parentheses. Percentage distributions of specific types of exports were estimated from bar charts and are only meant to illustrate the general magnitude involved, as are the dollar values of specific types of exports.
Source: Adapted from data in the *Statistical Handbook of Japan*, 1985.

United States by diverting some Japanese exports to developing countries rather than to U.S. markets. The import capacity of these developing countries would be enhanced by directing the Japanese saving surplus to finance the deficits of developing countries. Such a proposal was made in a report by a study group of the World Institute for Development Economics Research in April 1986.[20]

Although creative and novel, this appears to be a plan whose time has not yet come. Only when the economies of developing nations are sufficiently mature to provide markets and investment opportunities that are reasonable substitutes for those available in the United States can one meaningfully speak of resolving U.S.–Japan trade imbalances by diverting Japan's exports and capital outflow to places other than the United States.

For the next several years, at least, it is most unlikely that developing countries will be able to absorb Japanese exports on a scale large enough to significantly reduce the U.S.–Japan trade imbalances by diverting Japan's exports and capital outflow to places other than the United States.

For example, as Table 7.11 indicates, the value of Japan's exports to the United States is more than twice the value of Japan's exports to its next four largest markets combined. It is also unclear why capital should suddenly flow from Japan to developing countries when the current flow from Japan to the

Table 7.12. *Market shares of selected successful American businesses in Japan*

Product	Name of manufacturer	Market share (%)
Carbonated beverages	Coca-Cola	60
Powdered soup	CPC International Inc.	80
Canned soup	CPC International Inc.	30
Breakfast cereals	Kellogg	80
Ointment	Johnson & Johnson	31
Floor wax	S.C. Johnson & Son, Co.	30
Car wax	S.C. Johnson & Son, Co.	20
Deodorants	American Drug	59
Odorants	S.C. Johnson & Son, Co.	21
Bulldozers	Caterpillar Tractor	43
Panel heaters	Koehring Hosty Corp.	50
Computers	IBM	40
Instant cameras	Polaroid	45
Instant cameras	Eastman Kodak	45
Stem wine glasses	Owens-Illinois Inc.	60
Tupperware	Rexall Drug & Chemical	30

Source: MITI.

United States indicates that better investment opportunities exist in the United States.

Speaking of capital outflows, another alternative for reducing the U.S.–Japan trade imbalance is simply to restrict capital outflows from Japan. To the extent that such outflows tend to depreciate the yen, their elimination should decrease the U.S. trade deficit. This solution, however, is at odds with long-standing U.S. efforts to deregulate and liberalize Japan's capital markets. It could also lead to substantially higher interest rates in the United States, and even a recession. This policy would be so negatively received in the United States that it is most unlikely to be implemented. Even if this were not the case, Japan appears unwilling to undertake actions that might further appreciate the yen, as noted earlier.

Increased imports of American goods and services do not appear to be a promising option for alleviating the trade imbalance, at least over the short run. American newspapers concede that the Japanese are importing much more; however, in comparison with other countries, the growth in U.S. imports has lagged behind growth in imports from other countries. The May 16, 1987, issue of the *New York Times* reports that although the Nakasone government's campaign to buy foreign goods has been successful, imports from the

Table 7.13. *Sources of Japan's real GNP growth (percent, annual averages)*

Year	GNP	Domestic	External
1966–71	10.2	10.2	0.0
1972–4	5.5	5.9	−0.4
1975–9	4.7	2.4	0.5
1980–4	4.3	3.1	1.9
1985	4.6	3.1	1.9
1986	3.4	3.2	0.2

Note: Derived from national accounts data in 1975 prices
Source: World Financial Markets, Morgan Guaranty Trust Co., November 1985.

United States have not increased dramatically.[21] Imports from Europe and such newly industrializing countries as Taiwan and South Korea have shown far larger gains. The explanations for the relative lag in American imports vary widely, but American goods face a distinct image problem in Japan. Where European goods have an image of luxury and craftsmanship and Asian goods have compelling price advantages, the Japanese suspect the quality of American goods with higher prices – American goods do not have a brand-name image.

In addition, some Japanese blame American companies for not trying hard enough to modify their products to Japanese taste. But there are success stories in Japan. Mister Donut, which has changed its doughnut recipe to make its product less sweet in Japan, is one of the most successful companies in Japan. Table 7.12 shows examples of successful American businesses in Japan.

Exchange rate realignment and domestic demand stimulus emerge as the two options Japan may resort to in redressing the trade imbalance. Since exchange rate realignment has apparently been implemented to the extent feasible, however, fiscal stimulus to expand Japan's domestic demand looms as the lone viable option for Japan to help further reduce the trade imbalance.

There is every reason to believe that such a policy can succeed. That Japan must depend on exports for growth is a myth. As Table 7.13 indicates, only in 1980–4 did exports account for a substantial proportion of Japan's overall growth in real GNP. There is no reason why the pattern in earlier years, when real GNP growth was driven domestically, cannot be repeated in the future.

Despite its seeming promise, strong fiscal stimulus remains an option that Japan will resort to only if sufficiently pressured by the United States.

Whether such U.S. pressure arises depends, in turn, on the success of U.S. policy initiatives like Gramm–Rudman in reducing government spending and, ultimately, the trade imbalance.

Conclusion: Implications for the trade imbalance and trade friction

Some encouraging signs on the horizon point to a reduced trade imbalance. Trade statistics released by the U.S. Commerce Department in the beginning of May 1987 show that American exports to Japan continued to increase in March 1987, rising to $2.14 billion, up from $2.03 billion in February. Japan bought 12.6 percent more goods from the United States in 1986 than in 1985. The strong yen is causing many Japanese companies to "reimport" their own products from the United States. For example, the Honda Motor Company is considering reimporting passenger cars produced in the United States.

In spite of these encouraging signs, substantial improvement in the trade imbalance without concurrent escalations in trade friction between the two countries seems a distant hope. The United States is hell-bent on reducing its trade deficit with Japan. This will eventually be accomplished, one way or another. The most benign scenario would be that the policy initiatives of Japan and the United States are spectacularly successful in reducing the U.S. trade deficit, so that the trade imbalance is resolved without further U.S. pressure on Japan.

On the other hand, if the U.S.–Japan trade imbalance does not improve, protectionist sentiment will flare up in the United States. Japan will respond to mounting U.S. pressure by playing its last card – substantial fiscal stimulus. Most likely, this stimulus will first come in the form of greater efforts to expand public works. Tax cuts, removal of the tax-exempt status of personal saving, and the like may follow if the public works expansion fails to abate mounting U.S. protectionist sentiment. Under either scenario, the trade imbalance will be substantially reduced.

More ominous, however, are the implications for trade friction. It is probably true that, other things remaining the same, a decline in a trade imbalance would result in a decline in trade friction. But, in reducing the large trade imbalance between Japan and the United States, "other things," such as mutual trust and respect and a sense of international economic cooperation, may fall by the wayside. It is even conceivable that, in reducing the trade imbalance, Japan and the United States will intensify their trade friction.

Many of the factors that could induce this unhappy result are already present. On the one hand, we see the United States pressuring Japan to open its goods and capital markets while at the same time threatening Japan with increased protectionist measures. Although this may be an expedient way to reduce the trade imbalance, it is glaringly hypocritical and hardly conducive to mutual trust and respect.

For its part, Japan seems too slow to realize that "If one country's economic performance moves against the interests of the world economy, that country will be asked to change course."[22] Rather than accepting small trade surpluses as an exogenous political constraint in formulating domestic policy, Japan decides domestic policy as it sees fit, making significant changes only when countervailing actions by its trading partners seem imminent.

Exacerbating these basic problems is the fact that yen appreciation apparently has not been a strong force in reducing the trade imbalance. Masaya Miyoshi of the Keidanren has remarked that "the United States attaches importance to the results while Japan . . . places importance on good intention more than anything else."[23] If there is some truth to Mr. Miyoshi's observation, the salient effect of exchange rate realignment might lie not in decreasing the trade imbalance, but in increasing trade friction.

In fact, aside from harming Japan's export sector directly, the strong yen is prompting many Japanese companies, particularly those in the critical automotive and electronics industries, to establish plants at locations abroad, including the United States. From the standpoint of economic theory, these responses result from the firm's desire to maintain international competitiveness. From the perspective of the average worker, however, this means fewer jobs. Hence, the popular terms for relocation of Japanese plants abroad are "deindustrialization" and the "hollowing out" of Japanese industry. To the extent that relocation is viewed as "hollowing out," it is likely to increase friction between Japan and the United States.

Like many trading partners, however, Japan and the United States have been conducting business under less than ideal circumstances for a number of years, and will likely continue to do so. Interestingly, the very fact that there remains much room for improvement in cooperative efforts and freeing of markets between the two nations helps prevent trade friction from really getting out of hand. As long as trade imbalances and trade friction can be blamed on relatively benign factors like policy coordination failure, closed markets, and the like, the possibility of mutually beneficial trade remains. But imagine what might happen if the United States, for example, incurred substantial trade deficits with Japan in a world in which both countries behaved cooperatively, policies were perfectly coordinated, and all markets were open. In such a world, U.S. deficits would be attributed to a pervasive lack of competitiveness. Trade friction on a scale we have not yet observed would ensue.

This does not imply that we should not seek to reduce the trade friction that is present today through policy coordination, open markets, and the like. Nor does it imply that substantial trade friction is inevitable. We merely wish to

Appendix 1 The increase in Japan's trade surplus attributable to the yen's appreciation is calculated from the following table.

The J-curve effect

Period	Item	October-December 1985	January-March 1986	April-June 1986	1985
J-curve for October-	Exports	1,293	2,178	1,018	3,471
December 1985	Imports	81	220	386	301
	Balance	1,212	1,958	632	3,170
J-curve for January-	Exports		938	1,580	938
March 1986	Imports		58	159	58
	Balance		880	1,421	880
J-curve for April-	Exports			968	
June 1986	Imports			58	
	Balance			910	
Combined	Exports	1,293	3,116	3,566	4,409
J-curve	Imports	81	278	603	359
J-curve	Balance	1,212	2,838	2,963	4,050

Source: See Economic Planning Agency (1986).

point out that, although Japan and the United States should work together to achieve better coordinated macroeconomic policies and more open markets, each country must remain acutely aware that maintaining the international competitiveness of its industries is a fundamental ingredient in healthy trade relations. If international competitiveness is not maintained, very serious trade friction will emerge.

Notes

1 R. Sato and G. Suzawa, *Research and Productivity,* Auburn House, 1983, p. 159.
2 Although these results are suggestive, they must be viewed with caution. Positive first-order serial correlation appears to be present in most of the EPA's regression results, as indicated by the low values for the Durbin-Watson statistics they report. Unfortunately, the researchers did not correct for first-order serial correlation.
3 Charles Y. Horioka, "Household Saving in Japan: The Importance of Target Saving for Education and Housing," paper presented at the Japan Economic Seminar, Washington, D.C., September 21, 1985.
4 Jeffrey A. Frankel, *The Yen/Dollar Agreement: Liberalizing Japanese Capital Markets,* Institute for International Economics, December 1984, p. 61.

5 "The G-5: Meaning and Mission," *World Financial Markets*, Morgan Guaranty Trust, November 1985, p. 7.

6 Eishiro Saito, as quoted in "Keidanren Will Endorse Fiscal Rehabilitation," *Japan Economic Journal*, June 7, 1986, p. 4.

7 "Bulging Money Supply Sparks Fears of Inflation at Central Bank," *Japan Economic Journal*, May 31, 1986, p. 23.

8 K. Suzumura, and M. Okuno-Fujiwara, "Industrial Policy in Japan: Overview and Evaluation," in *Trade Friction and Economic Policy*, ed. Ryuzo Sato and Paul Wachtel. Cambridge University Press, 1987.

9 Frankel, *The Yen/Dollar Agreement*, pp. 47–8.

10 Ibid., p. 13.

11 R. Komiya, "An Economic Analysis of the Japan–U.S. Trade Problem: a Japanese View," translation of an article published in Japanese, in *Shukan Toyo Keizai*, June 7 and June 9, 1986.

12 Ibid.

13 "The Yen Shock," Japan Institute for Social and Economic Affairs, Tokyo, Japan, March 1987.

14 The standard explanation for this pattern is the so-called J-Curve effect. According to this theory, foreign goods ordered before a plunge in the value of the domestic currency *but paid for after* the drop in that currency increase the cost of imports, temporarily increasing that country's trade deficit. This has surely been part of the reason why yen appreciation did not reduce the Japan–U.S. trade imbalance in the first half of 1986. Eventually, however, yen appreciation should bring some improvement in the Japan–U.S. trade imbalance. How much improvement depends upon factors such as the determination of Japanese firms to maintain export market shares by avoiding price increases. Another important factor is that, although the dollar has depreciated substantially against the yen, the dollar's trade-weighted decline against 25 currencies dropped by only 5 percent from September 1985 to July 1986 (see *Business Week*, July 28, 1986). Thus, even if yen appreciation eventually improves the Japan–U.S. trade imbalance, the United States may remain in deficit vis-à-vis other trading partners.

15 "The G5: Meaning and Mission," p. 8.

16 *Statistical Handbook of Japan 1985*, p. 116.

17 Ibid., p. 116.

18 Ibid., p. 113.

19 "The Week," *Japan Economic Journal*, July 12, 1986, p. 2.

20 "The Potential of the Japanese Surplus for World Economic Development," *Report of a Study Group of the World Institute for Development Economics Research* (WIDER), for the United Nations University, Tokyo, Japan, April 18, 1986.

21 S. Chira, "Why the U.S. Lags in Japan," *New York Times*, May 16, 1987.

22 "Mayekawa Report Should Have Been Implemented Three Years Earlier" (interview with I. Miyazaki), *Japan Economic Journal*, May 31, 1986, p. 7.

23 M. Miyoshi, "Economic Friction between the United States and Japan – Illusion and Reality," in *Trade Friction and Economic Policy*, ed. R. Sato and P. Wachtel, Cambridge University Press, 1987.

Index